STILL RIGHT

STILL RIGHT

An IMMIGRANT-LOVING,
HYBRID-DRIVING,
COMPOSTING AMERICAN
MAKES THE CASE *for*
CONSERVATISM

RICK TYLER

THOMAS DUNNE BOOKS
NEW YORK

First published in the United States by Thomas Dunne Books, an imprint of
St. Martin's Publishing Group

www.thomasdunnebooks.com

Library of Congress Cataloging-in-Publication Data

Names: Tyler, Rick, author.
Title: Still right : an immigrant-loving, hybrid-driving, composting
   American makes the case for conservatism / Rick Tyler.
Description: First edition. | New York : Thomas Dunne Books, 2020. |
   Includes bibliographical references.
Identifiers: LCCN 2020016423 | ISBN 9781250256492 (hardcover) |
   ISBN 9781250256508 (ebook)
Subjects: LCSH: Conservatism—United States. | United States—Politics and
   government—2017-
Classification: LCC JC573.2.U6 T95 2020 | DDC 320.520973—dc23
LC record available at https://lccn.loc.gov/2020016423

Our books may be purchased in bulk for promotional, educational, or business use.
Please contact your local bookseller or the Macmillan Corporate and Premium Sales
Department at 800-221-7945, extension 5442, or by email at
MacmillanSpecialMarkets@macmillan.com.

First Edition: 2020

10 9 8 7 6 5 4 3 2 1

To my wife, Tamara. You are the love of my life.

CONTENTS

PREFACE

On New Year's Day 2020, when I arrived in the greenroom at the Washington bureau of NBC News, Ruth Marcus, *The Washington Post* opinion columnist was already there. She was scheduled to appear ahead of me on NBC's cable news network, MSNBC. We exchanged New Year's greetings, then with a mischievous smile she asked me if four years ago I would have thought that we would have such similar opinions about Donald Trump. What went unsaid but understood was: "despite our political differences." I responded by quoting the Eagles' Joe Walsh: "Everybody's so different. I haven't changed."

And I'm not about to change. I have been a conservative my whole life. And for several decades I've actively championed conservative principles by working on political campaigns at all levels of government.

My first political job was managing a campaign for governor, which, admittedly, I had no business doing. At the time, I was managing a restaurant along the coast of Maine near Bath. One of the waitresses who was working to put herself through college introduced me to her mother, who was the minority leader in the Maine Senate. She was running for governor but was not attracting talent to her campaign. She asked me if I would be her campaign manager. I refused the offer, saying I knew nothing about running for office. She then asked if I would be willing to be a volunteer on her campaign. I accepted and soon thereafter, despite my protestations, I became the campaign manager anyway.

Early on in the campaign, I called Fritz Rench, a family friend who was the secretary at the Heritage Foundation. Fritz had written the first business plan for the conservative think tank and had deep roots in and ties to the conservative movement. During our call, he kept repeating the refrain: "This is impossible." He was referring to me running a statewide campaign with no political experience. Nevertheless, he agreed to help. I was immediately enrolled in a Washington-based campaign school organized by Paul Weyrich's Free Congress Foundation. I got in my pickup truck and drove to DC for a week of intensive political training. By the end of the school, I had absorbed a lifetime's worth of experience from seasoned campaign professionals. But the most significant thing I learned was: we were going to lose.

Everything that I now understood about campaigns from the Free Congress Foundation campaign school, we weren't doing, and it was too late to make up lost ground. It was a hard lesson.

So by early 1994, the year of the Republican Revolution, I was just cutting my political teeth by running a statewide campaign for governor. I ran it right into the ground. We placed dead last in a nine-way Republican primary.

This sounds awful, but the thing is that in the political world, losing can be the best thing that happens to you. When you win, you learn almost nothing. There is no reflection or looking back on what went wrong. You just assume you did everything right. When you lose, losing is all you think about. So I would spend the next several years learning all there was to know about how to win campaigns. I was hooked and there was no going back.

Soon, I was working for the Maine Republican Party, where I eventually became the state director. I held that position for nearly five years. One of my key objectives was getting our candidates and their campaigns trained. I brought in GOPAC, a well-known conservative political training organization and we trained and trained. In November of 1996, when Republicans were following our presidential nominee, Kansas senator Bob Dole, off a cliff, Maine was one of the few states where he gained seats in the state legislature.

While still working for the Maine GOP, I started training candidates and volunteers for GOPAC around the country. At first, I used the material they had developed. But it wasn't long before I was developing my own presentations and talks because while GOPAC's were good, I thought they could be better.

So besides training in the nuts and bolts of campaigns, I focused on three neglected areas: leadership, communications, and messaging. I believed (and still believe) that the conservative message was a winning message, but it was not being explained or presented in a way that attracted people to its philosophy. I wanted to change that.

By 1998, my fifth year as ED of the Maine Republican Party, I was getting a little too comfortable. I openly supported a conservative candidate for state chairman, a state legislator who had been termed out. By the time he committed to run, we only had two weeks to campaign. Our opponent, a moderate, had been the vice chairman of the party for the last four years and had been actively campaigning for the top job for nearly two years. We lost by two votes and I lost my job.

Speaker Newt Gingrich also lost his job earlier that same year when he failed to meet expectations in the 1998 elections by losing four House seats, even though the GOP had held the majority in the House for three consecutive elections. He was giving up the speakership and would resign from Congress.

Despite failing to meet expectations in 1998, Newt solidified his position as the dominant conservative since Ronald Reagan having created a movement that brought the GOP out of the wilderness and into a congressional majority for the first time in four decades. My sense at the time was that he wasn't going to retire quietly and that he still had much more to offer.

I called Joe Gaylord, Gingrich's senior adviser, whom I had met while attending his weeklong Campaign Management College. I was curious about what Newt's next adventure might be. As everyone was exiting Newt world, I seemed to be one of the few who was asking to come on board. By July of 1999, I was on team Newt and moving to Washington, DC, arriving serendipitously on July 4. For the next decade, life with Newt was one never-ending grand adventure. I loved working for Newt. I never stopped learning, because Dr. Gingrich, PhD, never gave up teaching.

We traveled all over the country, mostly by private jet, to paid and some unpaid speaking events. We published thirteen books; made several movies; secured a Fox News contract; consulted with for-profit and nonprofit companies; developed conservative policy, especially in healthcare and national security (Newt even invented the Department of Homeland Security); campaigned for Republicans; oh, and we ran for president.

Although Newt never did become president, he remained and still remains relevant after relinquishing the speakership more than two decades ago. That's not easy to achieve.

I last saw Newt in Rome where his wife, Callista, serves as the ambassador to the Vatican. She was hosting an Independence Day party at the residence. I think it is fair to say that Newt and I don't see eye to eye on President Trump. We never discussed it. I think preserving relationships is more important than political disagreements.

This was emphasized by my send-off from the Ted Cruz presidential campaign in 2016. I have to admit I did not want to go. As was expected of key staffers, I had moved from my home in Virginia to Houston, where his campaign headquarters were. Most weeks, like so many on the campaign, I had worked all seven days, and most days I worked every waking hour, only finding time off on Sundays for church and the occasional Astros game. As the Cruz spokesperson, I made the case for him specifically and conservatism in general on TV and in person around the country. The mission was personal. But on my last day I was reminded that the mission was also social. The campaign and our shared principles had made us a family. So I found myself crying and laughing in turn as dozens of my colleagues from headquarters said good-bye with rounds of drinks and "Rick Tyler stories."

Prioritizing relationships is, I think, what is lacking in our political discourse. Since the founding, our nation has been divided, starting with the loyalists and the patriots. Later it would be the Yankees and the Confederates. Today, it's the Democrats and the Republicans, and while political poles have been with us since the founding, the division seems so vast now that partisans are more willing than ever to simply ignore facts and truth to advance political objectives. To be fair, that's not exactly new, either, but it is much more widespread, and it seems to come with no consequences. That is a dangerous road.

Despite our political disagreement, Americans have managed to remain a nation under the same Constitution for more than two centuries. Political differences will always be with us, but we need to find a better way of respecting those differences and get back to the central theme of a self-governing people—and that is to compromise. Without the willingness to compromise, the United States is in danger of traveling down the same dark road of every other failed nation, often with violent consequences seen so vividly in the last century.

This is why I leaped at the chance, offered immediately after I left the Cruz campaign, to become a contributor on MSNBC.

I had done nearly a decade of political commentary on all the cable networks but mostly on Fox News, where it wasn't a real challenge to argue a conservative position to their conservative audience. Getting the center-left viewers of MSNBC to understand and appreciate it, though, and maybe getting them to at least understand the conservative position and maybe even agree with it: that appealed to me.

I have to credit Chris Matthews with giving me my first chance there. I had watched him for almost as long as there has been cable news. I always had respect for Matthews because he knows the political game better than anyone else. He's worked on the Hill for four members of Congress, including Speaker Tip O'Neill. You have to do your homework, know your stuff, and do good television because Matthews doesn't suffer fools, so when he invited me on the first time my goal was simply to survive. But for years I was asked to come on again and again. Doing his show made me better at explaining what I believe and why, especially as the conservative brand has been tarnished and remade into something it's not, and for that I'm grateful.

This brings me back to Ruth Marcus's observation that no one would have predicted how dramatically Donald Trump would flip the political landscape, making for some very unlikely allies. What has disappointed me the most about this period in history, however, is how many members of my party were willing to give up on conservative positions in order to stay in good stead with President Trump. As we will see in the following chapters, the Republican Party has eschewed the conservative governing philosophy it had clung to since Reagan. It has abandoned the virtues of a free market and free trade for import taxes on consumers and protectionism. The GOP no longer welcomes immigrants willing to trade labor for a better life and a dramatically better future for their families. It has abandoned smaller limited government and balanced budgets. Our foreign policy—the prophylactic of war—is in shambles. Have there been some good policies? Yes, and we shall discuss them, too, but on balance the Trump presidency has been both a policy and political setback for advancing conservative principles. I'm not a Trump critic because I've become a liberal. I'm a critic because I remain a conservative.

That is to say, I'm "Still Right."

STILL RIGHT

INTRODUCTION:
THE IDEOLOGICAL FOSTER CHILD

Look for the narcissist. The most obvious target in today's lineup is, of course, Donald Trump. When he looks at a glass, he is mesmerized by its reflection. If Donald Trump were shaped a little differently, he would compete for Miss America. But whatever the depths of self-enchantment, the demagogue has to say something. *So what does Trump say? That he is a successful businessman and that that is what America needs in the Oval Office. There is some plausibility in this, though not much. The greatest deeds of American Presidents—midwifing the new republic; freeing the slaves; harnessing the energies and vision needed to win the Cold War— had little to do with a bottom line.*

—William F. Buckley Jr., 2000[1]

After Bill Clinton's election in November of 1992, conservative William Bennett suggested that the Republican Party had lost its way and had failed to communicate a coherent, conservative message in the presidential campaign for George Bush. Bennett's answer was that the Republican Party needed the "political equivalent of the Council of Trent,"[2] the gathering of Catholic bishops in 1545 who assembled to restate the fundamental teachings of the Church. The doctrines had remained the same, but leadership—composed of priests, bishops, and cardinals—had lost its way and openly lived lives and promoted ideals that ran counter to their stated beliefs. Thus, a council was called to answer a fundamental question: *what is it that we believe?*

After President Bush's defeat in 1992, Bennett suggested that the Republican Party needed to ask the same question: *what is it that we believe?*

Of course, one could make the argument that the *primary season, or nomination process,* serves every four years—albeit clumsily—as Trent served the Catholic Church. The subjects of foreign policy, immigration, trade, healthcare, and taxes are debated by various Republican candidates on a national stage. The year 2016, however, was different. More than during any primary season in modern times, *policy* was largely moved off the table. The central issue wasn't an issue at all; rather, it was a person: Donald Trump. As leading conservative opinion writer Thomas Sowell observed, "In a country with more than 330 million people, it is remarkable how obsessed the media have become with just one—Donald Trump."[3] Trump's ridiculous theories and/or belittling comments about every other candidate became news. All of Donald Trump's press conferences were covered, while other candidates found it nearly impossible to get airtime—even when they were winning primaries and caucuses. Largely, and certainly on a comparative basis with other election cycles, policy debates almost never happened.

As the national spokesperson and communications director for the Ted Cruz presidential campaign, I had a front-row seat in the 2016 presidential primary. Political coverage of campaigns focuses almost exclusively on the horse race, campaign strategy, and fund-raising and very little on policy anymore. Appearing regularly on the various news networks, I would make the case for a Cruz presidency. Even so, most of the discussion was not about what our campaign was doing but rather what was our reaction to Donald Trump's latest tweet or utterance. I spent most of my airtime explaining the fact that Trump had little history or connection with the party he was trying to win the nomination from. Before his candidacy, his stated views most often were in conflict with the Republican Party. He was pro-choice. He declared support for a single-payer healthcare system. He wasn't aligned with any conservative group, issue, or cause. The case against Trump being a credible candidate for the party of which conservatives mostly found their political home seemed solid and un-assailable. Yet, after his much-hyped descent on an escalator in a Man-hattan skyscraper bearing his name, Trump never lost his lead in any national poll. This was pretty frustrating. But as a conservative, there was something even more frustrating going on: Donald Trump was being billed as a conservative—as *the* conservative in the race.

This was an intellectually bizarre claim, and, of course, I was not the only one pointing it out. Many of the other campaigns were, too. But one significant voice who was having none of Trump's attempt at rebranding himself as a conservative was the *National Review,* the magazine founded by William F. Buckley. The conservative maga-zine echoed what I had been saying for months. The *National Review* pointed out that "Trump donated to both the Clinton Foundation and Hillary Clinton's Senate campaign, as well to Nancy Pelosi, Harry Reid, Chuck Schumer, and other Democrats." According to public disclosures available to anyone, the vast majority of his politi-cal contributions had been to Democrats—some of whom composed the *Far* Left. On the topic of fiscal policy, conservative radio talk show host Glenn Beck pointed out that Trump had supported "the stimulus, the auto bailouts, and the bank bailouts." Another noted his "passionate defense of eminent domain" and history of favoring higher tax rates. On the subject of trade, David Boaz of the Cato Institute referenced his "protectionism," while others wrote about his endorsement of tariffs. On being pro-life, conservative and media critic Brent Bozell pointed out that Trump had been supportive of Planned Parenthood; indeed, in a Republican debate, Trump ar-gued that Planned Parenthood did a lot of good. Theologian Russell Moore reminded his readers that Trump had even been in favor of partial-birth abortion.[4]

Of course, Trump is not the first person who claimed to be conser-vative while holding positions that are antithetical to conservatism. Among self-proclaimed conservatives who ignored or dismissed the points raised by the *National Review* was the late Phyllis Schlafly, a recognized leader of the conservative movement since the days of Barry Goldwater. Schlafly not only endorsed Trump in the general election, she also endorsed him very early in the *primary* season. This is a key point. It is one thing to argue in favor of Trump over Hillary, but it's quite another to argue in favor of Trump over proven conservatives still in the race. Why would Schlafly do that? Because her *own* positions had changed. This became clear in a book that Schlafly later wrote to support him, *The Conservative Case for Trump*, which she refers to as "the culmination . . . of more than seventy years of active involvement in Republican politics."[5] Given Schlafly's background, you might think that she would frame pro-life as the premiere issue, yet the pro-life issue does not even get its own chapter. Instead, Schlafly's first two chapters—"Immigration Invasion" and "Rotten Trade Deals"—evidenced a fundamental shift in conservative priorities.

While she assured readers that Trump "could be the most conservative president we've had since Ronald Reagan," the Trump/Schlafly positions on both immigration and trade bear no relation to Reagan's policies (as I will examine later in this book). On the topic of immigration, Schlafly mimics the Trump quasi-logical narrative: (1) you cannot have a nation without borders; (2) you cannot have borders without walls; and (3) therefore, you cannot have a nation without walls. Of course, by that logic, the United States of America has *never* been a nation. (For all their greatness, that's a point apparently missed by the founders of America.) Also, by that logic, a wall must be built on the northern border with Canada as well, not to mention a wall on the eastern and western coastlines, the Alaskan peninsula, and the chain of islands that constitute the state of Hawaii. Going to the beach might never be the same again, but at least we can dig our feet in the sand and stare at a big wall, confident that America is finally a nation.

Regarding free trade, Schlafly writes: "'Free trade' is not necessarily a 'conservative' issue given that so many liberal Democrats are in favor of it." That's her argument? Setting aside the fact that the human freedom to exchange with one another is *the* fundamental economic principle of conservatism, was Schlafly suggesting that any issue agreed on by liberal Democrats *cannot* be conservative? If that's the principle, she might as well have said, *Prosecuting bank robbers is not necessarily a conservative issue given that so many liberal Democrats are in favor of prosecuting bank robbers.* This kind of argument appears throughout the book. In doing so, Schlafly reduced conservatism to a *reactionary* position—that is, a system of belief that is borne of opposition—rather than a *fundamental* position that stands on its own.

Schlafly was one of the first conservatives to endorse Trump in the primary season, but others soon followed. On January 19—two weeks prior to the Iowa caucus—Sarah Palin came out with a ringing endorsement of Trump at Iowa State University, assuring the crowd that Trump was a "family man" who would "kick ISIS' ass."[6] (After watching her shrieky endorsement speech, I was happy she didn't endorse Cruz and that her endorsement was not worth very much after all.) Pat Buchanan, former White House communications director under Reagan, frustrated with "trade deficits" and the "pervasive presence of illegal immigrants," endorsed Trump in mid-January of 2016.[7] Buchanan, a lifelong traditional Catholic, seemed untroubled that Trump had made comments in favor of abortion on numerous occasions. Alabama senator Jeff Sessions endorsed Trump on February 28, 2016—just two days prior to Super Tuesday, the biggest day of the primary season. To this list, we can add those Evangelical leaders who announced their support of Trump over a number of devout Christians who were still in the race (this will be discussed in detail in Chapter 11).

But far more impactful than old-school conservative endorsements was Fox News. The Fox News network is almost universally recognized as a conservative media outlet, and it gave Trump very favorable coverage—even hosts like Sean Hannity not only supported him but acted as a campaign adviser.[8] (In contrast, Fox hosts who refused to endorse Trump, most notably Megyn Kelly, were ostracized.) Nearly every morning and night, Fox News gave extended airtime to Trump and his spokespeople, like Kellyanne Conway, National Spokeswoman Katrina Pierson, and Omarosa Manigault. Beyond that, Fox would generously cover news stories reinforcing the

Trump campaign's political narrative. For instance, part of candidate Trump's message was that "sanctuary cities" are dangerous, so Fox headlined news broadcasts about the crime taking place in sanctuary cities. Conservative radio talk show host Mark Levin referred to Fox as a "Trump Super PAC." Former Fox host Steve Deace claimed that Fox was nothing more than a shill for Trump.[9] More than any other single factor, it was Fox News that won the election for Donald Trump. And perhaps more than any other single factor, Fox News changed the very definition of conservatism.

In can be rightfully said that—in the persons of Schlafly, Sessions, Palin, Buchanan, many members of the Christian Right, and the network they all seemed to love—conservatism experienced a hostile takeover from within.

After the 2016 election, the redefinition of conservatism continued. Even the *National Review* softened, and along came a book by one of its authors. Victor Davis Hanson wrote *The Case for Trump*. (Apparently, Hanson could not bring himself to include the word "conservative" in the title.) The soft-spoken Hanson seemed impressed by Trump's brash style—the way that he "tells it like it is." I've heard that expression hundreds of times in the past few years: "He tells it like it is." Only nobody has been able to tell me what "it" is. In his book, Hanson goes on and on, essentially rearguing the 2016 election and why Trump was better than Hillary. At this point, that's a pretty fruitless discussion. The binary justification argument has made the conservative philosophy an unwanted, foster child.

During Trump's presidential campaign, "conservative" had come to mean "supporting of the policies uttered, however incoherently, by Trump. That meant adopting an unshakable belief in a wall on America's southern border, banning immigrants based on religion, a single-payer healthcare system, an affection for tariffs, a radical skepticism of free trade, withdrawing from NATO, kowtowing to dictators, and promoting inflationary easy-money policies from the Federal Reserve. Today it has also meant something else, and I've seen this firsthand as well: castigating anyone who refuses to go along with these newfound "conservative" policies. Nearly every day on Twitter, someone calls me out for not going along with some administration policy. They say something along the lines of: "You claim to be this great conservative, Rick! But look at you now, criticizing the president's policies on MSNBC!" And yet, I challenge them to name a position that I have changed on. Pro-life? Free trade? Immigration? Taxation? Foreign policy? Deficit spending? As of yet, no one has been able to name a policy that I've changed my mind on. I'm sure there's legitimate criticism of what I believe, but it's not legitimate to say that I've significantly changed my mind on any policy issue since the 2016 election. In fact, listening to my fellow Republicans today defend policies antithetical to conservative principles is like watching someone gnaw on a piece of raw meat while telling you they are a vegan.

Ultimately, these criticisms and the fact that conservatism has been so distorted by not only those supposedly opposed to it but its self-proclaimed adherents led me to write this book. I believe that I speak for many true conservatives who have been asking: *what the hell is going on?*

My hope is that by helping people understand conservative principles and how they apply to public policy, they might come to see why conservatism remains an attractive governing philosophy.

This book is not intended to be a refutation of Donald Trump and the policies of his administration; nevertheless his policies will be examined through a critical conservative lens. George Will recently wrote a book about conservatism but avoided mentioning Trump altogether. That's clever, but I've found it impossible to explain conservatism and avoid the mention of Donald Trump—if for no other reason than understanding what conservatism *is* sometimes requires understanding what conservatism *is not*. It is true that conservatives can disagree on minor points and the implementation of conservatism to particular policies (after all, a "Goldwater conservative" might disagree with a "Reagan conservative"). Nevertheless, there are elements of conservatism that have long been considered essential, and the chapters in this book seek to highlight those elements. But if conservatism no longer professes any of those beliefs, the term "conservatism" is rendered meaningless. To use the term "Trump conservative," for instance, is not to nuance an existing belief but to deny conservatism altogether. In order to distinguish ourselves, maybe we should call ourselves the "Still Right."

This book is for an audience of conservatives who identify and define themselves as such because of *principle* rather than personality or party affiliation. It's also for those who may never identify as conservative and yet seek a better understanding of those of us who do. My hope is that this book will rise above the current level of political discourse and do something that is rarely done today: examine actual issues from a conservative perspective.

My hope is also that the reader becomes more familiar with the rationale for conservative philosophy and why it deserves consideration and thought. But perhaps even more so, I wish to identify for the reader what conservatism is not. While many want to paint conservatism as ugly and unwanted, she is neither. She is the progenitor of a free people.

I

WHAT IS CONSERVATISM AND WHERE DID IT COME FROM?

In the 1932 presidential election, President Herbert Hoover, whose relative hands-off approach to the economy provided an opportunity for Franklin Delano Roosevelt, whose relationship with another former president would cause him to upset traditional ideological alignments and brand the Democratic Party with a new and surprising label.

FDR's political career nearly mirrored that of his fifth cousin Theodore Roosevelt but without the legendary antics. TR lost a run for mayor of New York City but then rose through the political ranks serving as governor of New York and vice president under William McKinley. TR was a Republican and a progressive who unexpectedly became president when McKinley was shot by a deranged man in Buffalo, New York, in 1901. TR was forty-two when McKinley was assassinated, making him the youngest person ever to serve as president. Not dissimilar to today's progressives, TR governed by the philosophy that government was a tremendous force for good.

After winning the presidency in his own right in 1904, TR promised he would not seek another term. Though he came to regret it, true to his word he supported William Taft in the 1908 presidential race, who, once elected, began to unwind Roosevelt's progressive agenda. TR tried to deny Taft a second term by challenging him for the 1912 Republican Party nomination, but he was deftly outmaneuvered at the Republican National Convention. So enraged by the tactics of the Taft campaign, Roosevelt refused to have his name put in nomination. Weeks later, TR launched a progressive party that came to be known as the Bull Moose Party, and TR became its first and only presidential nominee.

The 1912 Democratic presidential nominee was another progressive: Woodrow Wilson. The race was largely a battle between two competing progressive agendas, Wilson's New Freedom and Roosevelt's New Nationalism. Wilson won with 41.9 percent of the vote, followed by Roosevelt with 27.4 percent, the largest third-party vote for president in American history. (Taft got 23.1 percent. The Socialist Party candidate and labor leader, Eugene Debs, got 6 percent.) Wilson, however, won an impressive 435 electoral votes compared to 88 for Roosevelt and 8 for Taft. Having restored a mandate for his brand of progressivism, Wilson would serve for two terms.

After Wilson's eight years in the White House and the First World War, America was ready for a change. They found it in Republican Warren Harding, who won the 1920 campaign on the slogan "Return to Normalcy." He died less than two years into his presidency. Calvin Coolidge, his vice president, succeeded him. After six years as president, serving out the two-year remainder of Harding's term and his own four-year term, Coolidge decided not to seek reelection.

Herbert Hoover was elected in the 1928 presidential campaign on the slogan "A Chicken in Every Pot and a Car in Every Garage." Herbert Hoover's slogan is both ironic and appropriate on several levels. First, the slogan was appropriate because before the stock market crash that began the Great Depression, Hoover had earned a solid reputation as a humanitarian. He led food-relief efforts in both China and Europe as a private citizen and a businessman. So impressive were his efforts that Wilson asked him to lead the United States Food Administration, which provided American farm products to American troops serving overseas during the war. Second, Hoover's slogan implied the continuation of good economic times; it did not imply new government programs to provide poultry and automobiles. Finally, his slogan would come back to bite Hoover as the Great Depression dragged on and led to his defeat and the subsequent expansion of the welfare state. Hoover would live three decades after leaving the White House. His reputation, however, would never recover from the 1932 campaign.

FDR modeled his political path after that of the patriarch of the Oyster Bay Roosevelts. The family relation invited comparisons of which there were many similarities. FDR, a Democrat, did not support his Republican cousin's 1912 quixotic quest for another term but instead campaigned for his party's nominee, Woodrow Wilson. FDR's partisan loyalty was rewarded, and Wilson appointed him assistant US Navy secretary, a post TR occupied fifteen years earlier. FDR by all accounts was his cousin's ideological twin and had admired TR's agenda, but by 1932 a darker side to progressivism had emerged under Wilson.

The progressive movement spearheaded women's suffrage (giving women the right to vote), created the National Parks System, and sought to tame free market excesses and champion the rights of workers, but progressive policies also led to the 1913 passage of the Seventeenth Amendment, severing the 125-year constitutionally designed influence state legislatures had in the federal government by moving to a popular vote to elect US senators. Progressives also passed Prohibition in a time of prosperity, promoted foreign adventurism in an era of isolationism, and fostered racism and its handmaiden, eugenics.

Woodrow Wilson, a dedicated racist like many progressives at the time, put his faith fully in contemporary scientific conclusions to provide solutions to a host of societal ills from health to crime to poverty. In the late nineteenth and early twentieth centuries, Social Darwinism was largely accepted as "settled science" providing the justification for the horrendous practices the eugenics movement was advocating in the name of humanity. Their firm belief was that scientists and their evidence should be the dominant factor in determining socioeconomic policies based on scientific consensus. In the case of eugenics, the consensus was that defective traits like impaired cognitive ability in human beings could be eliminated within a generation if the government—through the practice of forced sterilization—were legally authorized to regulate procreation and decide who could and could not produce offspring.

By 1932, the evolution of progressivism had run its course. Beginning at the turn of the century under TR, progressivism went from advocating government expansion as a positive force for good to a pernicious proliferation of government power under Wilson. And that might have been the end of it. But it got a new life under a new name.

FDR, who could easily have been labeled a progressive—the moniker advanced and worn proudly by TR—rejected the label: First, because FDR was a Democrat who could ill afford to be seen following in his cousin's footsteps, a Republican, the party of Hoover. Second, since progressive policies so dominated the early twentieth century, the case might be convincingly argued that they had been the root cause of all the country's current economic woes.

So Roosevelt did something clever: he rebranded himself. FDR sold his "New Deal" progressive policy solutions to fix the economic crisis, and he sold himself as "liberal," a word stemming from the word "liberty." The branding stuck. Up until Roosevelt reappropriated the word to himself, it had most strongly been used to identify those who adhered to Edmund Burke's philosophy—liberalism.

The opponents of FDR's liberalism began calling themselves conservatives, thus the traditional ideological labels reversed themselves in the American political system. Liberals who advocated limited government power were now conservatives, and conservatives who argued for stronger centralized government power were now liberals.

At the same time, to confuse matters more, the Communists that grew out of the Bolsheviks in the Russian Revolution were protecting their ideological brand as well. Their main European ideological competitor was the National Socialist German Workers' Party—the Nazis. The Communists were competing to own the left end of the spectrum; in order to distinguish themselves as the true party of "workers," they branded the socialist Nazis as "the right." It stuck.

Both Communism (not in its pure and unattainable form but its stepchild Marxism) and Socialism rely on a powerful centralized government structure to organize every aspect of society. They are Leftist philosophies. Conservatism advocates limiting the power of the state specifically so it does not grow to resemble the rejected twentieth-century philosophies of Communism and Socialism that led to so much suffering and death.

Let's be clear, however. No one should attempt to brand the left end of the political spectrum or the political party—the Democrats that mostly occupy that space—as anything close to the Nazis. But what needs pointing out is that Socialism—as the ideology that adheres to the political philosophy that government and not the private sector should control the commanding heights of industry and distribution of resources—was also the philosophy of the Nazi Party. The point is that today, the "right" branding by the Communists—who wanted to be and still are ideologically left of the Socialists—allows ignorant talking heads on television to declare that right-thinking conservatives are the same as Nazis. In fact, though, classic liberalism—or American conservatism, which embraces freedom and the free market—has absolutely nothing in common with Nazi governing philosophy.

Similarly, it would be absurd to make a case that Vermont senator and twice presidential candidate Bernie Sanders would advance a revolution, as he's prone to call it, to bring about a government resembling the Third Reich. However, Sanders—the son of Jewish refugees who fled Poland to escape the Nazis—rose to become a US senator and was in the most advantageous position to have availed himself of the twentieth century's greatest lessons in governance which were the epic failures of centralized power. He did not.

During the unprecedented twelve-year presidency of FDR, "conservatism" was being replaced by Socialism's lesser twin, Collectivism, the belief that society should be directed by big government and enormous social programs.

Fast-forward fourscore and four years and another master of

rebranding similarly won the White House with a clever deception. Donald J. Trump was for most of his life a registered Democrat. He at one point enrolled in Ross Perot's Reform Party, where he briefly sought the party's nomination for president. Then he joined the Republican Party and won the GOP nomination in 2016. Party switchers are not entirely unusual. Winston Churchill famously switched allegiances when it suited his political purposes. But Trump wasn't just selling himself as a Republican; he was branding himself a conservative.

For most of Trump's life, he never spoke for the conservative cause. He was not known to have supported conservative candidates for office. In fact quite the opposite, he made numerous contributions to liberal Democrats. He also never attended events where conservatives gathered—most notably CPAC, the Conservative Political Action Conference—until 2011, when he spoke as a reality TV star, beginning his courtship with conservatives.

People change and positions change and converts to the cause should always be welcome. But Trump never acknowledged that he changed his positions on abortion, trade, federal spending, the deficit, the debt, foreign policy, healthcare, property rights, free markets, and monetary policy—in every one of these policies Trump was 180 degrees out of phase with commonly understood conservative thought. Instead, candidate Trump asked us to accept a different reality—his reality. When Trump became president, he simply redefined what conservatism was. Shockingly, most self-identified conservatives cultishly accepted the new ambiguously twisted conservatism and jumped aboard the Trump train. Left behind were the guiding principles of conservatism that gave the Republican Party its governing philosophy. Left standing on the station platform were a relatively few who, rejecting the politics of personality, didn't heed the "all aboard" call and refused to board.

Politicians most often allow their desire for reelection to trump their desire for good and wise leadership. Edmund Burke said that these politicians simply "make themselves bidders at an auction of popularity," in order to "outbid" political rivals with false promises.[1] That's another of Burke's observations that's as true today as it was yesterday. And will be tomorrow. Politicians routinely make promises based on two fears. The first is safety, which involves issues ranging from neighborhood crime to global war. The second is predictability, which involves issues related to health, the economy, jobs, inflation, and interest rates. On those two unknowable future conditions hang all the fears most Americans have. Yet, as COVID-19 searing illustrates, no politician can guarantee safety or make the world more predictable. They can promote policies that might reduce crime, keep us out of war, grow the economy, create jobs, or stave off a pandemic, but it is foolish to believe political promises provide immunity from adverse future events.

In the 1980s, Ronald Reagan's stances on pro-life, low taxes, limited government, parental rights, free trade, and Second Amendment freedom advanced the conservative cause from the White House. One of the reasons for his policy success is that unlike previous Republican presidents who came to Washington, Reagan had the benefit of a previously nonexistent entity: a conservative policy think tank that set up shop on Massachusetts Avenue, just steps away from the Senate side of the Capitol. The Heritage Foundation, founded in 1973, began to provide conservatives in Congress sound research to support conservative policy solutions. By 1980, Heritage published *Mandate for Leadership: Policy Management in a Conservative Administration,* which was largely adopted by the Reagan administration. Even today, Reagan is still known as the most conservative president in modern history. But he was also the most likeable. (Lest we forget, in Reagan's reelection of 1984, he managed to win forty-nine states.) Even many of those who publicly castigated Reagan's policies privately admitted that they liked him. Today, for the most part, he is remembered fondly—even affectionately. For instance, a 2018 poll of Americans aged fifty-four to ninety asked the respondents who they considered the best president in their lifetimes. Overwhelmingly, it was Ronald Reagan.[2] Republican candidates are aware of polls like this, as they are aware of the fact that Reagan is considered the most conservative president ever. Therefore, the recipe for Republican candidates seemed rather obvious: especially among older voters, compare yourself to Reagan whenever you can and claim you're a conservative just like him.

From the perspective of crude politics, it worked; from the perspective of honesty, it's often pure nonsense. Today, fewer and fewer Republicans claim to be Reaganites, and that is expected as time passes, but many who claim to be conservative haven't the foggiest notion about what conservatism is. Of course, that won't stop people from making the claim. The problem is that these comparisons damage not only the memory of Reagan but also the conservative brand. Though not all conservatives agree on every minute detail of every policy, it is dishonest (not to mention simply incorrect) to ascribe conservatism to someone who disregards or disbelieves its fundamental tenets (as we will explore in the subsequent chapters). And if the moniker "conservative" can be assigned to anyone regardless of his or her political stances, then the word "conservative" loses its meaning altogether.

One further point I want to emphasize here regards the nature of government. Conservatism advocates limited government, but that does not mean the absence of government. Conservatism is about ordered liberty with the recognition that order requires a properly functioning government, and liberty requires it to be limited to stay within those proper functions. Put another way, while conservatives do believe in a smaller, less powerful centralized government, they are not anti-government. They are simply pro–limited government. That brings us to the topic of libertarianism.

The word "libertarianism" is so widely defined that it has come to mean almost anything (an unfortunate circumstance that it shares with conservatism). It can simply mean the desire for less government and more individual freedom. If so, conservatives and libertarians might find themselves in virtual agreement; in the premiere issue of the *National Review*, Buckley identifies with this libertarianism.

But the sort of libertarianism that calls for the total absence of

government—anarchy—finds no agreement. This hard-core libertarianism was advanced by Ayn Rand, author of *Atlas Shrugged*. Ayn
Rand's name sometimes arises in conservative discussions and *Atlas Shrugged* often appears on the bookshelves of conservatives. One
hopes that it appears alongside Marx's *Communist Manifesto* as the
result of carefully deliberated cataloguing. Ayn Rand was not a conservative any more than Karl Marx was a conservative. Ayn Rand
not only rejected religion as a dangerous force in society but also
went even further, claiming that altruism—kindness and generosity
toward others—should be rejected by society. A proponent of abortion, she was also a materialist, meaning that she believed there was
nothing beyond this life and certainly no immutable moral order. In
Atlas Shrugged (a political screed masquerading as a novel), Rand's
character directly mocks Christianity writing a dollar sign in the
dirt as a final act of defiance.[3] In fact, Ayn Rand frequently wore
a dollar sign as a lapel pin—her homage to American economic
freedom but it served as more of an illustration of her allegiance to
mammon. She not only rejected the recognized tenets of conservatism but also conservatism by name, saying that conservatism was
mired in "the God, family, tradition swamp."[4] It is said of Ayn Rand
that after achieving her fame she refused to enter any room in which
people did not recognize her brilliance. After the *National Review*'s
Whittaker Chambers wrote a scathing review of *Atlas Shrugged* in
1957, she also refused to go to any party where Bill Buckley might
be.[5] How Ayn Rand and her books found a way into conservative
discussions is curious; why conservatives might claim her as an advocate requires a serious misreading of her books and misinterpre-
tation of her stated views. But this is sure: at the point where Ayn
Rand is being called a conservative, the all-inclusive use of the term
has become ridiculous.

Much has been written about conservative philosophy by far more
eloquent writers. Most resisted speaking for all conservatives, and
I shall do likewise. But what conservatives do have in common—
some of which is not unique to them—is a reverence for life, a love of

liberty, and a belief in the power of the individual, which correlates nicely with life, liberty, and the pursuit of happiness.

Central to that pursuit is our ability to create. Our inherent creative nature takes on many forms from innovation and invention, to engineering and design, to art and music. To deny our right to create is to deny our humanity. That is why the conservative philosophy rejects government interference in the creative process. This principle is demonstrated in an immigration policy that recognizes the individual right to be free to improve one's circumstance rather than be limited by the coincidence of one's birthplace. The right to create is a trade policy that recognizes that consumers should not be denied the full range of products in the marketplace, and producers should have the right to compete globally and not have their markets arbitrarily limited.

Because the right to create is so central to being human, conservatives believe that it is the burden of the proponents of a new government program to prove that government involvement is necessary, and not the burden of conservatives to prove government involvement unnecessary. Moreover, conservatives support protecting life, justice, a strong defense, a leadership role in the world, low taxes, and maintaining a government with a firm check on power to its constitutionally prescribed limits. Neither the core tenets of conservatism nor the policies guided by them are new. They are tried and true. While conservatives are very willing to embrace new technologies, new ideas, and new strategies, conservatives view them through the lens of the core values to which they hold fast. So where did these ideas come from?

On March 22, 1775—at almost the exact moment Patrick Henry was giving his famous "Give me liberty or give me death!" speech in Richmond, Virginia—a member of the British Parliament rose to deliver a speech that infuriated his colleagues as much as Henry's speech electrified his fellow colonists. In the London Parliament full of MPs who were determined to seize even greater control of the American colonies, Edmund Burke, who never set foot in the Western

Hemisphere, for "two and a half hours" argued one of the most spirited defenses of America in history.[6]

Burke's speech focused on the unique character of the American people, observing that the "fierce spirit of liberty is stronger in the English colonies, probably, than in any other people of the earth." After all, Burke posited, the colonists were "descendants of Englishmen," who loved liberty.

He noted the Americans' fascination and proficiency in law: "In no country, perhaps, in the world is the law so general a study." American resistance was not mindless; rather, it was rooted in natural and divine law. The colonists' benevolent obsession with good governance made them natural objectors to government corruption—so much so that they could anticipate political injustice. Burke says the Americans "snuff the approach of tyranny in every tainted breeze," and they won't stand for tyranny. How do you conquer a people like that? Burke's answer was that you cannot.

As Burke put it, "Three thousand miles of ocean lie between you and them. No contrivance can prevent the effect of this distance in weakening government." (In doing so, Burke was making an argument against something that would later be called nation building.) Further, the British trade with America had been surprisingly beneficial, and a violent response by the British would have negative consequences for the empire.

The proper course of action Burke argued was not aggression but conciliation: "The proposition is peace. Not peace through the medium of war" but "peace sought in the spirit of peace."[7] Though his resolution for peace was soundly defeated in Parliament, his speech was a great source of encouragement to the American colonists.

Burke's ideas about society—conciliation over war if possible, the benefit of religion, limited government, economic freedom, the rights of family, and private property—were largely accepted and furthered by Americans in the decades that followed. But very early in the twentieth century this body of belief came into doubt. A number of developments driven by the progressive movement in America might have caused Burke to shudder: America's involvement in World War I, the passage of big anti-trade laws including high tariffs, the passage of the Sixteenth Amendment that created a permanent income tax, antitrust legislation, and currency manipulation that created (to borrow a phrase from former Federal Reserve chairman Alan Greenspan) "irrational exuberance" on Wall Street. All of these factors conspired to create the conditions that led to the Great Depression.

By the early 1950s, after the conclusion of the Second World War, it seemed as though conservatism didn't even have a voice in America. But it was about to have one, and it came from an unlikely source: a brash twenty-five-year-old recent graduate of Yale University named William F. Buckley Jr.

The publication of Buckley's 1951 book, *God and Man at Yale,* took him from obscurity to instant fame. In the book, Buckley observes that the curriculum and professors at Yale University had undergone a radical shift in recent years. Once, Yale had fostered a belief in Christianity, liberty, and human creativity; now it was casting those things into doubt even to the point of mockery in the classroom and replacing them with a belief in collectivism. The book caused an absolute firestorm in America, more by critics than defenders—at least initially. As you might expect, most of the faculty at Yale (especially those who were named in the book) weren't exactly ecstatic over Buckley's writing, but you also might wonder why a book like this would matter to anyone outside of Yale. The answer is that Buckley presented Yale as a microcosm of what was beginning to happen more broadly in American society.

Though Buckley doesn't mention Burke, many of his observations echo Burke—first and foremost that society was undergoing something akin to revolution. This was manifested in the fact that many of the stabilizing elements of society were becoming destabilized.

Government becoming more involved in decisions that had always belonged to families. He observed that the rights of private property were coming under attack while the entire free market system was looked at with increasing suspicion. On the subject of taxation, Buckley's view was that increasing taxation constituted a lack of representation because it shifted economic power from the individual to the government.

(Although he doesn't mention it in this book, but rather in subsequent writings, one issue about which Buckley was completely wrong in his younger years was segregation. By his early thirties, he realized he had been wrong. As a biographer of his notes, Buckley stated in a 2004 interview: "I once believed we could evolve our way up from Jim Crow. I was wrong. Federal intervention was necessary."[8])

Regarding the role of religion in society, Buckley announced, "I myself believe that the duel between Christianity and atheism is the most important in the world. I further believe that the struggle between individualism and collectivism is the same struggle reproduced on another level."[9] Put another way, if there is no God, the government is the highest possible authority; thus, government is given free rein to control the citizens' lives as best it sees fit. (In his introduction to the twenty-fifth anniversary edition of his book, Buckley observes that this belief has even crept into the minds of many Christians who believe "that the road to Christianity on earth lies through the federal government."[10]) With the publication of God and Man at Yale, a new political movement was born not out of a new philosophy but rather the restatement of lost ideas that had dominated political thinking a century earlier.

The dominant political framework up until the early twentieth century had been to allow citizens to pursue the practice of virtuous and wise liberty—both political and economic—while still maintaining order in society. Edmund Burke pointed out that since "liberty and restraint" are opposite elements, getting the balance right would prove to be no easy task for those in government. Nevertheless, Burke considered it impossible to achieve order in society without good government. But he also understood that not all those who serve in elected government are always so noble.

LOOKING FORWARD

In contrast to Rand's libertarianism, conservatism is largely *about* serving others. It is a caricature of conservatives that promoting free market capitalism means we only care about making money for ourselves. First, however, the reality is that many conservatives really do try to love one another. A blanket characterization to the contrary is not only unfair but also statistically inaccurate.[11] Second, making money is very difficult without supplying goods and services that will improve the lives of others. Third, if the goal is to help alleviate poverty, conservatives regard free market capitalism as the best way to fulfill that objective. The free market's detractors are quick to point to capitalism's flaws. Conservatives should be equally quick to concede that the free market is imperfect—but like just about everything in life—it is also imperfectible. As Antonin Scalia phrased it; our burden is not to show how the free market is *perfect* but rather to show how it is a *better* system than its rivals. There should be no doubt that the main attraction of free market capitalism is that it can broadly better human lives. Admittedly, conservatives too often do a lousy job of communicating that we care deeply about the lives of others. Instead of discussing the free market in terms mired in impersonal data and statistics, conservative need to learn to tell meaningful stories to make their arguments stick.

To further resist the hijacking of conservatism for political expediency, we must also call out those who claim to be conservatives and then spew anti-conservative nonsense. The previous few years have served to confirm that the words "Republican" and "conservative" are not synonymous. They found themselves most closely aligned during the Reagan years, but as with most planetary alignments, it didn't last for long. In fact, the transition started with George H. W. Bush.

Today, there are precious few voices that represent a conservative recognizable to those who founded the movement. Moving forward, the recipe is simple: to restate and advance a conservatism Edmund Burke would recognize. In this, I hope the chapters that follow are part of that process.

2

THE MORALITY
OF FREE TRADE

The story is told that Margaret Thatcher was once sitting in a high-level meeting of Britain's conservatives. At this gathering, a tepid politician made a speech about how the Conservative Party should timidly approach the subject of economics and fiscal policy. The politician was being very careful not to upset the applecart of British politics by embracing an openly pro-market stance. One can only imagine how infuriated Thatcher became during this monologue, growing more exasperated with each concessionary syllable. As the politician hemmed and hawed to try to decipher what it is that he and his party believed, droning on about a third way between Socialism and free market capitalism, Thatcher could take it no more. She sprung from her seat, grabbed a book from her purse, held it up high, and solemnly announced: "*This* is what we believe!" After pronouncing her pro-capitalism verdict, Thatcher threw down the book like a gavel on the table. The book? Friedrich Hayek's *Constitution of Liberty*.

Hayek's central economic thesis in that book is that wealth is the result of liberty, not government coercion. As Hayek puts it, "The argument for liberty is not an argument against organization, which is one of the most powerful tools human reason can employ, but an argument against all exclusive, privileged, monopolistic organization, against the use of coercion to prevent others from doing better."[1] No matter which government imposes it, it is nevertheless true that government "coercion to prevent others from doing better" serves as a definition of anti-trade policies. Free trade is a principle of conservatism because it places individual liberty in society over the collective power of government. Free trade is about individual liberty, while tariffs are about governmental power. For conservatism, foreign trade has always been considered an essential ingredient of liberty.

If the belief in the rights of private property serves as the heart in the body of economic conservatism, the belief in free trade serves as its head. After all, if man does not possess the right to voluntarily exchange goods, is his property private after all? As conservative philosopher Russell Kirk put it, radicals love to "hack at the institution of private property."[2] And the imposition of trade restrictions is one of those hacks, as Hayek and Thatcher observed.

Of course, they weren't the first to recognize this; although we could say that the importance of free trade goes back to Aristotle and even further, we could say that the conservative view of free trade has a proud origin in Adam Smith. Whether by divine guidance or sheer coincidence, Smith's book *The Wealth of Nations* was published the same year that America declared her independence from the British. Half a world away, the same year Adam Smith was highlighting the virtues of free trade, Thomas Jefferson was condemning the vices opposed to free trade, listing "cutting off our Trade with all parts of the world" as a line item in his list of grievances against King George in the Declaration of Independence.

Both Smith and Jefferson were objecting to the same basic philosophy: mercantilism, which was the belief that wealth is a zero-sum game that is won by having more materials—in some cases specifically gold and silver—than your neighboring countries. Under that scenario, trade was considered a bad political policy because it enriched a country's neighbors. Thus, mercantilism professes that trade must be prohibited, even if it hurts the economic good of the home nation. Adam Smith takes umbrage with this philosophy, writing:

> *A nation that would enrich itself by foreign trade, is certainly most likely to do so when its neighbors are all rich, industrious, and commercial nations. A great nation surrounded on all sides by wandering savages and poor barbarians, might, no doubt, acquire riches by the cultivation of its own lands, and by its own interior commerce, but not by foreign trade . . . The modern maxims of foreign commerce, by aiming at the impoverishment of all our neighbours, so far as they are capable of producing their intended effect, tend to render that very commerce insignificant and contemptible.*[3]

In short, if we want to be prosperous, we should want our neighbors to be prosperous; we can help each other by trading freely. In terms of economics, this is clear; the problem is that we don't always use the principles of economics to formulate our opinions. Something in fallen human nature seems to root against the prosperity of our neighbors. In *Wealth and Poverty*—the book that served as the philosophical underpinning for Reaganomics—George Gilder writes: "The belief that the good fortune of others is also finally one's own does not come easily or invariably to the human breast. It is, however, a golden rule of economics, a key to peace and prosperity, a source of the gifts of progress."[4]

But if we are to table our vices, we can make further discoveries of economics, namely: it is not just that trade is good; it is that trade is one of the biggest wealth creators of them all. And refusing to trade is one of the biggest sources of poverty. Smith writes:

> *By means of glasses, hotbeds, and hot-walls, very good grapes can be raised in Scotland, and very good wine too can be made of them, at about thirty times the expense for which at least equally good can be brought from foreign countries. Would it be a reasonable law to prohibit the importation of all foreign wines, merely to encourage the making of claret and Burgundy in Scotland? . . . Whether the*

advantages which one country has over another, be natural or ac-
quired, is in this respect of no consequence. As long as the one coun-
try has those advantages, and the other wants them, it will always
be more advantageous for the latter, rather to buy of the former than
to make.[5]

Smith's logic is sound: why halt the import of something that costs thirty times less than it can be produced in the home country? Of course, in response to Adam Smith's question, we could think of one group who might benefit from a wine tariff or embargo: the winemakers of Scotland. But they may not benefit, either. Why not? Because at a certain price, almost no one will buy wine at all. If the average bottle of wine costs $10 and a tariff escalates the price to $300, there will be less wine sold; this is a simple matter of price's effect on demand. There exists the idea that protection- ism protects the industry, but very often it destroys the industry. (The Trump administration's steel tariffs put some smaller steel companies out of business.[6]) It also prompts the question: Which industries should we protect? Should we protect some industries and not others? And why *not* those? If you're going to protect the wine industry, why not protect the greeting card industry? Many times, it's not a matter of economics that determines those answers but who lobbies the hardest. If an entire industry needs protection, that's a clear sign that we should let someone else produce and im- port their product or service.

And there's another problem: inflation. The prices of goods in protected industries will rise. After all, that's the stated intention of protective tariffs: employees ostensibly will make more money. But the inescapable downside to this is that the prices of these goods will rise. Every human *producer* is also a *consumer,* and while he or she as a producer has higher wages, he or she as a consumer will pay more for tariffed goods. As classical French economist Claude- Frédéric Bastiat put it: "Is it true that the policy of protectionism, which admittedly makes you pay higher prices for everything, and in that respect harms you, also brings about a proportional increase in your wages?"[7] But if nations simply followed free trade, this should allow wealth to boom.

What's the logic in domestically producing a product that could be imported more cheaply? According to nineteenth-century economist David Ricardo, it doesn't make much sense at all. Adam Smith had argued that a free market creates an invisible hand that guides the economy to efficient production. With his law of comparative advantage, Ricardo takes that concept a step further by applying it not to just one nation but to all of them. Ricardo writes: "Under a system of perfectly free commerce, each country naturally devotes capital and labour to such employments as are most beneficial to each."[8]

As Ricardo explains, free trade stimulates people to specialize—to produce goods and services that they are best at producing. This promotes their inherent strengths, taking into account their unique skill sets and their geographical resources. Ricardo uses the example of French wine, but he could have used Swiss watches, Brazilian sugar, Italian suits, or California avocados. Because each person and each group of persons are doing what they are best at, not only does the nation itself benefit, but the other nations benefit as well. By contrast, the lack of free trade brought about by tariffs impels and compels people to attempt to produce goods and services for which they are inefficiently suited, hurting all countries involved. Obviously, free trade is not the only factor in the success of an economy—as things like overregulation, overtaxation, inflation, and Wall Street cronyism can stifle an otherwise brisk economy—but free trade contributes to the maximization of overall productivity.

The quote by Ricardo above also leads to another aspect that has long been considered a chief good of free trade: peace. Ricardo's comments that trade "binds together, by one common tie of interest and intercourse" and fosters a "universal society of nations throughout the civilized world" is a pretty big claim.[9] Yet his claim is not only backed up historically but it can also be observed currently. In 1996, perhaps as a result of his travels across the globe, *New York Times* columnist Thomas Friedman noticed a bizarre pattern among the nations of the world—or at least one that seemed bizarre at first glance. It was an insight about the relation between free market capitalism and peace. When Friedman made the pithy observation, it must have been maddening to others that they had not seen it first. Friedman expressed it thus: "No two countries that both have a McDonald's have ever fought a war against each other."[10] Dubbed "the golden arches theory of conflict prevention," critics were quick to point out the few cases where this rule did not apply, such as the 1989 US military action in Panama. The critics, however, were far too dismissive of Friedman's underlying thesis: free market nations do not tend to go to war with each other.

The key part of the equation is not that those who enjoy Big Macs suddenly discover an existential affinity with each other but that those who *trade* with each other develop a symbiotic relationship. Importing scarce and/or expensive goods into your own country while reciprocally exporting goods that are scarce and/or expensive in another is the greatest recipe for friendship in the history of international relations. Trading partners are just that: partners. With a slight adjustment to Friedman's point, what prevents conflict is not French fries but free trade.

Thomas Friedman can take only so much credit for this insight.[11] After all, the same basic observation was made centuries earlier by a figure who proved influential to America's founders. His name was Charles-Louis de Secondat, Baron de La Brède et de Montesquieu. Known to his contemporaries simply as Montesquieu, he was repeatedly mentioned and quoted at length by both Alexander Hamilton and James Madison in *The Federalist Papers*. For his part, Montesquieu opined that "peace is the natural effect of trade."[12] And attached to that positive observation, Montesquieu had a negative warning: "When two nations come into contact with one another they either fight or trade. If they fight, both lose; if they trade, both gain."[13] Back to Thomas Friedman's point, the reality is not simply that McDonald's-loving countries do not fight with each other but that countries without McDonald's do.

"If they trade, both gain."

That seems about as intuitive as economics gets, yet it's worth remembering: every tariff, at some level, is a rejection of that principle. Clearly, that does not prevent leaders and congresses from imposing them, as the American people discovered in the 1920s and 1930s.

THE SMOOT-HAWLEY TARIFF ACT

There was a time in America when imposing a tariff on worm gut, which was used in fishing tackle and surgical sutures, was considered so essential that it warranted an act of Congress and the signature of a president. Of course, it wasn't just the producers of worm gut who were seeking protection; it was the producers of thousands and thousands of other products. And the logic was that trade restrictions against foreign imports of these products was the best way to protect Americans and the American economy. It was called the Smoot-Hawley Tariff Act, named for two Republican senators, Reed Smoot and Willis Hawley.

Reed Smoot had represented the state of Utah in the US Senate since his election in 1902. Utah had become a state just six years prior to his election, and Smoot promoted himself as the state's biggest defender. Already by 1914, Smoot's fawning biographer lists "The Tariff" as Smoot's main legislative interest, viewing trade restrictions as the optimal way to protect Utah's wool and mining industries.[14] Smoot is generically remembered as being a "businessman," but Smoot's business was (as you might have already guessed) wool and mining. The Republican Party was pro-tariff, but much of that was due to the influence of Smoot, as he was the chairman of the Senate Finance Committee for the decade leading up to the legislation that bears his name.

Prior to his election as a congressman and then as US senator from Oregon, Willis Hawley had served as the president of Willamette University. Prior to that, Hawley had been a teacher of mathematics, history, and economics—three disciplines that should have discouraged him from attaching his name to tariff legislation. Yet, something trumped all this knowledge: reelection. Hawley served in an agricultural district that demanded protection from European farmers. (That might explain the existence of the worm gut tariff.) No tariff against foreign farmers—however high it may have been—seemed to satiate the farmers in his district, who seemed to prefer skipping the tariff altogether and just embracing a full embargo.

Smoot-Hawley's potential merits and demerits were argued from the floor of Congress for many months before its passage. Eventually passed by the House of Representatives in 1929, the tariff act began to do damage before it was even signed into law. In the light of history, the official congressional description of Smoot-Hawley—"To provide revenue, to regulate commerce with foreign countries, to encourage the industries of the United States, to protect American labor, and for other purposes"—is dripping with irony.[15] In truth, Smoot-Hawley angered allies, obliterated the stock market, vaporized wealth and capital, led to widespread unemployment, and mercilessly drained the oil from the engine of American capitalism.

When the Affordable Care Act, known also as "Obamacare," was up for debate and vote, there were those who complained that the bill was long, boring, and nonsensical. In its defense, however, the Smoot-Hawley Tariff Act made the Obamacare bill look like a Tom Clancy thriller. Smoot-Hawley consisted of thousands of paragraphs complete with an array of dizzying subsections, providing a tariff schedule for seemingly every commodity known to man—as well as a few theretofore unknown commodities. For instance, paragraph 1,533 of Smoot-Hawley provides the tariff rate for a certain group of items that most Americans may not have even known existed: "Catgut, whip gut, oriental gut, and manufactures thereof, and manufactures of worm gut, not specially provided for, 40 per centum ad valorem."[16] A 40 percent additional tax seems pretty steep, but after all—the logic went—we need to protect American workers. Of course, this prompts the question: was there a time when America was leading in the worm gut industry, and Republicans were afraid that the United

States might be relegated to second place? I can see it now, passing into Bad Axe, Michigan: "Welcome to Bad Axe. Population 1,129. Third-largest producer of worm gut in the Tri-State, and mighty proud of it!"

In title 1, section 1, paragraph 34, Smoot-Hawley lays out a 10 percent tariff schedule for "drugs, such as barks, beans, berries, buds, bulbs, bulbous roots, excrescences, fruits, flowers, dried fibers, dried insects, grains, herbs, leaves, lichens, mosses, roots, stems, vegetables, seeds (aromatic, not garden seeds), seeds of morbid growth, weeds, and all other drugs of vegetable or animal origin."[17] The moral of the story? Worm gut has four times the tariff duty of dried insects. (Unless they're *aromatic* dried insects. That's a whole different story.)

Smoot-Hawley was exacting in its madness.

That brings us to another issue with Smoot-Hawley in particular and tariff ordinances in general: namely, the arbitrary nature of the tariffs. Everyone knows that most bills—to a more or less degree—are the result of lobbying Congress. After all, we are a nation of pork barrel projects. But Smoot-Hawley was uniquely shameless in the arbitrariness of it all. Even if one admits the need for tariffs, why the enormous gap between the tariff on one product versus another? Smoot-Hawley was bantered about for eighteen months, which must have been the glory days of lobbyists—each one trying to get a higher tariff imposed for the foreign versions of his company's product. (It is forever a blight on the worm gut lobby that they were unable to persuade Congress to raise the ad valorem tariff on their flagship product.)

One group that wasn't laughing was America's trading allies. In fact, though it's difficult to anger all your allies with a single piece of congressional legislation, Smoot-Hawley came pretty close. Charles P. Kindleberger, author of *The World in Depression, 1929–1939*, notes that no fewer than thirty foreign powers made formal complaints against the act.[18] Author Amity Shlaes reminds us that as late as May 5, 1930, a group of more than one thousand "economists signed an open letter urging the president to veto the tariff legislation—and published the letter in the *New York Times*."[19] Essentially, the letter argued from the standpoint of classical economics that tariffs would be inflationary and "subsidize waste" and ultimately that "few people could hope to gain from such a change."[20] In the light of history, it can probably be said that these economists were never more right in their lives.

In the end, however, the input of thirty trading partners and one thousand economists wasn't enough to sway Congress or President Hoover, who signed Smoot-Hawley into law in 1930. After its passage, many affected foreign powers of the world punitively assessed their own retaliatory tariffs against the United States and all but refused to trade with the United States at all. Countries adopted the attitude that they would either produce it at home or not have it at all. As financial writer and retired neurologist William Bernstein put it: "By 1933 the entire globe seemed headed for what economists call autarky—a condition in which nations achieve self-sufficiency in all products, no matter how inept they are at producing them."[21]

Even those who attempted to trade found a difficult time doing so. It seems that in their desire to protect American jobs, the politicians forgot something: in a world of machinery, manufacturers rely on many different tools and parts from many different countries in order to make finished products. For instance, car companies didn't make their own screws; they bought the screws. And they didn't produce their own paint; they bought the paint. If it were as simple as screws and paint, they might easily be sourced in the United States. But with thousands of parts made all over the globe, it's easy to see how that could be a problem. In fact, the act increased the import tariff on more than eight hundred items that were used to build the American automobile. Of course, then the carmakers had an even bigger problem: retaliatory tariffs. Other countries decided to tariff American cars, and the buyers stopped buying. In 1929, Chevrolet and Ford combined to produce more than 2.8 million cars; by 1932, they produced just under 525,000.[22]

And it wasn't just the car industry that was being hurt by tariffs;

almost every manufacturing industry encountered similar challenges. Unable to obtain the necessary materials to finish their projects, business deals and contracts collapsed like dominoes falling across the world. Passed ostensibly to help the American workers, in reality the act had made it impossible for many Americans to work by limiting the material building blocks available to them.

The US stock market, always forward-looking and the most reliable leading indicator of America's economic health, almost immediately crashed. And that was only the beginning. History remembers 1929 as the year the market crashed, yet that fails to give a full and accurate accounting of what happened and why. The year 1929 saw the Dow Jones Industrial Average down 17 percent—certainly no banner year, but hardly apocalyptic. In the year 1930, however, something quite unpredicted occurred: between January and April, the stock market *rose* by about 20 percent. Whether it was rising on the hopes that Hoover would refuse to sign Smoot-Hawley into law is speculative, but this is certain: to that point, Hoover had not yet signed the legislation, and the market was rallying. It was in the weeks after Hoover signed Smoot-Hawley that the market fell off the table. Though the market had rallied in the first quarter, the full year 1930 saw the index lose more than 33 percent of its value. And yet the pain had still not subsided. In 1931, the first full year of Smoot-Hawley's implementation, the index lost almost 53 percent of its remaining value.

Many people—then and now—have blamed the stock market, but the market was only telling a truth, and the truth was that American productivity was almost unimaginably bad. The gross national product was plummeting. Specifically, in the two years following Smoot-Hawley, foreign imports fell more than 40 percent. And according to supply-side economist and senior Cato Institute fellow Alan Reynolds in the *National Review*, within a three-year span from 1929 to 1932, American exports fell from $7 billion to $2.5 billion.[23] Although the bill was envisioned to help the American worker, American unemployment numbers rose to a staggering 25 percent as soup lines replaced assembly lines.

In another historical irony, the three men chiefly responsible for the most damaging piece of anti-trade tariff legislation in history—a piece of legislation that had promised greater employment in America—lost their own jobs as the voters saw the tariff legislation play out. In 1932, American voters decided that they couldn't "use a man like Herbert Hoover again," and they weren't shy about telling him as much—in droves. Hoover lost in an epic landslide that saw Roosevelt receive almost 45 percent more popular votes than the incumbent president. But the repercussions were much more far-reaching than a single election: the election also saw a shift in power from the Republican Party to the Democratic Party that lasted generations. One can feel a sense of pathos for Hoover because even though the voting ballot said Hoover/Curtis, it might more appropriately have said Smoot/Hawley.

Of course, in the same election cycle, Smoot's name did appear on a ballot—on which he lost royally.

Hawley's reelection campaign didn't even get that far. Five-term incumbent senator Reed Smoot lost in the general election; thirteen-time incumbent representative Willis Hawley failed even to be renominated by his own party for the 1932 election. In another twist of historical irony, both Smoot and Hawley died within a few months of each other in 1941, just missing the onset of a world war that Montesquieu might have predicted their legislation had eventually helped cause. Montesquieu's observation that "when two nations come into contact with one another they either fight or trade" was proving itself right yet again. Nationalistic trade restrictions had made a toxic international situation even worse, and the world went to war.

Although economic historians have disagreed as to the extent of Smoot-Hawley's damage—some pointing to other carcinogenic factors at play, such as the bad monetary policy of the Federal Reserve and a politically disruptive Europe—there is essentially universal agreement among economists that Smoot-Hawley had a malignant impact on America's economy. In her book *The Forgotten Man*, Amity Shlaes writes that while there were various significant elements involved in the Great Depression, "the deepest problem was the intervention, the lack of faith in the marketplace."[24]

Ultimately, from a conservative perspective, this is the problem: there is no escaping the fact that tariffs, whomever may impose them, exhibit a lack of faith in the free market.

THE ARCHITECTS OF TARIFFS

As economist Milton Friedman has observed, the idea that free trade is an economic good is the most agreed-upon—and historically defensible—position among modern economists. Free trade is where the vast majority of classical economists and Keynesians—unable to come to terms on so many other issues—find common ground. The mountain of evidence in free trade's favor is impossible to ignore. Nevertheless, there are those who now reject free trade outright as a selling out of American sovereignty. There are also those defenders of President's Trump position on trade who continually make the argument that we can't look at what is going on *today;* we have to look at his long-term plan. In that spirit, there are those who argue that tariffs are a necessary evil, but they will eventually result in the good of free trade.

Here's the problem with that argument: President Trump has largely appointed those who are philosophically opposed to free trade. In fact, those most adamantly opposed to free trade achieved the highest positions in his administration, most notably Steve Bannon, Peter Navarro, and Wilbur Ross.

First White House chief strategist and perhaps the chief architect of Trumponomics, Steve Bannon is an outspoken anti–free trader.[25] Though one must apply a filter to Bannon's comments once it is recognized that he speaks almost exclusively in superlatives (Bannon has publicly proclaimed that Donald Trump was "the single greatest candidate in American history"[26] and "Donald Trump has done more for freedom and anti-racism in this country than anybody!"[27]), he used the term "economic hate crime" in reference to a policy that allows manufacturing jobs to move overseas,[28] and has referred to free trade as "a radical idea."[29]

Much of Bannon's antipathy toward free trade seems to center on an event concerning his father, Marty Bannon, that shaped Steve's political and economic worldview. As Steve Bannon relates this story, he speaks about the pivotal impact it had on him. So what happened that so profoundly affected this once-Reaganite thinker? The story goes like this. During the stock market panic of 2008, Marty Bannon had become increasingly worried that his stock in AT&T (also Marty Bannon's former employer) was falling in price. Unable to stomach the stock loss any longer, in desperation, the senior Bannon decided to sell his stock at around $26 a share, reportedly taking a capital loss of more than $100,000. "The only net worth my father had besides his tiny little house was that AT&T stock," Bannon insists. "And nobody is held accountable? All these firms get bailed out. There's no equity taken from anybody. There's no one in jail." This incident changed Steve Bannon's outlook on American capitalism. As he puts it, "Everything since then has come from there," there meaning that incident.[30]

While I wholeheartedly agree with his disconnected point about corporate bailouts, there was no bailout in this case juxtaposed to Bannon's loss. But more to the point, it was not the arguments of Adam Smith, David Ricardo, or Milton Friedman that formulated Bannon's outlook on capitalism and markets; it was a bad trade his father made. That stock trade would go on to influence trade policy in the United States.

There are many clear lessons in this story: understand principle preservation, diversify your portfolio, avoid companies with lousy management, and don't sell out of desperation. Columnist Froma Harrop posits a very natural question: "But where was Steve Bannon—his big shot son, a former Goldman Sachs banker and now political adviser to Donald Trump—when he unloaded his life savings at the bottom of the market? Apparently not calling home and saying, 'Dad, don't sell your stock now.'"[31] What's difficult to see is how this incident translates to concluding that the free market is bad. If Bannon's point was that bank bailouts are bad, it's clear that a conservative economist would agree; however, why would this story *change* Steve Bannon's mind about bank bailouts? Didn't he *always* think that bank bailouts were bad?

There is a moral to this story that Bannon might consider; it is one that he seems to have pondered but that did not seem to resonate. That moral is this: it is not only "Wall Street fat cats" who lose money when other people make bad decisions; real people, like retirees who may depend on their stock dividends for food and rent, suffer as well. Consider this. In early 2018, as the stock market plummeted after a new round of tariffs was announced, Steve Bannon not only cheered on the tariffs, but he also told Reuters: "Ask the working people in Ohio, Pennsylvania and Michigan about Wall Street. Wall Street supported and cheered on the export of their jobs. To hell with Wall Street if they don't like it."[32] Ironically, after that tariff announcement, AT&T stock proceeded to lose more than 20 percent of its value on the year, closing at around $26 per share.

Though Steve Bannon is no longer working in the administration, the fact that he was so influential is a testimony to the pro-tariff position of Donald Trump.

Informally, Peter Navarro is the "trade czar" of the Trump administration; officially, he is director of the Office of Trade and Manufacturing Policy (OTMP); practically speaking, he is the most powerful voice in the Trump administration when it comes to trade (or lack of trade). When Navarro, who holds a PhD in economics from Harvard, was chosen for his new executive position, conservative talk show host Hugh Hewitt said that the administration should be congratulated for its diversity in appointing him. Hewitt wasn't kidding: Navarro is diverse. Dr. Navarro has been a registered Republican, a registered Independent, and unsuccessfully ran for office five times as a Democrat. Actually, he once swam for office—literally. As a San Diego mayoral candidate, Dr. Navarro was scheduled to debate his opponent at a waterfront restaurant in La Jolla, so he decided to swim about a mile to the event. Emerging from the surf thirty minutes after the debate's intended start time, Navarro put on a pair of shorts and a sweatshirt and delivered his responses, still shivering from the cold. If you can make sense of that, making sense of his trade policy is a breeze.

Due to his powerful position within the administration, Navarro may be the most relevant proponent of tariffs in America. But Navarro did not always subscribe to the pro-tariff position. Quite the contrary: in 1984, Navarro issued a book that contains some of the best free trade arguments in modern times and refutes Trump's often repeated argument that foreign nations pay tariffs. They don't consumers do. It was called *The Policy Game: How Special Interests and Ideologues Are Stealing America*. In that book, referring to tariffs and protectionism, Navarro writes:

> *If the world is, in fact, sucked into this spiral, enormous gains from trade will be sacrificed. While such a sacrifice might save some jobs in sheltered domestic industries, it will destroy as many or more in other home industries, particularly those that rely heavily on export trade. At the same time, consumers will pay tens of billions of dollars more in higher prices for a much more limited selection of goods. Sacrificed, too, on the altar of protectionism will be the very heart of an international world order that since World War II has successfully changed the aggressive struggle among nations for world resources and markets into a peaceful economic competition rather than a confrontational political or military one.*[33]

Here, Navarro makes the classical arguments for free trade: first, trade results in "enormous gains" of wealth; second, protectionism causes a net loss of jobs in the home country; third, tariffs are inflationary; fourth, some products will no longer be imported at all; fifth, free trade fosters peace while trade restrictions lead to war. Those are some damn good arguments for free trade. So good, in fact, that some or all of them are held by nearly every economist in the Western world. For instance, *Bloomberg Businessweek* points out that "in 2012, 95 percent of leading economists surveyed by the University of Chicago Booth School of Business agreed with the following statement:

'Freer trade improves productive efficiency and offers consumers better choices, and in the long run these gains are much larger than any
effects on employment.'"[34]

Why did Navarro jettison the free trade arguments? When you
hear Navarro's current explanations, you begin wondering which of
his five previous pro-trade arguments, in his mind, no longer apply.
Do tariffs now result in enormous wealth gains? Does protectionism
now bring a net gain in American jobs? Are tariffs no longer inflationary? Do all tariffed products now make it to America's shores? Do
tariffs—*not trade*—now foster peace? Does history fail to confirm
the efficiency of free trade? So why the sea change? How does a Harvard economics PhD apostatize from the faith in free markets? In an
interview with *Axios*, Navarro says his views began to change in the
early 1990s when he "began to learn the importance of a strong manufacturing base."[35] (By his own words, Navarro had apparently not
considered a strong manufacturing base to be very important prior to
the 1990s.) He continues: "The turning point in my trade thinking
came several years after China joined the World Trade Organization in 2001 and began dumping heavily subsidized products into our
markets."

Dumping? That's not a term of economics. "Dumping" is simply
a pejorative term intended to give weight to the protectionist position. But it is his use of words like this that illustrates how Navarro
got his job in the first place. He's the trade czar whose credential is in
economics, but he doesn't believe in free trade, and he doesn't make
arguments having much to do with economics. He wasn't hired for his
PhD in economics; he was hired to bring some credibility to words like
"dumping." He was the one needle in a haystack of economists who
actually opposes free trade.

Though Navarro's criticism of free trade has largely focused on
China, he has become an outspoken proponent of broad and wide
tariffs, recently commenting:

"While critics may question how these metal tariffs can be imposed in the name of national security on allies and neighbors like
Canada, they miss the fundamental point: *These tariffs are not aimed*

at any one country. They are a defensive measure to ensure the domestic viability of two of the most important industries necessary for United States military and civilian production at times of crisis so that the United States can defend itself as well as its allies."[36]

While Navarro once maintained that free trade fosters peace, he now concludes that tariffs foster peace.

Wilbur Ross, the US secretary of commerce, seems adamant that foreign countries do not get a leg up on America's steel industry. Steel tariffs are the way to go he insists. In a self-congratulating op-ed of July 15, 2018, Ross wrote, "Despite objections over the Section 232 tariffs from foreign producers and governments, the tariffs are on track to accomplish what they were intended to do. They are helping re-establish two vital industries for our national security."[37] This is a bit ironic considering his background with the steel industry.

In 2002, Ross founded a company called International Steel Group, which bought up the assets of several troubled and/or bankrupt American steel companies (of which Bethlehem Steel was one) and combined them into one large steel outfit. To his credit, Ross was able to combine the assets, renegotiate contracts, and sell the company three years later for a tidy profit of about $2 billion. The buyer? Mittal Steel of the Netherlands. Ross saved American steel— just in time to sell it to overseas buyers.[38]

Bob Woodward reports: "On July 12, 2017, 15 former chairs of the Council of Economic Advisers, the high-powered, formal advisory group of academic economists, had sent a letter to Trump urging him not to 'initiate the process of imposing steel tariffs' because it would harm relations with key allies and 'actually damage the U.S. economy.'"[39] But Wilbur Ross persisted, writing a note to the president that the United States must persist.

The steel tariffs went forward. And Ross seemed eager to go on national television to defend them. On March 2, 2018, Wilbur Ross appeared on CNBC, holding up a can of Campbell's soup. In an awkward interview in which Ross repeatedly looked down at his notes for basic information, Ross assured viewers that the tariff would increase the price on the steel in the can by less than one cent.

"Who in the world is going to be too bothered by six-tenths of a cent?" Ross asked.[40] Though the question was probably intended to be rhetorical, there was an answer as to who would be bothered: the CFO of Campbell Soup. After the stock plummeted by May, Campbell's CFO Anthony DiSilvestro said on a conference call: "The issue is primarily one of cost inflation. And we're seeing and expecting an acceleration on the rate of inflation across a number of ingredient and packaging items. For example, we expect double-digit increases on steel and aluminum. A lot of that driven—or *all of it driven by the impact of anticipated tariffs.*"[41]

DiSilvestro had alluded to something that Wilbur Ross had apparently not considered: commodity prices tend to rise and fall together. It was not just that a 25 percent steel tariff would likely raise the price of steel; it would raise the price of many, if not most, commodities. It's not just the price of the can that was likely to rise but the price of what goes *into* the can. Between March and September of 2018, the price of steel rose by more than 35 percent, but the prices of other commodities followed. And even as commodity prices have risen, Wilbur Ross continues to defend tariffs.

TARIFF MAN

The Trump administration not only promoted anti-traders such as Bannon, Ross, and Navarro, but those in favor of free trade also quickly lost their jobs.

One of the most interesting pieces of the tariff and trade puzzle involves Gary Cohn, director of the National Economic Council. In Bob Woodward's recent book *Fear: Trump in the White House,* he outlines that Gary Cohn felt like the lone free marketer in the White House, frequently getting into verbal skirmishes with Peter Navarro and other proponents of tariffs. In one such exchange, Gary Cohn made three factual—yet unpopular—observations: First, America is a service economy, as 84 percent of our GDP is service related, and largely we are admired by the rest of the economic world because of it. Second, trade deficits—not surpluses—are actually positive for America because they bring more wealth into the country. Third, the main reason that manufacturing numbers are down is that people are voluntarily leaving manufacturing jobs. Cohn, according to Bob Woodward, phrased it thus: "I can sit in a nice office with air-conditioning and a desk, or stand on my feet eight hours a day. Which one would you do for the same pay? . . . People don't want to stand in front of a 2,000 degree blast furnace. People don't want to go into coal mines and get black lung. For the same dollars or equal dollars, they're going to choose something else."[42] Great point and one that just about every American understood. But on March 6, 2018, it was announced that Cohn—perhaps realizing that his position of free trade was not going to be taken seriously—was resigning from his position. Now, with the most ardent supporter of free trade no longer part of the administration, the tariffs began in earnest.

In 2018 alone, the Trump administration imposed more tariffs than did the Smoot-Hawley Tariff Act. Beginning on January 22, 2018, the administration proudly announced a tariff on washing machines and solar panels. The effect? The Bureau of Labor Statistics' CPI data reported that the cost of laundry equipment rose more than 9.6 percent in the month of April alone, followed by another rise of over 6 percent in the month of May.[43]

On April 3, 2018, the Trump administration announced a $50 billion tariff; this included a 25 percent tariff on about thirteen hundred Chinese products covering a wide swath of materials including machinery, chemicals, and medical products. A full forty-five pages of tariffed goods including Coenzyme Q10, dental cements, sewing machine needles, flight data recorders, and X-ray tubes. (At least worm gut was let off the hook.) By the end of 2018, the Trump administration had imposed tariffs on a quarter trillion dollars of Chinese imports. Imported steel was slapped with one of the more ruthless tariffs. Less than twelve hours after Trump announced the tariff on Chinese steel, China responded with a 25 percent tariff increase on $50 billion worth of goods on US imports to China. Following this, President Trump announced that he was considering another round of tariffs—this time a $100 billion round of tariffs.

What happened next was predictable to just about any economist outside the administration: American steel companies began to tank. In a Wilbur Ross/Steve Bannon/Peter Navarro world, the stock in U.S. Steel should see a rally after a big steel tariff. Of course, we don't live in that imaginary world. In January 2018, stock in U.S. Steel was trading at more than $40 per share; by late 2019, shares traded under $10 a share. By October of 2019, Wall Street wasn't rosy on the prospects for steel going forward. On October 3, 2019, Moody's downgraded the US steel industry to "negative," citing the fact that the steel tariffs had caused price distortions and disturbances. In 2016, Donald Trump had run a campaign promising that people would be "tired of winning." The entire American steel industry, crippled by market-distorting tariffs, looked well past tired, all the way to damn near exhausted.

Though steel got the lion's share of attention, agricultural tariffs had a much wider scope. Tariffs on produce from Mexico drove up the prices on many food items including raspberries, strawberries, tomatoes, and avocados.[44] The countries on which America imposes tariffs, like Canada and Mexico, retaliate with their own tariffs. For instance, Canada retaliated with a 20 percent tariff on American orange juice. This means that American citrus farmers export less orange juice, which puts people out of jobs and hurts the Florida economy. America doesn't like that, so we respond with more retaliatory tariffs, and so the vicious circle continues. The common denominator is misery. But it's the poor who are most miserable. A 25 percent rise in the price of tomatoes is immaterial to wealthy Americans, but for poor families, they just go without.

The discussion of agricultural tariffs leads us to one of the more bizarre aspects of tariff legislation. Since retaliatory tariffs have significantly hurt American farmers, the Trump administration has been writing checks to farmers who have been negatively impacted by these tariffs. In July of 2018, the Trump administration announced $12 billion in aid to American farmers whose former foreign buyers have dried up. Ben Sasse, Republican senator from Nebraska, summed it up well, commenting that this overall program was "cutting the legs out from under farmers," then spending "$12 billion on gold crutches."[45] Noting the unmistakable similarity between this administration's policies and those during the Great Depression, Sasse observed: "This administration's tariffs and bailouts aren't going to make America great again, they're just going to make it 1929 again." As it turns out, this $12 billion payment was only the beginning of these payments. In 2019, the administration announced another $16 billion in aid, most of which was simply cash payments. In effect, the Trump administration is paying farmers not to grow food, while the poor people in America can no longer afford to buy produce. To borrow a phrase from George Bush, if that's not "voodoo economics," what is?

On December 4, 2018, President Trump tweeted: "I am a Tariff Man. When people or countries come in to raid the great wealth of our Nation, I want them to pay for the privilege of doing so. It will always be the best way to max out our economic power. We are right now taking in $billions in Tariffs. MAKE AMERICA RICH AGAIN."[46]

This tweet goes right to the heart of the issue. In President Trump's view, the government's imposition of tariffs—and not free trade—is and "will always be the best way to max out our economic power." This tweet illustrates a deep misunderstanding of basic economics at the transactional level. The way some politicians talk, you would think that trade is something that occurs at a governmental level between America and other nations. But as Daniel J. Ikenson of the Cato Institute writes, "Trade is not conducted between countries. Rather, trade is the culmination of billions of daily transactions between individuals around the world seeking to obtain the most value from that exchange."[47] Free trade allows consumers to search globally for the best price. Tariffs, however, gum up the system and disallow you and me from purchasing the products we want and paying the lowest price. Countries don't pay tariffs. In most cases, you and I (the consumers) pay them. In other cases the manufacturer lowers their cost, if there is enough margin to do so, to offset the tariff. If it is a publicly owned company, the shareholder may bear the cost in the form of a lower stock price or dividend. Sometimes the seller will eat the tariff or some combination of the three; the consumer, the seller, and the manufacturer. In all cases, someone pays. The tariff is collected at the point of entry and the money goes directly into the treasury where it creates nothing. Tariffs are effectively a sales tax that hurts everyone; consumers, shareholders, manufacturers, and retailers. Everybody loses.

LOOKING FORWARD

Of all the changes that have taken place in the Republican Party's transition to the party of Trump, the about-face in trade is one of the starkest.

On April 21, 2015, Ted Cruz and Speaker Paul Ryan coauthored an op-ed for *The Wall Street Journal* which began: "The United States is making headway on two historic trade agreements."[48] (Although neither agreement was named in the op-ed, they were clearly referring to the Transatlantic Trade and Investment Partnership, or TTIP, and the Trans-Pacific Partnership, or TPP.) The statement argued in favor of granting fast-track authority, or Trade Promotion Authority (TPA), to President Obama and future presidents.

Since 1974, TPA legislation has set the objectives and priorities of a potential trade agreement but gives the president authority to negotiate and execute specific trade deals with one or more foreign governments. Why would Congress grant that authority? Because without it, Congress would need to reconvene for every minor foreign trade deal—a practical impossibility that would inevitably result in less free trade.

In the piece, Cruz and Ryan touted the incontrovertible benefits of free trade agreements, including better wages, lower trade deficits, and "greater access to a billion customers for American manufacturers, farmers and ranchers." Seems like a no-brainer. The benefits of

NAFTA negotiated by the Clinton administration and passed by a Republican Congress far outweighed the negatives. In the aggregate, NAFTA created millions of American jobs, increased wages, lowered inflation, and created the biggest bull market in American history. Cruz was a Republican candidate for president, and traditionally modern Republicans support free trade. Or so we thought.

Two months after the *Journal* piece, I got a call from Jon McClellan, who worked in the political division of the Cruz campaign. He wanted me to join a state leadership call on TPA and TPP. Though the term sounds redundant, "political" is the organizing arm of a campaign responsible for recruiting volunteers, assigning tasks to volunteers, and recruiting leaders and local chairpersons among many other responsibilities. They organize coalition groups like Women for Cruz, Second Amendment supporters, pro-life advocates, and so forth.

An important function of the political division was to make sure everyone in the organizational chart had access to talking points about issues. The policy division was in charge of setting the official policy of the campaign with the candidate's approval. The communications shop would translate policy language into talking points or simple-to-understand language our volunteers could use when asked where Cruz stood on an issue and be able to communicate those positions to voters.

On June 10, 2015, I joined the state leadership call to discuss TPA and TPP. Cruz had already voted in support of TPA in May and based on his op-ed with Paul Ryan, he seemed to support the TPP. But after some opening remarks and questions, I realized we had a problem: most people on the call opposed free trade agreements in general and/or vehemently opposed trade agreements that Barack Obama would make.

Some on the call confused the similar-sounding TPA with TPP. And then there was the corresponding issue of TAA (only politicians could create an alphabet soup out of something as simple as the free exchange of goods and services without government interference). Many understood the difference but were upset that Cruz would give Obama blanket authority to negotiate a trade deal. Some had wild conspiracy theories ranging from TPA being unconstitutional (it is not), to giving the president extraordinary powers to unilaterally make immigration laws, to TPP overriding American sovereignty.

What was remarkable about all the comments was that although each had heard that these provisions were in the TPP agreement, there was no final TPP agreement as of then. No one had any firsthand or reliable account of what was going to be part of the TPP. What we *did* have was a toxic mix of ignorance, distrust, conspiracy, and people who were not free traders. In fact, so toxic was the issue that free trader Ted Cruz took a "wait and see" approach, and his campaign issued this statement:

> *Sen. Cruz has not taken a position either in favor or against TPP. He will wait until the agreement is finalized and he has a chance to study it carefully to ensure that the agreement will open more markets to American-made products, create jobs, and grow our economy.*[49]

By November, trade was a sharp dividing line in the Republican primary. Trump positioned himself as—if not fully "anti-trade"— certainly someone who was consolidating voters who were in the "the-globalists-are-screwing-us" camp. At an Iowa event on November 20, 2015, Cruz for the first time publicly opposed TPP. On the CNN debate in March 2016, Jake Tapper asked why Cruz had changed his position. Cruz then used the TPA/TPP confusion to his advantage. Cruz said, "There are two different agreements. There's TPA and TPP. I opposed TPP, and have always opposed TPP, which is what you asked about."[50] While it is true—Cruz never directly supported TPP—his *Wall Street Journal* piece with Speaker Ryan made his support for free trade sound unequivocal, and moreover he was advocating for a TPA specifically tied to TPP.

On May 22, 2015, Cruz had voted for fast-track Trade Promotion Authority for the Trans-Pacific Partnership trade deal as well as Trade Adjustment Assistance (TAA) for the same. But by June,

Cruz had reversed himself and voted no on a procedural vote to clear the way for TPA, claiming that he had become aware of new details in the TPA that "smacked of a backroom deal," and he would have no part of it. It passed anyway. Clearly, the political calculation of losing voters to Trump was the driving force in opposing the same TPA he advocated for in his op-ed with Speaker Ryan.

On January 23, 2017, three days into his presidency, Trump signed an executive order withdrawing the United States from the TPP. Six months later in July, eleven nations reached an agreement on TPP without the United States. The world might start trading more freely, but it would do so without the United States. In the course of a few short months, Republicans had decided against free trade.

We live in an age in which one political group tends to demonize the other; that's part and parcel of American politics, and that's a shame. We can assume that those who are in favor of tariffs and those who are in favor of free trade both want an America that is strong, whose people are paid good wages, and that the workers of America are able to make a good living doing jobs that they actually enjoy and that are fulfilling. The question is how do we get there? In large measure, the response of the Trump administration has been to impose tariffs—and plenty of them. And as we've seen from his top advisers, their ultimate goal is not free trade but protectionism.

In the third presidential debate in 2016, candidate Trump said, "Because I did disagree with Ronald Reagan very strongly on trade. I disagreed with him. We should have been much tougher on trade even then. I've been waiting for years. Nobody does it right."[51] Presumably, what we have seen so far is considered right, but it certainly has not been conservative. And it's worth saying that the free trade position is not correct because it is conservative; it is conservative because it is correct. The conservative arguments are backed up—in the aggregate—by all of recorded economic history.

Of course, it would be better if all nations traded freely; that is our essential argument. But, as Milton Friedman likes to point out, why must the stupidity of one nation become our own stupidity?[52]

Why extend bad policy of foreign nations to our own nation? Maybe we can force other countries to the bargaining table by applying tariffs—so the logic goes. Historically, the answer is quite the opposite: the best way to force a country to halt tariffs of American imports is to halt their tariffs coming into our country.

From a conservative perspective, there's an even more fundamental question: where does the government get the right to prevent a free market transaction in the first place? As Amity Shlaes pointed out, the very existence of tariffs and protectionism exhibits a distrust of the free market.[53] Ultimately, a tariff is a transfer of power and money from private hands to the government. That's the tradeoff, but it's a trade we shouldn't make.

3

KNOWING OUR PLACE
IN THE WORLD

For many Americans, the term "foreign policy" rarely conjures happy thoughts and images; rather, it serves more as a wistful lament and a source of confusion. To be sure, it's not always easy to make sense of America's foreign policy, which is the nice way of saying it. A more honest way of putting it would be that it's damn near impossible to make sense of it. Not that coming up with a comprehensive foreign policy is something you can do over a cup of coffee, but America's foreign policy often looks random. Even its greatest apologists would have to admit some seeming oddities, like the following. After initial short-term goals are achieved in various military deployments, the Pentagon routinely adopts long-term goals. The United States extends foreign aid to the governments of about half of the nations on earth, some of which are governed by leaders who conduct substantial and ongoing human rights abuses. As the late *Washington Post* columnist Charles Krauthammer once put it, "The essence of foreign policy is deciding which son-of-a-bitch to support." With one hand, the American government chooses some countries to stiffly tariff so that the American worker can "more fairly" compete against them; with the other hand, the government sends hundreds of millions of dollars in cash to these same countries—the net result is that American consumers pay more for products *and* pay higher taxes.

Does any of this make sense?

Not only could the subject of America's foreign policy fill volumes but America's policy toward *each* nation of the world could do so; indeed, a plethora of such volumes exist. Therefore, it's not my intention to lay out a complete foreign policy in this chapter but rather to examine the conservative position on foreign policy and highlight a few significant areas of focus going forward.

THE MILITARY STRENGTH OF AMERICA AND NATO

From a conservative perspective, a strong military is essential. Without a force to properly defend a nation, the presence of "ordered liberty" is tenuous at best because the citizens would live under constant fear of attack and invasion. And because of the essential nature of defense, conservatives have historically been willing to pay significant costs to maintain a strong military. Yet, it's a dicey proposition, because if our military becomes too large, America runs the risk of becoming a modern-day Sparta, that is, a society that revolves around war rather than peace. And in the age-old economic conflict between guns and butter (the decision whether to devote resources to consumer goods or military defense), conservatives recognize that military spending can quickly get out of control. It's a delicate balance. For conservatives, much of the answer to these questions lies in conducting sound diplomacy and meaningful foreign policy.

Foreign policy can be a dizzying subject, but at its core foreign policy has the same essential goals as domestic policy: peace, order, and prosperity. And one essential ingredient of a successful foreign policy is a strong military force. Some might say that the fundamental purpose of the military is to conduct war. However, it serves a prior purpose: *preventing* war. Some might say that preventing war is not the function of the military but rather of politicians and negotiators. To be sure, good diplomatic negotiators are essential to America's overall program, but diplomatic negotiations are a hell of a lot easier—that is to say peace is much easier to achieve—if your military is strong, ready, and willing. That's a sentiment that's been addressed many times over the years by various presidents of both parties. In his inaugural address of 1961, referencing how to deal with America's military adversaries, John F. Kennedy warned the American people: "We dare not tempt them with weakness. For only when our arms are sufficient beyond doubt can we be certain beyond doubt that they will never be employed." A generation later, Ronald Reagan would promote the same message with a more pithy slogan: "peace through strength."

Of course, the argument that America should have a strong military is not without its detractors. Whereas Kennedy had warned that a weak military would tempt other nations to war against America, some argue that a strong military will tempt America to make war against other nations. In fact, if you watch cable news shows on the subject of foreign policy, you don't have to wait long for someone to appear and tell you why America shouldn't be the "world's policeman." Though, in the right crowd at the right time, that kind of talk can serve as great rhetoric. It's an unfair caricature that suggests that America and American troops are just walking the global beat, anxiously looking for someone to arrest and detain for minor crimes and misdemeanors. Often dubbed as "noninterventionists" to friends and "isolationists" to foes, they suggest that America should rarely, if ever, become involved in foreign affairs. To their thinking, America and foreign entities don't mix. (Of course, this argument is not without some historical irony; after all, it is unlikely that America would have won the Revolutionary War without the foreign aid of France. Had it not been for the French advisors, as well as naval and military ground assistance in battles, including the siege of Yorktown, Jefferson's Declaration would be only a dead letter from the losing side.)

Many isolationists believe that America's foreign policy should take its cue from Switzerland, a country whose foreign policy is essentially to have no foreign policy. For a number of reasons—including geography, demographics, and its relative importance on the world stage—Switzerland might have that luxury. But it is impossible for a country the size of America to have no foreign policy. Even for basic reasons of self-defense, America must conduct a foreign policy. As Barry Goldwater, author of *Conscience of a Conservative*, wrote, "American freedom has always depended, to an extent, on what is happening beyond our shores."[1] There is an inescapable reality to the fact that even if America takes no interest in the world, the world takes an interest in America—and very often, an unhealthy interest. Thus, America needs a strong military and a powerful intelligence community. It also needs to maintain its standing with other nations by conducting itself with fairness, and it needs to foster relationships by trading with other nations.

Beyond that, America needs meaningful global alliances, and from the years following World War II to the present day, the most vital alliance has been NATO (the North Atlantic Treaty Organization). Formed four years after the end of World War II, the goal of NATO was to keep the peace against the rising influence of Russia and its empire of satellite states. And for good reason.

Since the "Red October" revolution of 1917, Russia has proven to be one of the most notorious global terrorists in world history. For instance, there was Lenin's grain confiscation program that caused the starvation of more than 2 million people in 1919; the farm collectivization program starting in 1928 in which millions were shot or starved; Stalin's forced starvation of 6 to 7 million Ukrainians in 1932; the World War II–era invasions of eastern European countries, which saw millions of innocent women and children kidnapped and shipped to Soviet concentration camps; the attempted starvation of Berlin in 1948; the funding of North Korea's invasion of South Korea in 1950; the supply of missiles to Castro's Cuba in 1962; the invasion of Afghanistan in 1979, in which the Soviets dropped bombs disguised as toys for the purpose of blowing off the arms of innocent children; 1986's Chernobyl disaster and subsequent "cleanup," which poses a radiation threat to this day. And as any Sovietologist could tell you, this is just a partial list of atrocities—merely the tip of the Cold War's iceberg—leading up to the Soviet Union's failed state status of 1991. A detailed list would be impossible in a book of this size.

The seventy-year regime was a campaign of lies, and everyone knew it. There was a narrative then—and now—that Soviet leader Mikhail Gorbachev recognized the error in the Soviet ways and therefore instituted *glasnost* and *perestroika* (political and economic reform programs) as a goodwill gesture to help the Russian people. That was another lie. The truth is that the Soviet Union ran out of money and could no longer fund their seventy-year Marxist experiment.

When Russia fell, there was a man who found himself out of a job as a KGB officer who, at the time, was working as a Soviet spy in Germany. Sharing a first name with Lenin, the original Soviet Communist who murdered his way to power, his name was Vladimir Putin. While the world was cheering the fall of Communism, Putin was regarding the fall of Communism as a devastating event. But— and this is the key point—not as the final chapter in Soviet history. As one expert on Russia put it, Putin viewed the fall of Communism merely as "a pause" in Russia's global dominance.

Because of his connections and his extraordinary ability to form an alliance of oligarchs and former KGB officers, he quickly took the helm as deputy mayor of St. Petersburg. From there, he wielded power and peddled influence to ascend to the office of prime minister of Russia from 2008 to 2012, then to the office of president, where he still served as the de facto prime minister.

There are those who think Putin is a different kind of leader for Russia. Is he? He has annexed Crimea, a strategic part of Ukraine principally because of its location on the Black Sea and the Sea of Azov; invaded Georgia; funded Bashar al-Assad's chemical-weapons regime in Syria; stifled media to the point of murder (likely including the murder of Russian journalist and human rights activist Anna Politkovskaya); assassinated political adversaries; seized private industry; rigged Western elections (not to mention his own); consolidated money and power to himself and a few oligarchs who assist him. In a speech in 2018, Putin criticized the United States as the global aggressor for pursuing its missile defense program. While he wags a suspecting finger at America's and NATO's military presence in Europe, he has built a military force that has more combat tanks, armored fighting vehicles, and aircraft carriers than the United States.[2] According to Putin, Russia also owns a vast array of intercontinental ballistic missiles (ICBMs) of which more than one hundred are launchable by three Russian nuclear submarines. Many of these weapons are clearly designed as "first-strike" weapons. In fact, in a 2018 speech, Putin proudly catalogued the current Soviet arsenal and took a threatening posture toward Western nations—a familiar theme.[3]

A different kind of leader?

Which aggressive and murderous instinct of his Stalinist predecessors is Putin lacking? The only thing that he may be lacking is funds. Though we often regard Russia as a global powerhouse, its economy is a disaster and surprisingly small. In fact, though it once may have been considered the chief economic rival of the United States, Russia's GDP now falls under South Korea, Italy, and Canada. In fact, the state of California has roughly twice the GDP of Russia.

Though the Cold War is said to be over, the relationship between America and Russia hardly constitutes anything resembling spring. Vladimir Putin is bragging about rebuilding Russia's military and criticizing America with the same breath. NATO was formed for the allied protection against Russia, and while some—including, of course, Putin himself—are calling for America's withdrawal from NATO, the importance of that alliance may have never been stronger. Putin represents America's biggest worry.

The key point is that America must maintain a powerful military against established enemies as well as potential future hostile adversaries. More recently, we've had to meet the challenge of non-state hostile actors who have the capability to wreak havoc on an open society with relatively few resources. American policymakers would be well served to reconsider Kennedy's admonition: "We dare not tempt them with weakness." And this applies not only to Putin and similar tyrants but also to America's war against terrorist states.

THE MILITARY WAR ON TERROR

Most wars can be traced back to a particular event, on a specific date, by easily identifiable sides. For instance, the Civil War began at Fort Sumter on April 12, 1861, as Confederate forces attacked the Union; the Revolutionary War began with shots fired by colonists and British loyalists at Lexington and Concord on April 19, 1775; World War II began with Germany's invasion of Poland on September 1, 1939. When we speak about America's "war on terror," this conflict is markedly different in each of these respects: the event, the date, and the sides. Reflexively, most people would choose 9/11. Yet, citing its initial severity, its psychological impact and influence on America, and the message it sent to the people and countries involved, some have speculated that the opening salvo was the 1983 bombing of a US Marine barracks in Beirut. As Reagan put it, "There was a time when our national security was based on a standing army here within our own borders . . . The world has changed. Today, our national security can be threatened in faraway places."[4]

During the 1982 Lebanon War, President Ronald Reagan had sent eighteen hundred members of the US military to Lebanon in a vague peacekeeping mission after a confluence of events including the attempted assassination of the Israeli ambassador to the United Kingdom, Shlomo Argov, in London. That event was used by Israeli Prime Minister Menachem Begin to justify sending Israeli Defense Forces (IDF) into southern Lebanon. The supposed short incursion expanded from ejecting military assets from southern Lebanon to set up a security zone to the IDF advancing all the way to Beirut and attempting to set up a government. It was quickly discovered that Beirut and peace didn't easily mix. In April of 1983, the US embassy in Beirut was attacked, killing seventeen Americans. After that attack, Reagan stood firm, asserting that if America left the country now, it would send a message to terrorists that America was weak in its resolve. Six months later, however, terrorists would strike again with a massive explosion at a marine barracks on the early morning of October 23, 1983—this time killing 241 and injuring 100 others. Though many of the American soldiers wanted to stay and fight, Reagan pulled them out. The problem was that Reagan had been right in his statement six months earlier—it sent a message to terrorists that America was a weak nation whose resolve could be shaken—a belief that would inspire future conspirators against America.

One who seemed to take the lesson that American would cut and run was Muammar al-Gaddafi, but the leader of Libya would soon learn a radically different lesson. Though terrorism occurred on many fronts in many places during Reagan's presidency, Muammar al-Gaddafi, would be the first to experience meaningful retaliation. By Reagan's first year in office, it was clear that Gaddafi was involved in a vast network of global terrorism that stretched into no fewer than forty-five different countries and had funded or supplied weapons to just about everything from the PLO to the IRA.[5] It seemed that whenever a terrorist act occurred in Europe, it could be linked to Gaddafi. After a 1986 terrorist bombing in a Berlin nightclub that killed two Americans and injured dozens more, Reagan decided he'd had enough. Days after this bombing, more than one hundred US planes carried out a major strike against Libya's government, pounding military targets in Tripoli and Benghazi.

One of those chosen targets was a military residential zone where US intelligence showed Gaddafi lived. According to one Reagan biographer, had Gaddafi had been killed in the attack, the Reagan administration was prepared to deliver the message that the Libyan leader's demise was "a fortuitous by-product of our act of self-defense,"[6] which would have amounted to a fancier way of saying: *Who cares?* Though Gaddafi survived the attack (his daughter did not), the message was unmistakable: this time, the bomb is in your front yard. Next time, it'll be in your living room.

Reagan would go on television later that night to explain to the American people what and why military action was taken against Gaddafi. Explaining that there was clear evidence against Gaddafi in the attack and that America bore no ill will toward the citizens of Libya, Reagan stated that Gaddafi "counted on America to be passive. He counted wrong. I warned that there should be no place on earth where terrorists can rest and train and practice their deadly skills. I meant it. I said that we would act with others if possible and alone if necessary to insure that terrorists have no sanctuary anywhere."[7] For Reagan, the matter was simple: "America will never make concessions to terrorists. To do so would only invite more terrorism."[8] In the light of history, the story of Gaddafi seems distant. Though Gaddafi was the biggest sponsor of terrorism in the world (other than the Soviet Union), Gaddafi's Libya became so quiet that the Western world all but forgot about it for about twenty years. Reagan's response proved definitive.

These two events—the withdrawal of troops from Beirut and the successful bombing of Libya—marked the two most significant happenings during Reagan's administration regarding terrorism. One was terribly tragic; the other was an enduring success. Valuable lessons can be learned from both.

Regarding the Beirut withdrawal, it is clear that the mission was doomed to failure from the beginning. Caspar Weinberger, who served as Reagan's secretary of defense, later stated that the Beirut withdrawal "was an absolutely inevitable outcome of doing what we did, of putting troops in with no mission that could be carried out."[9] Though Beirut was intended to be a peacekeeping mission, he asserted that this mission was impossible. Weinberger assessed that "there's nothing more dangerous than in the middle of a furious prize fight, inserting a referee in range of both the fighters, both the contestants. That's what we did."

By 1984, Weinberger had developed a six-point plan for foreign intervention—later known as the Weinberger Doctrine—that would serve not only as a guiding policy against the war on terror today but also on a broad foreign policy scale. The Weinberger Doctrine states that: (1) "the United States should not commit forces to *combat* overseas unless the particular engagement or occasion is deemed vital to our national interest or that of our allies; (2) there must be a "clear intention of winning"; (3) there must be "clearly defined political and military objectives" along with a plan to "accomplish those clearly defined objectives"; (4) the mission's "objectives and the forces we have committed" to achieving those objectives "must be continually reassessed and adjusted if necessary"; (5) "there must be some reasonable assurance we will have the support of the American people and their elected representatives in Congress" prior to troop deployment; (6) "the commitment of U.S. forces to combat should be a last resort."[10] Since it was outlined, the Weinberger Doctrine has been even more relevant, and it seems that when our foreign policy has gone wrong, it has violated one or more of these precepts. As a whole, the doctrine seems consistent with conservative ideals, including discouraging something a conservative would never attempt: foreign nation building.

AMERICA CANNOT BUILD NATIONS

During almost every election cycle since World War II, someone has had the nerve to promise to bring peace to the Middle East. But the last time there was peace in the Middle East (the so-called Pax Romana, which, even then, was only peaceful on a relative basis) someone wrote a book about it. It was called *The Gospel of John*. The total absence of conflict is unrealistic in a fallen world—and perhaps most unrealistic in this region that not only has deep divides across geopolitical lines but also across cultures and religions dating back two millennia or more. To all that, throw in vendettas that originate to the time of the First Crusade. How do you go about changing all this? Inevitably, the response amounts not to tinkering but to nation building.

There are those who believe that the concept of nation building is a relatively recent development—that America essentially invented the idea. However, the term "nation building" itself dates back at least decades, and the concept dates back centuries. In fact, the colonialization of the Western Hemisphere and parts of Asia conducted by Spain, France, and England in the sixteenth century and the centuries following were an early form of nation building.

In modern times, there is both an *intentional* and then an almost *accidental* process of nation building. As Francis Fukuyama, an American political scientist describes it, nation building normally occurs as a two-stage process: the first involves "stabilizing the country," and the second involves "creating self-sustaining political and economic institutions" in which self-governance can flourish.[11] It would be more accurate, however, to say that nation building is what often follows *after* the initial intervention. If a foreign power enters another nation for purposes of conducting a military campaign against its government, that is not nation building. That is an important distinction. Protecting a nation against hostile foreign invaders—especially if that is done so at the urgent request of the legitimate leaders of that nation—is not nation building. For instance, 1991's Operation Desert Storm—in which an American-led coalition of forces freed Kuwait from Iraqi invaders—was not nation building. Nor was landing troops on Omaha Beach in 1944, nor was the Berlin Airlift in 1948, nor was repelling the Communist forces from invading South Korea in 1950.

It is on Fukuyama's second point, when foreign powers go from stabilization to not only the micromanaged creation of a new government but also an insistence on that type of government, that nation building often begins. And it is at this stage, well intentioned though it may be, that America's foreign policy often runs amok. At any given time in the past several decades, America has been building a nation somewhere.

Nation building by a foreign power is inconsistent with conservatism. Conservatism is about fostering order in society and much of that order springs from a people's belief and trust in those governing. If the form of government and those governing them are not chosen by the people *without outside interference*, the government is likely to fail. This is a founding lesson of America, and it still holds true.

Although society and government are not synonyms, the government is, ideally, a reflection of that society. And, this is a key point, it need not be a democratic government to accurately reflect it. Plenty of good governments are established as monarchies or aristocracies. To impose a democratic state on a society that has known only monarchy does not necessarily help the citizens. As Margaret Thatcher put it, "Attempts to suppress national differences or to amalgamate different nations with distinct traditions into artificial states are very likely to fail, perhaps bloodily."[12]

One of the best examples of this is illustrated by America's involvement with Afghanistan. The country of Afghanistan is nomadic and tribal, and its most effective form of government over the centuries was probably its monarchical period. But even that overstates the case, because monarchy presumes a central government—a foreign concept to many Afghans. Over the centuries, much of Afghanistan has been a country of tribal rule—something that foreign powers have discovered. When the Soviets established a puppet government in Kabul in the late twentieth century, they essentially asked the same question that the then-controlling British asked in the nineteenth century: "OK. We have control of the central government. Now what?" America's attempt at nation building has led to a similar question: "OK. We established a democracy. What does that mean?" As it turns out, it has led to a government unwilling and/or incapable of governing, it has led to corruption, and it has led to election fraud.[13] In fact, Afghanistan has the dubious distinction of throwing out more than 1 million popular votes.[14] Although the initial purpose of America's intervention in Afghanistan in 2001 was to overthrow the Taliban, the idea of establishing a democratic government with centralized power quickly became the secondary goal. And here's the real irony: these goals have proven contradictory. As of 2019, some politicians were moving toward establishing "an interim government that, as part of a peace deal, could include the Taliban."[15]

The longer the United States stays in Afghanistan (America's longest war), the more that stay invites comparisons with Vietnam (America's second-longest war). The comparison is even more fair when we consider a largely overlooked fact: namely, that America's conflict in Vietnam was a failed exercise in nation building. At one point, the United States had thousands of advisers in the country who were there for the express purpose of nation building and helping the non-Communist Vietnamese government gain legitimacy among its own people.[16] Of course, it didn't work; in fact, it almost never works. Imagine what would have happened if French advisers had stuck around after the siege of Yorktown to advise the colonists how to form a government. Instead, the French did something very wise: they left town when the battle was won and left the business of nation building to the colonists in their own young nation. That's a good blueprint for America going forward.

None of this discounts the fact that rebellions frequently take place around the world with the aim of removing totalitarian regimes. America may lend its support from public expressions up to the supply of arms and aid. But that is far different from nation building.

In the future, we must recognize the difference between *helping to liberate a country* from hostility, totalitarianism, or foreign invasion and *nation building*. One does not necessitate the other—far from it. Though it is often wise to remain in a country long enough to ensure humanitarian needs such as food and medicine are met, once clear military goals are achieved, American military should withdraw. Nation building has proven not only ineffective but also counterproductive for both America and for the foreign nation in question. Our foreign policy seems intent on establishing a system of democratic voting, but democracy goes well beyond that. It is about establishing individual liberty, a system of property rights, a free press, contract law, and freedom of religion. These are not things that can be quickly established; rather, they are achieved over a process of decades.

The insistence on nation building following a military success only serves to, as the saying goes, snatch defeat from the jaws of victory. And any coherent foreign policy going forward must recognize that reality.

HUMANITARIAN AID

Except under the rarest and most dire of exceptions, if America has the ability to halt genocide, prevent mass starvation, or stop a pandemic on foreign soil, it has the moral obligation to do so. Some argue that humanitarian aid does nothing to further American interests, and therefore these missions should not be pursued. Conservatives should not concede that argument; after all, extending friendship to people in dire need has positive reverberations in America on multiple levels. Humanitarian missions not only identify who we are to foreign powers; they also define who we are to *ourselves*. It is clear that humanitarian causes are consistent with conservatism. Conservatism professes that a moral order exists, and that moral order must include protecting life by accomplishable means. Sometimes this requires military intervention, and sometimes it requires shipments. Sometimes it requires both.

Perhaps the best example of this principle occurred with the Berlin Airlift, which served as a blueprint for humanitarian aid and is remembered as "America's finest hour." It also should be considered the first act of the Cold War. After the Allied forces toppled Hitler's regime at the close of World War II, it was agreed by the Allies that postwar Germany would be divided into four sections, with each controlled by a different country. Northern Germany was to be controlled by the United Kingdom, southwest Germany by France, southern Germany by the United States, and eastern Germany by the Soviet Union. The city of Berlin, Germany's most populous city by far with more than 2 million residents, was in the Soviet Union's sector; however, it was agreed that the city of Berlin would be divided into four parts with similar government allocations of control. Ostensibly, the notion was to help rebuild the country of Germany that had been so terribly devastated by war and then leave the country once a government was established.

Joseph Stalin had other ideas.

Stalin was a Marxist-Leninist whose stated objective was domination of the world, and it quickly became clear that Stalin intended for his portion of German control not to be provisional but to be permanent; not to be capitalist but to be Communist. He also intended to take over the rest of Germany—and Europe. Though Stalin pretended that he wanted to be part of reconstruction efforts at first, he made his intentions brutally clear in 1948. Up until then, the other three nations had been providing food to German families in Berlin, including those in the Soviet section. Stalin knew that he was being outclassed by the free nations, and he wanted to put an end to it. So Stalin established a blockade of Berlin and shut off electric power to the city. Soviet troops began to halt the movement of cars, trucks, trains—anything and everything—through the surrounding Soviet portion of Germany. Fathers and mothers immediately began to fear, with good reason, that they and their children would starve to death. But the Americans weren't about to let that happen.[17]

The problem was what should America do about it? President Truman realized the seriousness of the threat and the evil of Soviet Communism, but he also didn't want to go to war against the Soviet Union. So how do you feed 2 million people without road or railway travel? His advisers had a thought. The Soviets could block the ground, but they could not block the air. "We can supply the city by air!" they argued. Of course, there were two issues with that idea. First, the Soviets could decide to shoot down the American supply planes if they were so inclined. But the Americans were willing to take that chance; if Stalin insisted on shooting down planes full of food and medicine and start World War III, so be it. The thought was that America hadn't liberated Germany from Nazism only to lose it to Communism.

The second and bigger problem was a logistical one: supplying a city of 2 million people by air had never been done in the history of the world. Nothing even *close* had ever been done. Between food and energy supplies, it was estimated that Berlin would need roughly five thousand tons of goods *daily*. And the decision had to be made soon; the Germans had about one month of food left in their country. When that ran out, people would start dying. And there was little doubt that Stalin would not only let that happen but also that he was eager for it to happen. Stalin had used starvation as a political tactic in the past, including the forced starvation of between 6 and 7 million Ukrainians in 1932.

So, on June 28, 1948, just four days after Stalin had blockaded the city by ground, Americans and their allies began supplying Berlin from the air—calling it Operation Vittles. The campaign was not only courageous and ingenious, it was also incredibly well orchestrated. The United States formed a coalition to accomplish this task, organizing a team of pilots not only from America but also from the UK, South Africa, Australia, New Zealand, and Canada. At one point, doing daily what was widely thought impossible, the combined air forces were arriving in Germany at the rate of two planes per minute, dropping supplies such as flour, sugar, cereal, meat, and coal. Most of the pilots on these missions are largely unknown to history. One pilot, however, is known to history, along with the rather unique cargo that he dropped.

After flying in the air force (then it was called the United States Army Air Forces) in World War II, Lieutenant Gail Halvorsen again took the skies to partake in the Berlin Airlift. Delivering supplies both to West and Soviet-controlled East Berlin, Halvorsen noticed one day that about thirty children had lined the Soviet fence to see him. He says that they never asked for anything, but he felt compelled to give them something. All he had to hand them through the fence were two sticks of Wrigley's Doublemint gum. The children tried to divide the two pieces as equally as they could, carefully tearing each stick of gum into smaller strips. Those who did not get a tiny piece of gum passed around gum wrapper so all the children could smell the scent of sugar and mint.

Halvorsen was so moved by the children's act of selflessness that he promised he would bring more gum the next day and drop it from the air. The children believed him but considering that so many planes were always flying overhead, they asked, "How will we know it's your plane?" Halvorsen promised, "I'll wiggle the wings of my plane." And that's just what he did, not only the next day but for the months following—dropping candy in little parachutes to the children below. Of course, this was completely against air force regulations, but when the air force saw the effect it was having on the German children and the American pilots, they initiated Operation Little Vittles. In all, they dropped more than twenty-three tons of gum and candy from a quarter million little white parachutes, and Halvorsen was dubbed with the nickname "the Candy Bomber."[18]

As the days and weeks of the Berlin Airlift wore on, it became increasingly clear to the international community that Soviet Communism was a morally bankrupt system, intent on injuring anyone it its way—including innocent children. It also became clear that America aiding the liberty-loving people of the world wasn't just talk. It was action. Whatever propaganda the Soviets tried to push on the world was drowned out by the valorous and generous actions of the West. Thus, eleven months into the blockade, the Soviets stood down and agreed to discontinue the blockade. In sum, the Berlin Airlift delivered more than 2.3 million tons of food and supplies to Berlin.

There would have been every reason to believe that Americans and Germans would have had an adversarial relationship in the post-war years. Even Halvorsen later admitted to growing up with a lack of fondness toward the Germans, but he realized on his very first flight how important his new mission was and how much he liked the German people.[19] For their part, many of the German children were frightened when they first saw American planes flying overhead in 1948, only to cheer them on in the coming months as they saw candy fall from the sky. The humanitarian Berlin Airlift changed what could have been an adversarial relationship to a friendly one. And it will forever stand as a powerful argument against the idea that humanitarian efforts should not be done because they do not advance American interests.

Going forward, humanitarian relief efforts can and should play a significant role in foreign policy. Though the circumstances are different in each case, America should welcome the opportunity to illustrate to the people of the world that the United States is peopled by those who still believe in life, liberty, and the pursuit of happiness—and not just for American citizens but for the people of the world. John Lenczowski, foreign policy specialist and former lead expert on Soviet Communism under President Reagan, points out that the perception of America by the outside world is often based on the American movies they see—movies filled with "sex and gratuitous violence."[20] That's somewhat understandable; after all, if you've never been to America and you've never met an American, the entertainment America exports could mold your impression. As a refutation of this perception, Lenczowski says that some recent, well-designed humanitarian policies have illustrated America's goodness to the world and have exerted major influence on indigenous Muslims, even in those areas once considered strongholds of radical Islam.[21] These types of programs should continue to push forward.

A CLEAR STATEMENT OF TRUTH AND LIBERTY

Lenczowski's above point is that part of America's foreign policy must be to communicate to the world a proper notion of America, along with what it is that Americans traditionally hold dear—things like truth, free speech, political liberty, religious liberty, free press, the right to pursue happiness and the right to life that precedes it, the right to private property, justice, the right to a fair trial, and so forth.[22] If we fail to communicate that message to the world, it is an epic fail. It's hard to overstate the importance or influence of America articulating such a message to the world—most notably in the person of the president.

There was a time when presidents understood the enormous value of such positive communication. In the Declaration of Independence, Thomas Jefferson clearly and brilliantly laid out the reasons why the American colonists had no choice but to break with England. Essentially forming an address to the people of the whole world, Jefferson detailed a litany of British abuses and explained that political separation from tyranny is the inescapable reality of a freedom-loving people. Moreover, he made the case that everyone everywhere who was in favor of liberty should support the underdog colonists in their just cause. Although never again stated quite as eloquently, Jefferson's Declaration formed a template for explaining foreign policy. Roosevelt's Infamy speech after Pearl Harbor followed this template, as did some of President Bush's addresses after 9/11. But no one did it better than Ronald Reagan.

Ronald Reagan was the best apologist for American liberty since Thomas Jefferson. In a world that was afraid to upset the Soviets, Reagan boldly referred to the USSR as an "evil empire." To be fair, in some ways previous presidents had done some version of that. Indeed, President Kennedy's remarks toward the Soviets were also very strong and condemnatory. But Reagan went far beyond explaining merely why Communism was evil. He did something more impressive and more enduring: he articulated the reasons why liberty was good. That was his special genius.

Perhaps the best example of this was Ronald Reagan's commencement address at the University of Notre Dame in 1981. Appearing in public for the first time since the assassination attempt on his life, Reagan delivered one of the best speeches in American history. Reagan assured his audience that Communism was on its last legs: "The West won't *contain* communism; it will *transcend* communism. It won't bother to dismiss or denounce it; it will dismiss it as some bizarre chapter in human history whose last pages are even now being written."[23] Not only was this a daring statement; frankly, it seemed to be factually incorrect. After its recent invasion of Afghanistan and its successful installations of puppet governments in Latin America and Southeast Asia, Communism certainly *seemed* to be building a world empire. Even many of those in his own administration thought he was off base.[24] But, notwithstanding its successes, Reagan saw that Communism was already in a state of moral bankruptcy, and its failure was predictable and inevitable. Also inevitable was the triumph of liberty. Reagan continued, "For the West, for America, the time has come to dare to show to the world that our civilized ideas, our traditions, our values, are not—like the ideology and war machine of totalitarian societies—just a facade of strength. It is time for the world to know our intellectual and spiritual values are rooted in the source of all strength, a belief in a Supreme Being, and a law higher than our own."

Reagan knew he had allies in his message of liberty. In that same speech, Reagan affectionately mentioned Pope John Paul II, who—like Reagan—had also recently been shot (the evidence both then and now, pointed to a Soviet-inspired attack) and would go on to be perhaps Reagan's closest ally. Though his papal predecessors were anti-Communists (Pope Pius XI, for instance, had written an encyclical condemning Communism in 1937), Pope John Paul II understood the evil of totalitarian Communism firsthand. Born in 1920 Poland with the given name Karol Wojtyla, he had seen his country torn apart by Communist monsters under the leadership of Stalin. He was going to use the power and influence of the papacy to fight Communism. And the Communists knew it. As biographer George Weigel puts it, "A Slavic Pope, capable of addressing the restive people of the external and internal Soviet empires in their own languages, was a nightmare beyond the worst dreams of the masters of the Kremlin."[25]

But it was much worse than the Soviets thought.

The Soviets, like every Communist regime, sought to quash their citizens from practicing their faith. From the very moment he was elected, the Communist government tried to find a way to stop Wojtyla from returning to Poland as Pope John Paul II. The new pope declared his desire to come back to his native country for two days in May of 1979 for the feast of Saint Stanislaus, the patron saint of Poland. Stanislaus had remained faithful to Catholic teaching despite government interference and intimidation. John Paul's desire to come back for his feast day sent chills up the spine of Brezhnev and the Soviet leaders in Moscow and Poland, who suspected that John Paul simply wished this commemorative remembrance to stir up anti-Communist and anti-government sentiment with massive crowds of Polish Catholics. Therefore, the Communist government tried to negotiate against his arrival for that feast day. Instead, it was agreed that he would come in the month of June rather than in May. However, as part of that concession, the Pope would come not for *two* days, but for *nine*. And this two versus nine days accommodation proved fatal for Polish Communism.[26]

The Soviet and Polish Communist leaders had hoped that no comparison was made between the regime that martyred Saint Stanislaus and the current Communist regime in Poland. After all, that was the fervent hope behind their negotiations. Apparently, Pope

John Paul II didn't get the memo. For starters, the Catholic Church moved the feast day of Saint Stanislaus to June that year, infuriating the Communists.[27] And from his first homily in Warsaw on June 2 (in which he mentioned Saint Stanislaus seven times) to his farewell homily on June 10, he continually invoked the saint's memory. As author and professor Paul Kengor put it, "Throughout the nine-day pilgrimage, John Paul II avoided being explicitly political. Nonetheless, no one failed to connect the dots."[28] We might say that the pope's statements about the dignity of man *preceded* politics. For instance, in his opening homily at Victory Square, now Piłsudski Square, in Warsaw, the pope said, "Christ cannot be kept out of the history of man in any part of the globe, at any longitude or latitude of geography. The exclusion of Christ from the history of man is an act against man. Without Christ it is impossible to understand the history of Poland."

We could say that the pope's speeches were inspiring, but the word "inspiring" fails to capture the euphoria that Polish Catholics felt during those pivotal nine days. Day after day, the pope was drawing some of the largest crowds in the history of Christianity: his first speech drew a quarter million, and his final speech drew 2 million people, which was the largest public gathering in the history of the nation. By the time John Paul left Poland, the entire country was transformed, and Communism's days in Eastern Europe were numbered. The Polish people had been reminded of their inestimable worth and God-given dignity.

Reagan's other major ally in the battle against Communism was Margaret Thatcher. The prime minister built up her own military forces and let the Communists know that they could not extend their global reach on her watch—most notably through her liberation of the Falkland Islands but also in her commitment to NATO.[29] In her speeches, she was eager to condemn Communism, especially in her Conservative Party conference speech in 1980, in which she called Soviet Marxism "politically and morally bankrupt."[30] She also assured the world that she was prepared to fight Communism with all her might. "To those waiting with bated breath for that favourite media catchphrase, the 'U' turn, I have only one thing to say. You turn if you want to. The lady's not for turning. I say that not only to you but to our friends overseas and also to those who are not our friends."

Thatcher was not one to tempt her enemies with weakness.

Together—Reagan, Thatcher, and John Paul II—formed an alliance to bring down Soviet Communism with an unshakable resolve and a message of political liberty that was clear. Not only did they have a powerful message, they also had the integrity to make these claims. From time immemorial, the great orators have agreed that the integrity of a speaker forms a proof to the audience of the statement's truth. Today, we need men and women who can echo that message with the voice of integrity. But in recent years, the Jeffersonian template—the ability to champion the cause of liberty to the world—has been lost. It needs to be regained. America is currently failing in the war of words and ideas against those who reject and even hate liberty.

LOOKING FORWARD

In December 2018, I was invited to attend the eighteenth annual Doha Forum in Qatar. The slogan of the forum is: "Diplomacy, Dialogue, Diversity." Indeed, it would on the surface live up to its declared three Ds. But beneath the surface, the forum is a massive public relations campaign to generate positive press for Qatar. It succeeds there as well. Among the many notable attendees was António Guterres, secretary general of the United Nations. Shortly after his remarks, it was revealed that Qatar was making a $500 million donation to the UN. Qatar has pursued an aggressive strategy to build its prestige on the world stage, like hosting the 2022 World Cup, which they simply bought. Remarkable, given that Qatar is virtually isolated on a small peninsula. Its only land border is with Saudi Arabia, and that is closed. Saudi Arabia, along with its ally Bahrain to Qatar's north and the United Arab Emirates to the south, ceased all diplomatic ties with Qatar in June of 2017. There was speculation that Saudi Arabia might invade. A coordinated information campaign targeted Qatar as being a sponsor of terrorism, President Trump unwisely repeated these allegations but seemed to back off after realizing the United States has a military base in Qatar: Al Udeid Air Base, the largest US military base in the Middle East.

Saudi Arabia has closed its airspace to flights in and out of Doha. Flights to and from the West are routed around the Kingdom of Saudi Arabia. My flight into Doha flew south over Iraq and Kuwait and down the Persian Gulf. The flight home went over Iran to the Caspian Sea and over Russia to Estonia. Qatar has diplomatic relations with both Iran and Russia. It has a shared agreement with Iran to extract natural gas, from which it generates most of its wealth. So when I read in the agenda that one of the breakout sessions was called "Russia's Evolving Global Role," I should not have been surprised.

The panel was hosted by Timofey V. Bordachev, who is a director for the Center for Comprehensive European and International Studies at the National Research University Higher School of Economics in Moscow. During his opening and throughout the panel, Mr. Bordachev repeated the phrase "Russia's new role as a peacemaker" or some variation on that theme. So much so, I could almost lip-sync it. Did Professor Bordachev not realize his audience had access to the internet? His propagandistic case for Russia as a peacemaker was laughable. But I wasn't laughing. It was infuriating to have him attempt to present Russia in this light and even more so to have his selected panel echo his sentiments.

When it came time for questions, my hand instantly shot up. I waited patiently as others were called on. Each question seemed to start with a grandiose statement reaffirming Professor Bordachev's peacemaker premise and then went on to ask an insipid question prompting the panelists to build on the theme. My question, given Russia's limited resources and its new role as global "peacemaker," was what was Russia's plan to rebuild the Syrian city of Aleppo?

I didn't get the chance.

In a sense, this experience was a microcosm of foreign policy and

not just overseas but here in America in the sense that foreign policy, even otherwise good foreign policy, tends to be communicated
poorly, if it is communicated at all.

Whatever foreign policy America pursues, it must be communicated clearly and honestly to the American people. Reagan, Thatcher,
and John Paul II were convinced that Communism was based on a
lie and that societies built on lies cannot last. People simply get sick
and tired of the lies. Lenczowski reminds us of an observation of
Aleksandr Solzhenitsyn, a writer who served time in a labor camp
and later exposed the horrifying nature of Soviet Communism. He
talked about the physical brutality, the constant shortages of necessi-
ties, and so forth. Yet, Solzhenitsyn said that the worst part of Soviet
life was the "daily force-feeding of a steady diet of lies."[31] That, they
could not take. As Lenczowski notes, truth—in the war of ideas—is
the "most powerful weapon." There is a lesson in that for perhaps every politician but rarely more so than for politicians in our own time.

4

TAXATION *WITH* REPRESENTATION CAN BE WORSE

At midnight on June 30, 1997, the British flag was lowered for the last time in Hong Kong. Raised in its place was the Chinese flag, peacefully ending more than a century and a half of British rule. Beginning in the summer of 2019, Hong Kong was not at peace, as its streets were filled with protesters wanting to preserve something they had had for the last hundred years: freedom. Hong Kong is one of the world's most vibrant cities, densely populated with more skyscrapers than any other city in the world. Its 7.5 million residents of numerous nationalities would have the seventh-highest life expectancy of any nation, if it were a nation. With a GDP of $341 billion, Hong Kong alone would be the world's thirty-fourth most productive and the seventeenth wealthiest per capita country in the world. What makes these statistics astounding is that unlike the United States, Russia, Canada, Qatar, South Africa, or Saudi Arabia, Hong Kong has no oil, no coal, and no precious metals to be drilled or mined. It has no natural resources. Its wealth relies entirely on human productivity and innovation. So, how did Hong Kong become so rich while so many other nations, large and small, remain so poor?

As already stated, it's not Hong Kong's natural resources that made it rich. Other than its proximity to the South China Sea and its fishing and farming, Hong Kong has none. With people from so many diverse cultural backgrounds, we can only conclude that people from any background can assimilate into a wealth-creating society. To further make the point, we can use North Korea and South Korea as a model, as the populations in those two countries are genetically and culturally the same. With that in mind, North Korea lags far behind South Korea by every conceivable positive measure. In 1973, the north and the south's economies were both small and roughly the same size. Today, the South Korean economy is the twelfth-largest in the world, dwarfing North Korea. South Korea's GDP is nearly thirty-seven times greater at $1.2 trillion per year versus a paltry $33 billion for North Korea. The average South Korean has a life expectancy of twelve more years than the average North Korean. And because of food shortages, North Koreans are actually shorter by an average of several inches compared to their South Korean counterparts.

So what accounts for Hong Kong's incredible prosperity?

Before I answer that, I must address a question that should be coming into the mind of the reader. Am I about to advocate for the reinstitution of colonialism? Certainly not. I'll also readdress nation building and why it fails in a moment. But while Hong Kong was a British colony, it largely escaped the exploitations of its sisters, and without question Hong Kong was left astoundingly more prosperous than when the British found it.

Now before we look at what Hong Kong did do right; we should first look at how it came to be.

Hong Kong's extraordinary, prosperous rise began as the result of a trade war between the Qing dynasty and the British Crown. For mid-nineteenth-century British merchants, trade with China was hugely profitable, but trade with China, which is still familiar today, was largely a one-way street. Britain bought goods like tea, porcelain, textiles, and silk from China, but China would buy nothing in return. Moreover, China would only accept silver for payment of its goods from the British. The rate at which silver was being exported to China caused the British considerable alarm. In order to balance trade with China, the British began illegally importing into China a commodity the Chinese couldn't resist: opium.

In a mirror trade policy with the support of the British government, silver became the only acceptable payment for the illegal opium. It didn't take long for the opium imports to almost entirely offset the total Chinese exports to Britain and for millions of Chinese to become addicted. The Chinese needed to put a stop to the opium trade.

Thus, began the First Opium War.

By August of 1842, a negotiated peace between England and China ended the war. But the illegal trade continued, and after a Second Opium War the British gained control of not only Hong Kong but the entire Kowloon Peninsula region under the 1860 Convention of Peking that ended that war. Thirty-eight years later, the British obtained a lease from the Chinese for the New Territories that included Hong Kong and 235 other islands in the South China Sea for ninety-nine years.

Over the next century, the bucolic 422-square-mile region made up of farms and fishing villages transformed into one of the world's most vibrant and productive cities that would become an incontrovertible example of how free markets are created and how they lead to exponential wealth from virtually nothing. Land that had been sparsely populated and of little value became scarce and expensive as millions of people attracted by opportunity moved to the wealth-creating mecca.

Many point to reports that up to 20 percent of people in Hong Kong are living in poverty, and while the gap between the very rich and the very poor is wide, Hong Kong's poverty problem is one of relative poverty. Setting aside the fact that Hong Kong in 2016 changed its definition of poverty, doubling the minimum income of the new official poverty level, its residents who are poor, like in other free market societies, don't usually stay poor. Low-skilled workers, including many immigrants who come looking for work can immediately find low-paying jobs, but the opportunity is there to climb the economic ladder. There is no caste system, so while the poverty rate often seems stuck, it's not the same people who are poor. Hong

Kong is by no means a utopia—it will always have its share of poor people—but the measure of wealth creation and the ability to participate juxtaposed against any other economic system remains unrivaled.

If we had to distill what made Hong Kong so successful to a single word, it would be "freedom." It's what they had for more than one hundred years and what the protesters today are trying to preserve. While North Korea got tyranny and China got Communism, Hong Kong and South Korea got freedom.

Like nineteenth-century colonialism, the United States' foreign policy over the course of the last thirty years has exhausted its experiments with nation building—the idea that we can supplant a dictatorial or autocratic regime with democracy, and everything will work out. It won't. While it is historically true that democracies pose a substantially lower risk to our national security, it is futile to attempt to overlay a democratic system on an existing nondemocratic regime.

For example, let's take a fictitious country whose ruling class says they are open to democratic reforms and understands that by making changes they would allow their country to experience dramatic economic growth. But once our enlightened ruling class begins to understand that democratic reforms invariably mean giving up power, they balk. For instance:

We like the idea of a free press, but it wouldn't work here.

We support free elections, just as long as the right people remain in power.

We are happy to support freedom of expression but criticizing the government causes unrest.

We want our people to have more resources, but it's best if we decide for them.

We want more businesses, but we should decide the winners and losers.

I am not advocating a new mercantilism or even capitalism per se. Free market capitalism can exist only where government does not interfere with it and therefore distort the buying and selling signals inherent to a free market including industry-specific tax incentives or even incentives designed to benefit a specific company. Governments can provide tax incentives for companies to expand or hire, but they should be broadly available to any company.

The hard realities of why nation building fails are numerous and complex. The simple answer is that it is too difficult to entice the entrenched ruling class to give up power for the greater good. Embracing freedom partially or even halfway simply will not do. All its essential ingredients are necessary, or it will fail. Even China has recognized the miracle of Hong Kong by establishing the One Country–Two Systems constitutional principle created by Deng Xiaoping for the purposes of reunification in the early 1980s. Up until the 2019 protests—sparked by a change in the judicial process where a resident of Hong Kong could be extradited to face trial in the opaque mainland Chinese criminal justice system—China has had the wisdom to change very little in order to preserve the goose that keeps laying the golden eggs. But its resolve to maintain One Country–Two Systems is being severely tested. China seems to want to absorb Hong Kong into the old system but doing so will kill the goose. You simply cannot have the innovation and productivity that creates wealth without a system of freedom.

Hong Kong is prosperous because the British gave it:

- Respect for human life
- Democratically elected officials
- An appeal process
- Contract law
- Private property rights
- Intellectual property rights
- Freedom of the press
- Freedom of speech
- Freedom to file grievances with the government with a process for redress
- Freedom of expression
- Freedom of religion

- Civilian control over police and security enforcement
- Freedom to protest
- An independent judiciary
- And finally, capitalism

This is the recipe for economic growth. All of its ingredients are essential. Remove one and the dish is ruined. On its face, it appears that only a few of these items apply to economics, but free markets simply cannot function if protecting the rights of the individual are not central to government's purpose. The "pursuit of happiness" is not possible without "liberty," which is meaningless without "life." The hierarchy is deliberate. They must be protected in order: life, liberty, and the pursuit of happiness.

Two of these essential ingredients—an independent judiciary and the right to protest—are being tested in Hong Kong today. If China fails the test to preserve them, Hong Kong will begin its decline—if not collapse—as an economic power. Because when any of the prerequisites of freedom are lost, others are sure to follow.

FREEDOM AND THE FREE MARKET

At its core, the free market recognizes the right of human beings to create new ideas, new solutions, new products, new innovations, new music, or new art and be able to offer their creations to as large a market as possible. The free market is the manifestation of the human desire to be creative. The free market is free because all of its transactions are entirely voluntary. The system of trade between individual sellers and individual consumers is based upon both sides getting what they want from the transaction. If you have something to sell, you must convince a potential buyer that they want the product or service that you are offering more than the money they have in their wallet, bank account, or their ability to borrow. There is no requirement to buy. The buyer can simply decide not to buy or to buy elsewhere.

But true markets can function only when the consumer has information to compare and knows the real price. This is truer today than in all of human history. For most products and services, the internet has made it relatively easy to compare cars, hotels, flights, electronics, or cat litter. Although marketing budgets remain hugely unequal, everyone who has a product or service to sell has a plug-and-play distribution system through Amazon or eBay.

When I was growing up, we bought our music in a record store. The selection was limited to the size of the store. Most music for sale was heard on the radio. Obscure or alternative music was hard to find or had to be ordered. Today, consumers look for the music they want online in virtual record stores that have no limits on shelf space. This is true not only for music but for everything conceivable that we can purchase.

Yet today, governments still routinely distort the markets in any number of ways: Taxes on different products or services, tariffs on imports, regulations, compliance, bailouts, and more. Government interference in the market comes at an enormous hidden cost: laws like the Sarbanes-Oxley Act that create barriers to market entry; laws that create advantages for established companies with a lobbying arm over smaller companies and start-ups. This causes the loss of innovations that the normal chaos of the marketplace creates. When government creates barriers for competition, what is lost is the next Apple, Amazon, Google, the next innovation, the next cancer treatment, or the cure for Alzheimer's (a multitrillion-dollar problem over the next decade).

The 2008 bailout is illustrative of government intrusion. The American people were told over and over again that financial companies like AIG were too big to fail. While it is true that the government did not invent the bundling of high-risk loans as a security to be traded, they did sanction the practice when they bailed out the companies, arbitrarily in some cases, that sold them. In other words, millions of people who could not afford to buy the houses they bought qualified for them because they were essentially going in on the deal with a big backer. But when millions of Americans who went underwater did the rational thing and simply walked away from their mortgages (which they have a right to do under the mortgage contract), they lost their homes. Nevertheless, the government decided that the wealthy bankers should be reimbursed and not suffer the loss of their bad decisions. That is not only a government distortion of the market, but it is also morally reprehensible!

Similarly, GM—along with other auto manufacturers—took a bailout during the George H. W. Bush administration and again during the Obama administration. Last year, GM announced it would be closing five auto plants. Some would argue that taxpayers should be upset that the government bailed out GM and GM turned around and closed plants anyway. And they would be right to be angry. But why should we have bailed out GM in the first place? Or AIG? Or any other company?

It is true that the US Treasury collected positive revenue from the GM bailout. It is, nevertheless, classic market distortion. GM would not have needed a bailout if the company had not been mismanaged. But vastly more important, GM was not building cars consumers wanted. The Lordsville, Ohio, plant didn't close because of cheaper labor in Mexico or a government policy. It closed because people weren't buying the Chevy Cruze manufactured there. Just because the result was additional revenue to the treasury in this case doesn't mean it won't be in another case. But again, that's almost inconsequential compared to the larger issue. Should the government have bailed out Smith Corona typewriter manufacturers because they couldn't see the future in computing? If consumers choose not to buy GM cars, how is it justifiable that politicians take taxpayer money and give it to a company whose products they don't want?

The government bailed out GM for one reason—votes. But by picking winners and losers, the government distorted the automobile market by saving GM while disadvantaging its competitors and upstarts ready to sell consumers products they actually do want. Worse, it takes money from companies who are innovating and gives it to companies who are stuck in the past.

Would it have been financially catastrophic? Of course, especially for the people who work or are invested in those companies all the way down to the dealerships. It may seem compassionate to bail out GM and save all the jobs but is it compassionate to take taxpayer money and give it to a company where they don't receive a service or product in return? Is that the purpose of government?

Ultimately bailouts lead to propping up the past at the expense of the future. It steals from the innovators who are trying to compete with the established corporations. Moreover, I believe that despite the short-term pain, the US economy and displaced employees would be better off today, a decade later, if we just took the hit then rather than have wasted more than $3 trillion attempting to bail out the past. Too big *not* to fail should be the motto.

People do not fully reap the benefits of a free market as long as the government involuntarily takes their money and gives it to a company the taxpayer does not directly receive a service or product from. The government is a third party that distorts the seller-consumer relationship.

Conservatives had long championed these and other principles of the free market, but it seems that we have forgotten what we used to know so well. The lessons of Hong Kong are a vivid reminder of how the freedom to create creates wealth and the innovations that make our lives better and can sometimes actually save them. Governments cannot create wealth, nor can they manage the economy. The economy is simply billions of transactions that occur every day between buyers and sellers. In the web of transaction, innovators discover unmet needs, manufacturers find niches, and marketers use branding, price, and quality to appeal to different customers. The smartphone led to an explosion of applications never dreamed of two decades ago that are now common: apps that generate billions in economic activity that didn't exist just a few short years ago. All of this activity is unmanageable, chaotic, and unpredictable. Innovations are disruptive especially when consumers adopt them quickly, as in the case of the personal computer making the typewriter obsolete almost overnight. Laptops and then smartphones eliminated the need for desktop computers. The value of million-dollar taxi medallions—the required license to operate a cab in New York City—plummeted as soon as New Yorkers began to use ride services like Uber and Lyft from their phones.

All of this innovation could not take place without risk takers who invest their money either directly with a start-up or through one of the financial exchanges found on Wall Street in New York and elsewhere around the globe. Sometimes those investors—big and small—take big hits, at other times they reap huge rewards, as they should. Government can reasonably and evenhandedly regulate the well-established activities surrounding worker safety, market manipulation, consumer and environmental safety. What government should *not* do is rig the game in favor of an industry or company.

Although, I want to acknowledge that the government does do a great deal of beneficial scientific research, especially in health, it is absurd to think the government could create anything approaching the scale of innovation that happens in the private sector. While it is also true that ARPANET, the forerunner of the internet, was invented at the Pentagon to secure our nuclear offensive capabilities, they could not and would not have conceived of all the ways the internet is used today. No one could have. From a conservative's perspective, freedom and financial incentives to create have resulted in an explosion of activity that has dramatically improved the lives of people. Competition spurs more improvements, generates new ideas and markets, improves quality, convenience, options, and drives down costs.

New York mayor Bill de Blasio loves to lament that we have to get money out of the wrong hands; by that he means the rich and get it into the right hands, by that he means the poor. More accurately he means the money should be put in government's hands. But the mayor has it exactly backward. In order to foster innovation and wealth creation, we need a system that keeps as much money in the hands of those who know how to create wealth and out of the hands of government central planners who erroneously believe they can do more good with the money than the private sector.

Of course governments need money to function, and conservatives make a mistake positioning themselves as being anti-government.

Government provides essential services in society. Money is necessary to build and maintain infrastructure, provide for the common defense, education, law enforcement, and a myriad of other good government functions. However, government has a tendency to constantly expand into areas better left to the private sector because governments have no built-in incentives to be efficient, to be timely, to be helpful, or to innovate. Downward cost pressure or incentives to improve services, common in the free market due to competition, are absent in government.

Keeping as much money in the right hands, the private sector, and out of the wrong hands, the greedy hand of government, has made the United States a factory for innovation and since 1890, the world's largest economy.

WEALTH VS. POVERTY?

We hear a lot about the 1 percent. And while there is a yawning income gap between the very rich and the very poor not only in the United States but also across the globe, most Americans today live a quality of life their grandparents couldn't have imagined. And if you are reading this, you are likely in the global top 1 percent. Earnings of $32,400 a year puts you in the 1 percent of income earners worldwide.

Living near the poverty level has many challenges I've been familiar with in my own life. I'm not suggesting that any American should take satisfaction or be satisfied by being in the top 1 percent of wage earners globally. I'm simply providing context of where our capitalist system has brought us in comparison to other economic systems. While there is chronic poverty in the United States, it's relative and not absolute poverty.

When I was growing up, owning two cars, traveling on an airplane, going on vacation, owning more than one television, going out to eat (even fast food), or eating steaks on no special occasion were the things that only rich people did. Today, while the rich sit in first class or fly private, stay in nicer hotels, drink rarer vintages, and own more exotic cars, there really is not much the rich can do that is beyond the reach of most Americans.

By contrast, 84 percent of the world lives on less than $20 a day. By comparison, 12 percent of Americans are that poor. More than half of the world lives on less than $10 per day. In fact, the ability to work, create, and innovate, and subsequently profit and accumulate wealth from your efforts has been the single greatest attraction for people wanting to come to the United States.

The United States holds one-quarter of the world's wealth because of a system that has, on balance, allowed people with the willingness to persevere from any background the freedom to pursue not only a better life for themselves but a better country for everyone else.

Capitalism is the only major economic system that gives people the chance to rise from poverty to wealth. As economist Hernando de Soto put it, "Capitalism stands alone as the only feasible way to rationally organize a modern economy."[1] Critics often equate corruption, cronyism, and exploitation of workers with capitalism, but that's not capitalism. Do those things occur? Of course they do. But they occur in socialist systems or any other economic system you could conceive of because the one thing they all have in common is flawed human beings. People do not become angels under a capitalist system, but neither do they become saints under socialism. Central planning has never made a dent in chronic generational poverty; only a capitalist system allows poor people to liberate themselves from destitution. Capitalism's biggest beneficiaries are not the rich but the poor. In practice, true capitalism has lifted billions of people out of crushing poverty.

India provides a good example. When India received independence, the nation was led by Jawaharlal Nehru, who was a Socialist. For decades to follow, a tiny fraction of India's government officials commanded the nation's industrial production. It was not the free market but nepotism and cronyism and corruption that dictated the economy's winners and losers—mostly losers. The byzantine bureaucratic maze to get a business license was, to quote Elizabeth Warren, "a rigged system that props up the rich and powerful and kicks dirt on everyone else."[2] Needless to say, the few won, and the rest of India's billion-plus people lost. Under that system, poverty was a life sentence from which there was no escape.

But over the last thirty years, India has loosened its central-planning stranglehold and simply allowed the free market to operate. It has become easier to start a business, and India has made great strides—not by central planning, but by letting the free market, with all of its creative energy, allow people to escape poverty and accumulate wealth. Today, even in the poorest parts of India, people are freer to sell their products and services and are doing so. This is capitalism. By our metrics, these people are very poor, but the free exchange of capitalism is allowing them to move in the right direction.

The trajectory for eradicating poverty is moving decisively in a positive direction. The only obstacles preventing most of the world's countries from minimizing poverty are war and politics. Still, there is much to be done. The World Bank has defined extreme poverty as living on less than $1 a day. Today, the number is around $2 a day. No one would defend that level of income as anything more than subsistence. But everywhere large numbers of people are lifted from poverty, the irrefutable cause is economic freedom. We can't point to a single example where central planners have had anywhere near capitalism's level of success.

Much of the rest of the world has seen similar progress in that same time frame. East Asia and the Pacific region have made the most gains. As recently as 1990, 60 percent of the people living in East Asia and the Pacific lived in extreme poverty. Today, it is fewer than 4 percent. Sub-Saharan Africa has made the fewest gains, but even there, extreme poverty is being reduced. Many places in between have made dramatic gains. In 1990, 35 percent of the world lived in extreme poverty; today, less than 11 percent do. Yet, many people keep looking elsewhere than capitalism for answers to this global economic turnaround.

While I may never have even a fraction of the wealth of Bill Gates, I am grateful for all that I do have, and I am grateful for what others have that I don't. While I believe that the current gap between rich and poor is lamentable, I don't sit around trying to think up ways to make the rich get *poor*. Instead, I'd like to see the poor get *rich*. But too many actually believe that the poor are poor because the rich are rich. Like an epidemic, that fallacious idea can lead to a dangerous revolutionary outcome.

After World War II ended in 1945, American poverty was on the decline, bottoming out at about 13 percent in the early 1960s. In his State of the Union address on January 8, 1964, President Lyndon Baines Johnson famously declared his War on Poverty while introducing the Great Society, a set of welfare programs to combat racial injustice and poverty. While it was an exciting proposition to be sure, fifty-five years later, generational and chronic poverty proved to be a formidable foe. Building on President Roosevelt's New Deal programs, Johnson dramatically expanded the welfare state. But after spending $23 trillion on anti-poverty programs, America has been stuck at the same 13 percent.

What the government didn't try to do was to simply teach people how not to be poor. At the risk of sounding patronizing, I do think it's important for people to know how to leverage a free market to avoid being poor.

Dave Ramsey believed in helping people with their financial situations so much that he wanted to create a radio show to help people out of debt and on to wealth building. No one was interested in investing in his idea, but he believed in it so much he bought airtime on local stations to broadcast his show. Today, his show is nationally syndicated and a top performer that he owns outright. People want to know how they can create a better life for themselves and their families, and Dave helps them learn how to do it. You could call it Dave Ramsey's war on poverty, and it's doing more to combat systemic poverty than any government program.

Likewise, for all the criticism of Walmart and its competitors like Target, they have dramatically increased consumer buying power and thus have done more to raise the standard of living of the poor than all the government programs to combat poverty ever did. Some will retort that Walmart and other companies pay wages so low that many of its employees qualify for government aid, thus arguing that taxpayers are subsidizing their wages. While it's a valid point, the government's welfare policy has little to do with Walmart's business model. If anything, the government's welfare policy distorts that wage market, not the other way around. Further, it was a popular public policy decision to allow people who are willing to work to also collect public benefits in order to encourage work rather than have welfare recipients reject a job because as an employee they would lose their public benefits. The idea was that it was far better for someone to be acquiring new skills and good work habits than to stay home and collect benefits. Moreover, people who are employed are better connected to the network of opportunities that come from having a job and being around people who have jobs. That gives the working poor the best opportunity to find a better job and get off public assistance.

Here again, I'm not suggesting scrapping any particular welfare program (although I could think of a few). Welfare should be a safety net for when people truly need it. I don't think most Americans mind paying taxes that go to help the poor. But when too many able-bodied people end up on welfare, the truly needy get hurt the most.

My wife and I took in a woman who became homeless after she lost her home due to foreclosure. She has passed, so I don't mind telling her story. My wife met Beverly at church and found that she had some needs that we could help with. She needed things fixed around the house that she was unable to do herself or couldn't afford to get repaired. She had been a nurse in Massachusetts. She was very knowledgeable, articulate, and smart. But she was suffering from both physical and mental health issues that made it difficult for her to manage her finances. She could no longer hold a job. We helped her with living expenses. We made sure she was with us for Christmas dinner so she wouldn't be alone and so she would know that she was loved. Eventually, we learned that her house was in foreclosure, but it was too late at that point to try to help refinance or even to sell the house so she could get the equity out of it. She lost it and had no place to go.

We tried to get her to fill out paperwork so that she might qualify for disability and affordable housing. She would agree, saying she would get it done right away, but she was simply incapable of organizing the data she needed to fill out the forms correctly. We, as I came to find out, like most people, had to get a lawyer to complete the required paperwork and then we had to wait. Meanwhile, I ran into someone I knew and had asked what they were up to. During that conversation, I found out they had filed for and qualified for disability, so they were not working. I knew this person well enough to know that they were very capable and competent. There certainly was some kind of work they could do. In fact, competent enough, I thought, to get on disability when Beverly, who was not competent enough to fill out the forms, could not. I bit my tongue.

Beverly was not going to get better. She was always going to need help. But how was she ever going to get help unless someone like my wife, who routinely seeks out people to help, steps up? There was no one from the government that was going to find Beverly and help her. Worse, having people capable of work clogging up the system made Beverly even more invisible. We should have a safety net for people who fall on hard times but even more so for the chronically unemployable. But to deal with systemic poverty, we need an army of Dave Ramseys who can show people the best practices for being prosperous.

TAXATION

Being anti-government is not a conservative value. Government administration is necessary. The founders agreed and created our government, which is outlined in the Constitution. Contrary to what many think, the Constitution does not grant power so much as it explicitly limits it. It goes further to share governing power among three branches so that no single branch or tyrant could fully control it. Its function depends on cooperation and compromise. A necessary government therefore needs funding. It gets its funding through taxation. Taxation is not only fundamental to America; it was *foundational* to America's creation. The inescapable reality is that the origin of the United States will be forever linked to the British insistence on taxing nearly everything they could think of, including sugar, paper, paint, glass, coffee, and—most infamously—tea. In the Declaration of Independence, Jefferson insisted that "imposing Taxes on us without our Consent" amounts to tyranny and is a just cause for armed revolution." Whether taxation was the *largest* straw for the colonists will be forever debated, but this we know for sure: taxation was the *last* straw. As for the colonists, their victory over the British hardly put the matter of taxation to bed. Quite the contrary: it was in the ensuing discussion of whether to adopt the Constitution that a detailed philosophy of taxation really emerged. As one historian puts it, "Colonial politics were governed more by disputes over taxes and how they would be spent than all other matters, such as freedom of conscience, French threats on the frontier, and security of land titles."[3] That point is not lacking evidence. Written by Alexander Hamilton, James Madison, and John Jay, *The Federalist Papers* were a series of eighty-five newspaper articles that made the case for adopting the US Constitution. By my count, the document mentions the words "tax" and "taxation" along with synonymous words like "excise" and "duties" more than three hundred times. Another series of contemporary articles that came to be known as *The Anti-Federalist Papers* (written largely by Patrick Henry of "Give me liberty or give me death" fame) mentioned the subject of taxation at least as many times, if not more. Why the emphasis? Is there a link between taxation and liberty? Does the government even have the right to tax? And if so, at what point does overtaxation occur? What's the conservative position on this?

Americans were not the first to wrestle with the issue of taxation; nor were they the first to believe that taxation is a pretty big deal. In fact, there is a figure who appears and reappears in history who also thought it was a big deal: God. Recounted in First Samuel, the Jewish people were living under a theocracy, that is, government by God, but they were unhappy. They expressed their desire to Samuel that instead they wanted to have a human king like other nations. When Samuel spoke to God and relayed the people's desire, God told Samuel that if they had a king, terrible misery would follow. And God was specific about what that misery would look like: thousands of men would be made slaves and forced to fight and die in arbitrary wars, women would be made into servants (sexual slavery seems implied), and the king would steal their lands and vineyards.

And God told them something else: they would be overtaxed.[4]

Consider this litany of misery: slavery, forced conscription in needless wars, institutional rape, and, *overtaxation*? What's taxation doing in there? That last part doesn't seem to fit in. And yet, when you consider what taxation actually entails—the transfer of wealth from private hands to government coffers—it really does fit in. Whether or not you are a believer in Judeo-Christian revelation, this much is historically clear: many of the kings were brutal. As predicted, when the kings took power, they committed terrible atrocities, and this mayhem was financed with tax revenue. And as tax historian Charles Adams writes, Samuel hadn't even mentioned the scourging that awaited those who dared to evade the tax. One of the kings, Rehoboam, decided that tax evaders should suffer a uniquely brutal form of punishment nicknamed "the scorpion"—a leather whipping device that had metal hooks attached at the ends that were designed to tear away human flesh.[5] For obvious reasons, this had a scarring effect on the Israelites for many generations. How do we know that? Consider that a thousand years after the episode with Samuel, the New Testament recounts that it was not Judas of whom the disciples of Jesus were most suspicious; rather it was Matthew, for the reason that he was a tax collector. The people of both the Old and New Testaments agreed that taxation equals power and power equals taxation.

So when politicians says they want to raise your taxes, what they are really saying is that they want to take some measure of your freedom. After all, someone who gets to keep all their earnings would be considered free. Someone who is forced to give up all their earnings would be considered a slave. Raising taxes may be necessary, but the benefit should be carefully weighed against the loss of freedom. On the scale between freedom and slavery, conservatives lean strongly toward freedom.

In this, the founders of America agreed that a government's taxing powers must be severely limited. That point is made throughout their writing. They saw the unmistakable connection between taxation and liberty. For all their disagreements, they agreed on this fact: if money equals power, taxation equals the *transfer* of power. One such sentiment comes to us from Supreme Court Justice John Marshall. In the case of *McCulloch v. Maryland*, where the state of Maryland was attempting to tax a Federal Bank out of existence, Justice Marshall famously wrote that "the power to tax involves the power to destroy."[6] That's a powerful sentiment to be made by a sitting Supreme Court justice. And when you read that quote, it's important to consider that the IRS had not yet been established. And when it was, it proved Marshall correct in ways he could have never imagined.

THE IRS

Going back to the first days of his national campaign, President Trump has adamantly and consistently refused to show the American people his tax returns, criticizing those who call for their release as being motivated purely by politics. On the level of presidential politics, however, this could hardly be more ironic. Though the fact did not come to much public attention until the Nixon administration, for the past century, American presidents have routinely—albeit quietly—grabbed the tax returns of their political enemies in an effort to persecute and prosecute them. One IRS expert and historian notes that "almost every administration since the end of World War I has one way or another used the selective enforcement of the tax laws and the information contained in tax records for improper political purposes."[7] Though Nixon's articles of impeachment specifically cite the use of IRS audits and investigations against political adversaries, he was not alone, before or since. Franklin D. Roosevelt cracked down on those who dared criticize him and/or have more money than Roosevelt thought they should have, like Andrew Mellon. John F. Kennedy employed the IRS to go after right-wing groups.

Though Bill Clinton publicly denied having done so, his misuse of the IRS might have been the most obvious, if not outright brazen. The Clinton list of conservative firms under investigation included the NRA, the Heritage Foundation, *National Review*, *The American Spectator*, Freedom Alliance, the American Policy Center, American Cause, Citizens Against Government Waste, Citizens for Honest Government, Concerned Women for America, and others.[8] Another group that found itself under IRS investigation was the Washington, DC–based conservative group Judicial Watch, which had led dozens of lawsuits against Clinton. In the course of its investigation, a senior IRS investigator asked out loud: "What do you expect when you sue the president?"[9]

Of course, not all IRS corruption has been presidential in origin; nor does the IRS confine itself to political opponents; persecuting religious groups had grown increasingly common in recent years. The Thomas More Society, a not-for-profit law firm based in Chicago, notes that religious groups are commonly targeted by the IRS.

Peter Breen, the firm's senior counsel, noted in 2013 that "Despite claims to the contrary, the IRS continues to target and harass pro-life and conservative charities, illegally questioning their religious activities and withholding their tax exemptions."[10] In a 230-page document submitted to Congress, the society illustrated that the IRS often withholds tax exemptions from pro-life groups unless and until they can provide intimate details about their charities. For instance, during its nonprofit application process—which dragged on for months—the Coalition for Life of Iowa received a very strange demand from the IRS: "Please detail the content of the members of your organization's prayers."[11] One can only wonder whether the Hail Mary passes legal muster at the IRS Exempt Organizations Division.

The IRS has a history of abuse that is well documented from many different sides of the political spectrum. To be fair, the IRS does prosecute individuals who are clearly violating the law, but its history shows that it often goes after law-abiding American citizens who cannot afford to provide a decent legal defense. Congress is aware of this, so every few years, Congress holds a hearing at which IRS commissioners and agents are called to account for the injustices that seem rampant within the agency. The responses of the IRS officials range from dazed and confused to indifferent and indignant. In 2013, Steven Miller, the head of the IRS until that year, provided a series of responses to questions that suggested he knew very little of what had been going on in IRS offices.[12] To his credit, when he resigned from the IRS in 2013, he wrote to his fellow IRS employees that much work needed to be done "to restore faith in the IRS." He was perhaps referring to the fact that the Exempt Organization Unit of the IRS had targeted conservative groups and individuals under the leadership of Lois Lerner.

Perhaps even more important, the tax code is so confusing that many taxpayers are not able to complete their taxes on their own. Even a professional tax accountant may not completely understand it. You might use one of those file-it-yourself programs, but if your finances are complex, you cannot say with certainty that what you filed is correct or indisputable. The reason the tax code has become so complicated has more to do with politicians trying to rig the code in favor of their favorite constituencies or special interests. Decade after decade, layer after layer of complicated tax code is the result of politicians carving out exemptions and loopholes for their favored patrons. The tax code can be thought of as the code that pays off special interests in return for power when what is needed is a system that is flatter, fairer, and keeps more money in the hands of the taxpayers who earned it.

INCENTIVE-BASED TAXATION

The Laffer curve is often hailed as a principle of conservative economics; however, even though it is employed to make arguments for lowering taxes, there is nothing particularly conservative about promoting the Laffer curve. In case you were getting popcorn during the scene in *Ferris Bueller's Day Off* where Ben Stein explains the Laffer curve to his high school economics class, here's a refresher. If income tax rates are set at 0 percent, the government will collect zero in taxes. That's pretty clear: 0 percent of any dollar figure is $0. But what if the government has a 100 percent income tax rate? How much revenue will the government collect then? The answer is also $0. Why? Because, knowing that every dollar in income will go to the federal government, no one would work. The Laffer curve says that there is a point between 0 percent and 100 percent that will maximize government revenue. The Laffer curve is often cited by some people as an argument to lower tax rates—and thereby increase government revenue. Though the principle is associated with economist Arthur Laffer, it's one of the most intuitive and self-evident principles in all of economics. And though Arthur Laffer highlighted the principle in the 1980s—and has taken a four-decade victory lap ever since famously drawing it on a bar napkin—it was actually developed centuries ago (a point admitted by Laffer himself). It's even implicit in ancient texts.

Though the mere mention of the Laffer curve may peg one as a conservative, it is a problematic position for a conservative to advance. Yes, conservatism seeks lower tax rates. And in principle, the Laffer curve expresses a mathematical truth; that much is true. Insofar as it seeks to achieve the highest possible tax revenue, however, it violates conservatism's fundamental concern to limit government. P. J. O'Rourke once wrote that "giving money and power to government is like giving whiskey and car keys to teenage boys."[13] By seeking to enact the tax rate that maximizes government revenue, the promotion of the

Laffer curve into law seeks not only to increase my car payments but also to maximize the amount of whiskey for those teenage boys. The idea is about as ass-backward as things can get. There's a related problem with promoting the Laffer curve, and it's a big one. Once you concede that the ideal tax rate is the one that produces the highest tax revenue, you will wind up in a perpetual argument about what that rate may be. Is it 18 percent, 34 percent, or 70 percent? Who's to say? By the way, a number of progressive economists suggest that the proper tax rate is 70 percent. Yes, the logic of the Laffer curve is often employed to make an argument for lower tax rates, but I think it's a crappy argument because it can just as easily be used as an argument to raise taxes.

In whatever tax system we employ in America, the fundamental goal should not be how to achieve the highest possible revenue for the government, but how to restore and retain the highest level of liberty for Americans. We should seek to achieve the lowest possible financial governmental intrusion into the lives of Americans while funding only those government operations that are properly authorized—either directly or indirectly—by the Constitution.

That's it. Not a dollar more.

And to achieve that number, we should have an optional flat tax. Actually, I'd rather have a national sales tax that would replace the income tax, largely because I don't think it's any of the government's damn business how much money you or I make. But I think it's a political impossibility—at least for now. Plus, if a national sales tax like that were passed, we'd end up with *both* a sales tax and an income tax. That being the case, we need a flat tax. Many people make the argument for a flat tax because it seems "more fair." That's not why I make the argument, in part because it's impossible to know what fair is. I don't want to have that argument. Instead, I would argue that a flat tax encourages innovation.

Looking back to the *McCulloch v. Maryland* decision, let's examine Justice Marshall's full quote referenced earlier. Marshall writes that "the power to tax involves the power to destroy; that the power to destroy may defeat and render useless the power to create." If a tax system removes the power to create, it destroys an economy. A tax system must encourage innovation—or at a minimum at least not discourage it. That brings us to the notion of progressive taxation— that marginal tax rates should increase as one's income rises.

Increasing marginal tax rates might be a political winner, but it's an economic loser. As George Gilder puts it, "Steeply 'progressive' tax rates not only destroy incentives; more important, they destroy knowledge. They take from the givers and thus prevent them from giving again, from reinvesting their winnings in the light of the new information generated by the original gift."[14] Whether it's the invention of Wi-Fi technology, a better heart medication, or a way to make automobiles safer, we need creators creating, and we need investors investing, then reinvesting. To use Gilder's terminology, we want more gifts. It is an economic law that the more a thing is taxed, the less we'll have of it. Tax cigarettes more, fewer people will smoke. Tax innovation—which is what progressive taxation actually is—and you will have fewer innovations. Lest we forget, many of the innovations of the previous few decades have not only improved the quality of life but have kept people alive. I, for one, want those products and services that will better my life, and if someone makes a ton of money making my life better, hats off to him or her.

When we think of progressive tax rates, we often think they only apply to the überwealthy like Mark Zuckerberg and Warren Buffett. Some view progressive taxation simply as the most efficient way of sticking it to the rich. Problem is that's not what happens at all. Here's why. First, wealthy Americans can hire CPAs and tax attorneys to help them find ways to reduce taxes. They pay plenty of people to find loopholes, and if the loopholes don't yet exist, they lobby Congress for loopholes and tax shelters. That's how it works in the real world. It's not the überwealthy who suffer from progressive taxes; it's the middle class that gets stuck. Many Americans who are far from millionaires are disincentivized by a jump in tax rates.

LOOKING FORWARD

It's a little-known fact of American history, but our first income tax was a flat tax. Signed into law by Abraham Lincoln in 1861, the law imposed a 3 percent tax beginning with incomes higher than $800 and went progressively higher.[15] Lincoln was ahead of his time. And I suggest we go back to that original idea.

The institution of a flat tax would eliminate the need for the IRS (although there could be some meek tax collection agency in its place rather than the current leviathan). A flat tax would also create a massive and much-needed boon to GDP, to savings, to innovation, and to the personal liberty of Americans. Simultaneously, the capital gains tax should be eliminated, so that the government no longer penalizes risk-taking.

Though Lincoln's 3 percent and $800 income level is no longer realistic, it still works in principle. How about a 15 percent flat tax with a $25,000 single/$50,000 married exemption with another $3,000 per child under eighteen? Maintaining or growing population is essential to long-term economic growth, and its benefits are well worth incentivizing even for those who don't choose to have children. Anything you make above that, whether it's $1 or $1 million, you pay 15 percent. And no loopholes. Back in 1976, Milton Friedman called for a similar structure, and among his arguments he explains that a flat tax would significantly help poor families because it would encourage business investment. Milton Friedman once called the income tax system "an unholy mess" that "purports to tax people in accordance with their ability to pay, but it actually taxes people in accordance with their ability to find tax shelters and ways to get around the law."[16] His observation is verifiably accurate. The flat tax levels the playing field, finally granting Americans a fair tax system. And if 15 percent isn't enough revenue for the federal government, then might I suggest cutting spending?

5

SAVING THE PLANET OR THE HUMANS?

In the spring of 2007, I traveled to Las Vegas with former Speaker Newt Gingrich and his wife, Callista. We were there for an event where Newt was scheduled to speak, but we arrived two days early, which meant I had the full day off before the event. I decided to rent a car, get up very early, and make the five-hour drive to one of my favorite spots on earth: the Grand Canyon. I had been to the South Rim several times but always remembered the North Rim from the one time I had been there in the 1980s as being less traveled, with fewer people. So even though it was farther, I opted for the North Rim.

Being on East Coast time, I left the lights of the Las Vegas Strip in the rearview mirror before the sun came up. I plugged my destination into a Garmin nüvi GPS and settled in for the long ride. I was almost there when I started running low on fuel. Now I was looking for a gas station that was open on a Sunday. Finally, there it was, but I had just passed it. I made a U-turn, pulled into the station, and was now facing in the opposite direction. Relieved, I filled the tank. While the tank was filling, I noticed the GPS was showing the park's service roads, which appeared to be unpaved. I decided to do a little exploring. So instead of turning around to resume my journey, I drove about a mile back and turned right onto a dirt park road. The road wound through the woods, and it was a bit rough and steep in some places, but the rental car was doing fine. There were some off-the-grid camps back there that gave me pause, but I continued through the winding wilderness. I was now on a great adventure.

Eventually, I made it to a wide paved road, which was the main road to the Visitor Center on the North Rim. Having left the treacherous service roads, I accelerated toward the canyon. It was just about 10:00 a.m., and there would be plenty of time to enjoy it. Along the sides of the road, there was a lot of snow piled up—more than I would have expected for early May but it was now melting, and I didn't think much of it.

As I drove, I noticed something strange: there was no one else on this road except a couple of cars heading in the opposite direction. As the cars approached, the drivers would wave. I waved back. Friendly enough, but it seemed odd. Finally, I arrived at the gate that serves as the entrance to the park. There was no one there. When I reached the Visitor Center, the parking lot was nearly empty, with only a few cars. The few people I saw were working. Then I realized it. The park was closed. This was the spring opening crew. They thought I was just one of them. I was now simply trying not to look lost or obviously out of place.

I made my way past the Grand Canyon Lodge, which has a huge veranda overlooking the canyon, and headed down a path to a lookout point. When I got there, I realized what an amazing gift I had been given. I was able to look out over the canyon in the same way it had been discovered: no buildings, no cars, and no people. Just the magnificent canyon. I was alone. What a gift!

Driving back, I almost hit the locked gate. It was but a few hundred yards from the gas station where I filled up. I would have seen it from the other side if I weren't so focused on making the U-turn to get gas. I backtracked my way again on the dirt roads to get out. Had I not needed to get gas at that station, I would have also seen the conspicuous PARK CLOSED sign, given up, and gone back to Las Vegas—a wasted trip. But as it was, it will be one of my most memorable experiences.

ENVIRONMENTALIST *AND* SKEPTIC

My wife, Tamara, and I, and—until recently—my now-married daughter Briana, have lived in the same thousand-square-foot home on a dirt road among the foothills of the Blue Ridge Mountains in Northern Virginia for the last twenty years. Our property was once part of a large dairy farm. We live in the dairy keeper's house, which was long ago sold off with approximately two acres after the dairy ceased to exist. Today, we are bordered on two sides by sixty-six acres of pasture, where beef cattle now graze. There were ten calves born this spring. We share a seventy-five-foot fence line with another neighbor who owns a ten-acre horse farm. On the west side of the property is a three-acre pine grove. The owners of the grove cleared a path so that anyone can enjoy it.

We compost all organic waste material in a composter I made from a wooden lattice. It produces several yards of rich soil each year for our gardens. If you remove the top layer of the pile you can see thousands of worms doing their work making dirt. We also recycle all wastepaper, cardboard, plastics, glass, and metals. I take the recyclables to the local recycle station because I am highly dubious that my trash pickup contracting service actually recycles. I fired my last trash service because they couldn't reassure me that the recyclables were actually being recycled. I have my doubts about the recycle center, too.

I drive a plug-in hybrid. I installed the level II 50-amp charging station myself. Before I bought the hybrid, I was on probation for getting too many speeding tickets. Since I bought the hybrid, I have not gotten any speeding tickets because the desire to get there in the least about of time has changed to a desire to get there the most efficiently. My current gas mileage is 46.5 miles per gallon. My next step is to move to a fully electric vehicle. Similarly, I changed nearly all of the lights in our home to LEDs years ago.

Nick Holonyak was born in the little town of Zeigler, Illinois, in 1928—just a few months before the beginning of the Great Depression. It seemed preordained that Nick's parents would meet. Although they grew up in the same Carpathian Mountain region of eastern Europe, they never met until coming to America. His father immigrated in 1909, arriving in Baltimore; Nick's mother arrived at Ellis Island twelve years later. Like tens of thousands of immigrants from that part of the world, Nick's father worked as a coal miner—often working double shifts. Though he was uneducated himself, Nick's father believed that education was the way out for Nick and his sister. In school, Nick demonstrated an aptitude in math and science. Despite straight As in school, he had not planned on going to college; instead, he worked for a railroad. One time at that job, he worked a straight thirty-three-hour shift. That shift might have changed the world. Years later, he still recalls: "Thirty-three hours straight."[1] He says that when he finally returned home, he said to himself: "That's no damn way to live. That's no way to survive."[2] So he decided to enroll at the University of Illinois, where he earned a bachelor's, master's, and doctorate—and developed an interest of semiconductors along the way.

After a brief stint in the military, Holonyak went to work for General Electric—the company founded by the man who had invented the lightbulb, Thomas Edison. Young Edison had not had as much luck in school as Holonyak. The story is told that seven-year-old Thomas was sent home from school after only a few months in the classroom with the note: "This boy is addled. I cannot teach him." Edison's mother read the note to herself, and when Thomas asked her what the note said, she replied, "It says 'This boy is a genius. He is far too smart for me to teach. You will have to teach him at home.'" Whether the story of the note is true, we do know that his teacher described him as "addled" and that Edison's mother decided to homeschool him. Edison later recounted: "My mother was the making of me. She was so true, so sure of me: and I felt I had something to live for, someone I must not disappoint." The rest is history: Edison went on to light up the world.

But while Thomas Edison had invented the lightbulb, Nick Holonyak invented something that would perfect it—or at least produce something very close to perfection. When the government needed a solution to a particular problem, they went to the free market. In 1962, with a research grant from the air force, Holonyak invented the light emitting diode (LED) for a very specific application that required a visible light indicator that didn't produce heat. Today, LED lighting is commonplace in America. Though it was not first used to produce household lightbulbs, Holonyak predicted very early on that it would be. Turns out he was right. Today's LED lightbulbs emit much less heat, produce more light, last perhaps fifty times longer, and use a fraction of the energy versus incandescent bulbs. You can make them in any color, some you can change the color, and with your smartphone you can turn them on and off from half a world away. LEDs have been described as "the most efficient light source ever created."[3] That's a big achievement, but it's even more impressive when you consider that 20 percent of the energy used on earth is for lighting.[4] According to the Department of Energy, "Widespread use of LED lighting has the greatest potential impact on energy savings in the United States."[5] The Department of Energy says that in the next ten years, use of LED bulbs could save an "equivalent annual electrical output of 44 large electric power plants [1,000 megawatts each], and a total savings of more than $30 billion at today's electricity prices."[6] Of course, that number does not even count the energy saved by no longer mass-producing or recycling incandescent bulbs. Plus, they're getting cheaper all the time. As of this writing, you can purchase 60W-equivalent LED lightbulbs for about $1.

Who predicted this? Who predicted that the world would be lit by a seven-year-old second-grade dropout? Who predicted that the son of an uneducated coal miner would lead an energy revolution? No one. And that is the genius of it all. That is what the Austrian economists refer to as "spontaneous order."[7] You cannot legislate creativity and genius. You can simply create an environment for it to flourish.

As I write this, I can hear the call of a peacock belonging to a distant neighbor. He spend most nights high in the safety of our elm tree. His call is unmistakable. If you've never heard a peafowl's call (the peacock is a male and the female is a peahen) it can be quite startling. It sounds like Kevin, the snipe in the animated movie *Up*. So we started calling him Pete. One day I may ask the owner what his real name is.

In the winter when the ground is covered with snow, you can see our yard is a busy intersection for wildlife because of all the tracks crisscrossing our property. We routinely see deer, foxes, raccoons, and opossums. A neighbor saw a bear on the wooded lot next door. I missed that! I've seen coyote and bald eagles (until they fished the pond empty). Hummingbirds are common as are Canada geese. One morning, I counted fifty-two turkeys wandering around the backyard. On a recent cool, sunny day sitting on our deck looking out over the field, I said to my wife, Tamara, that if heaven were no better than this, I would be so happy.

I think it is in our DNA to have a deep desire to connect with nature. Hiking through the mountains or along the beach away from the noise and life's many distractions gives us the ability to recharge, to gain insight and perspective.

Growing up in New England, I hiked many of New Hampshire's White Mountains, including Mount Washington, which I hiked four times in one summer. I've hiked to the top of Mount Katahdin with a friend at the northern end of the Appalachian Trail in a wild rainstorm. Today, I live within a few miles of the same trail in Virginia. I tell you all this so that some of you might resist throwing this book across the room as you read further on in this chapter. I have a deep love of the natural world and believe that we have a responsibility to care for it. Indeed, caring for a garden was God's first charge to Adam and Eve. They blew it. We should not.

I am a conservative, and I care about the environment. To many, that may sound like a contradiction and not a surprising one given that it's hard to think of a single facet of life today that is not politicized, even a virus; seemingly every human action is viewed through a political lens. "All politics is local" has become "everything is political." Nowhere is this more obvious than in the sphere of the environment. Years ago, there was a theory advanced called the butterfly effect, which essentially stated that microscopic causes can produce catastrophic effects. The theory was so named because it posited that the mere flap a butterfly's wings can cause a tsunami half a world away. Conveniently for its originator and its adherents, the butterfly effect is impossible to either prove or to completely disprove. Nevertheless, the kind of thinking behind the butterfly effect forms the argument advanced by many climate change advocates. It's as though we're half expecting Wolf Blitzer to come on CNN one afternoon to report a story about a terrible tornado in Akron as: "A tornado ripped apart an entire community of mobile homes this morning in Akron because Robert Adams is still using 100-watt bulbs in Anchorage. What a dumbass!" Admittedly, that's hyperbole, but I have noticed the language used in advancing the issue of climate change is religious in nature. If you express the slightest skepticism about climate change you are labeled a denier, meaning you don't believe. In religious terms, it would be heresy: the same as denying a religious doctrine where there can be no room for debate. For me as a Christian, that would be tantamount to denying the virgin birth of Christ or the triune nature of God. There is no point in having the debate, and that it seems is how some climate change advocates want it.

For instance, on several occasions when I've talked about climate change with one of its religious adherents, they invariably use weather events to make their point. Yet, as I've learned, that if I cite a weather event to make my point, I will quickly get a lecture on the difference between weather and climate. What's more is that every weather event—an unusual hot spell or a cold snap, a record number of tornadoes or a lack of them, record flooding or record drought—except those that deniers cite, fits somehow neatly into their argument. It's all caused by climate change. And if you have the temerity to question any of the cause-and-effect assumptions of the climate change religious adherents, you'll hear that it's "settled science," and as I've been told that because I am not a scientist, I have no right to even an opinion about climate change, that is, unless it's the consensus opinion. It seems that what is settled is all the rules for discussion, which is to either believe in climate change or be a climate denier, or worse, a science denier. How convenient.

For the record, I'm neither a scientist nor a climate change denier. I can accept that the climate is changing and will continue to change as it has done since the big bang. I can also accept that human activity likely impacts the climate—but to what extent? I'm not sure anyone knows.

I describe myself as a climate skeptic. I think the idea of "settled science" is arrogant. Scientists are skeptical by nature. Settled science suggests there is nothing more to know. When it comes to climate, I doubt any scientist believes that there is nothing more to learn. Charles Darwin was no doubt a great scientist. Most of his scientific conclusions were at the time, conventional. In his book *The Descent of Man*. Darwin writes: "Man is more courageous, pugnacious, and energetic than woman, and has a more inventive genius."[8] He also concludes: "It is generally admitted that with woman the powers of intuition, of rapid perception, and perhaps of imitation, are more strongly marked than in man; but some, at least, of these faculties are characteristic of the lower races, and therefore of a past and lower state of civilisation."[9] Thank goodness that Darwin's belief that women are inferior to men never became "settled science."

I'm not suggesting people will use climate science to establish a master race; still climate science is undeniably being used to drive political agendas.

There no longer seems to be any purpose in debating the matter at all. The cataclysmic outcome of man-made climate change is routinely presented as a given reality. As the avuncular Bernie Sanders puts it, "The debate is over. The scientific community has spoken in a virtually unanimous voice. Climate change is real. It is caused by human activity."[10] Well, I guess that's all there is to say then. Bernie Sanders has declared the matter closed. There's a consensus, after all.

Of course, science doesn't have a damn thing to do with consensus. As Michael Crichton once put it, "Historically, the claim of consensus has been the first refuge of scoundrels; it is a way to avoid debate by claiming that the matter is already settled."[11]

More to the point, consensus has a way of destroying real science and kicking mankind in the ass. Case in point: Dr. Ignaz Semmelweis. A

Hungarian physician by profession, Semmelweis published a book of his findings in 1861 that showed that if an obstetrician merely washed his hands with antiseptics, the cases of infant mortality would drop considerably. During the time of his writing, cases of puerperal fever were killing a huge number of infants. Admitting that he wasn't exactly sure why it was the case, Semmelweis nevertheless maintained that the use of antiseptics could lower infant mortality by 90 percent. He was right. Known to history as a "pioneer of antiseptics" and a "savior of mothers," Semmelweis's research has saved millions of lives. Tragically, however, Semmelweis never lived to see many of those babies' lives saved. His research angered his anti-antiseptic colleagues, who had spoken—to use Sanders's terminology—"in a virtually unanimous voice." In the eyes of his fellow doctors, the debate was over. And so was Semmelweis. His fellow doctors conspired to have him committed to an insane asylum, where he died two weeks later after being beaten by guards. Semmelweis had gone against consensus—and paid for it with his life. Today, the "Semmelweis effect" refers to the automatic rejection of new findings or discoveries or hypotheses merely because they contradict scientific consensus.[12] As Crichton puts it, "The greatest scientists in history are great precisely because they broke with the consensus."[13]

Does that mean there is no man-made climate change? No. But it does mean that consensus is sometimes wrong. And statements like "the debate is over" are not simply anti–free speech; they're antiscientific.

But here's another problem with Sanders's consensus argument: there is no consensus. Rhetorically, it's easy to see why you might claim that all scientists agree about something; at a certain point, you no longer have to point to factual data. All you need to do is say that every scientist agrees. The consensus *is* your evidence. We've just seen how this is faulty. But is there a consensus? I'm not trying to single out Sanders, because there are many others who share the same position that there is scientific consensus on this. In fact, they even have an exact figure for that consensus: 97 percent. The problem is that no one can cite where this number comes from, and/or what exactly it refers to, and/or can't identify what constitutes a scientist in the first place.

In a 2012 letter signed by forty-nine former NASA employees, some of the most highly credentialed astronauts, meteorologists, and engineers in the world called out NASA for making a series of "unproven and unsupported remarks" in support of man-made climate change. The letter states: "With hundreds of well-known climate scientists and tens of thousands of other scientists publicly declaring their disbelief in the catastrophic forecasts, coming particularly from the GISS leadership, it is clear that the science is NOT settled."[14] It is fair to say that there are impressively credentialed people on both sides of the climate change issue.

Donald Rumsfeld famously coined the term "unknown unknowns," a term that refers to the fact that it's impossible to know which facts are the pertinent facts affecting a thing. There are many factors that affect climate—so many, in fact, that we don't even know them all. Roy Spencer, doctor of meteorology and former senior scientist for climate studies at NASA, writes: "Climate science isn't rocket science—it's actually much more difficult than that."[15] Spencer explains that certain branches of science tend to have few variables and are very predictable: rocket science, for example deals largely with gravity, which is very predictable. Planetary alignment is also predictable; you can predict whether there will be a full moon on a particular night decades in advance. Spencer says that when it comes to climate change, it's an entirely different ball game consisting of "gravity, the turbulent fluid flows of the atmosphere and ocean, evaporation, clouds, precipitation, ice sheets, vegetation, and a wide variety of processes that make a chaotic soup of competing forces and energy transfers."[16]

Think of the climate change problem as an algebra problem. In algebra, the student is asked to "solve for x," that is, solve for one variable. In the climate change problem, however, we need to solve for dozens, perhaps hundreds of variables or more. You can design computer programs to help you make assumptions, but they are really just guessing on some of the variables and these are just the *known* unknowns, and even these software models often disagree.[17]

The earth has warmed about 2 degrees Fahrenheit over the past 140 years. Why? The honest answer is that we don't exactly know. It's unsettled. And the honest answer—at least for now—is that we don't exactly know if the warming trend will continue.

Recently on Twitter I was asked: "Say Rick, an honest and innocent question: do you hold a similar point of view regarding climate change, [referring to my assertion that we are not in a constitutional crisis] meaning it's only currently a climate inconvenience, and not a crisis until Florida is underwater, the Midwest is in another Dust Bowl, and category 5 hurricanes are the norm?" I responded, "I don't know; are we trying to save the planet or the humans. I think we can do both."

It's a good question. Should we wait to find out if these cataclysmic events occur before we act? Note the questioner is emphatic that these events *will* occur. I'm neither convinced that they will, or they won't. What is still unknown is that if we eliminated to virtually zero, all carbon emissions from all human activity including and especially the burning of fossil fuels, can we know that Miami will be saved, droughts thwarted, and hurricane velocities diminished? No one can say.

A GREEN NEW DEAL

In February of 2019, New York Democratic congresswoman Alexandria Ocasio-Cortez and ninety-three cosponsors introduced a resolution to the House of Representatives called "Recognizing the duty of the Federal Government to create a Green New Deal." It may surprise you that I give credit to AOC (as she is commonly referred to) for creating a vision for a world beyond fossil fuels. Similarly, I've been critical of the Republicans for reflexively opposing any legislative action to protect the environment. What I find objectionable about the proposal itself is its apocalyptic specificity of outcomes should it not be adopted.

The resolution confidently asserts that over the past century climate change has resulted in widespread natural disasters including "wildfires, severe storms, droughts, and other extreme weather events."[18] It further warns that if the warming trend continues, a litany of disasters will ensue, including a doubling of the number of global wildfires and a "loss of more than 99 percent of all coral reefs on earth." Climate change, it states, will also lead to billions of dollars in property losses, widespread economic hardship, $1 trillion in damage to America's infrastructure, mass migration (as people from particularly hot areas relocate to cooler regions), as well as posing "a direct threat to the national security of the United States." Most of the dire predictions have a particular date attached: doubling of wildfires *by 2050,* $500 billion in lost revenue *by 2100.* Why is all this happening and going to continue happening? What is the cause of all this misery? For the answers, the report is very up-front about it; in fact, it's the lede. It states that "*human activity* is the dominant of cause of observed climate change over the past century." Moreover, the repeated claim that has a similar refrain to past unfulfilled predictions is that we only have twelve years to solve it.

The resolution does not provide the reader evidence to support its draconian environmental claims; rather, the resolution simply takes man-made climate change and its catastrophic consequences as a given reality.

As I've stated, I am open to being convinced that we must take urgent action, but as a conservative, my skepticism for the Green New Deal peaks when reading the proposed solutions to averting certain catastrophe.

What the Green New Deal does is outline a massive list of federal programs to address the climate change problem. And not just the types of programs you might logically expect—like a plan to ensure clean drinking water or reduce carbon emissions, for example—but instead you find programs that have long been a part of the progressive agenda suddenly being offered as a comprehensive solution to a crisis. Turns out that's quite a long list: the resolution specifically mentions healthcare, housing, education, race relations, transportation, jobs, farming, public transportation, retirement plans, and so forth. In fact, reading it through, it's difficult to think of an area of life that would not be affected somehow by the adoption and implementa-tion of the Green New Deal. It's all-encompassing prescriptions lack the credibility of a serious proposal. Pass this progressive legislative agenda or we will all die!

It's no coincidence that the name Green New Deal was chosen to echo President Roosevelt's New Deal, a huge blanket of social assis-tance programs issued by the FDR administration during the Great Depression. From the standpoint of economics, the New Deal made the Great Depression worse, not better. And, specifically, the New Deal was much harder on the poor than the wealthy.

What the New Deal *did* accomplish was a greater federal in-trusion into the lives of Americans. It forever changed American society with the federal government's new role. Thus, we might say that the Green New Deal is aptly named. The cynic might even say that the Green New Deal is a backdoor entrance into making tons of changes in American society. In fact, Ocasio-Cortez's former chief of staff, Saikat Chakrabarti, once described the Green New Deal as an economic plan rather than an environmental one, saying, "The interesting thing about the Green New Deal is it wasn't originally a climate thing at all. . . . (W)e really think of it as a how-do-you-change-the-entire-economy thing."[19] Like the original New Deal, the Green New Deal is aspirational, but its objective seems to have more to do with expanding government power than it has to do with the limiting threats to the environment. The vehicle to the expansion is the "settled science" of the climate crisis. But are we trying to save the planet or expand government?

The obvious concern to conservatives is that the environment be-comes a vehicle for an economic agenda by which the climate "crisis" is the forcing function through which the government attempts to regulate every aspect of society.

THE ENVIRONMENTAL VOTER PARADOX

Overwhelming consensus exists on the environment—not just among scientists but from the American people. When asked by pollsters if we have an obligation to protect the environment, Americans overwhelmingly agree. Moreover, the majority of Americans think the climate is changing but are split on the causes. Man-made causes edge out natural causes slightly, but it is still not a majority position. Despite this, Americans believe by large majorities that the government should take action. Just over half would even support a carbon tax.

Democrats seem eager to exploit such overwhelming political agreement and support for policies that protect the environment. Admittedly, they've been largely successful in positioning themselves as the party that cares for the environment, and polls confirm their success.

But there's been a persistent problem. Every month since 2001, the Gallup poll asks Americans to name their top issue concern, and in 2017 only 3 percent offered the environment.[20] That poll is not an outlier. In 2018, the environment didn't make the top four issues voters used to make their voting decisions. In the 2016 presidential race, the environment was the twelfth issue on voters' minds, and among Democrats it was only the seventh. While it is true that younger voters are more concerned about climate change, their age group is still the least likely to vote and it is still unclear whether their priorities will change as they get older.

Politically, the problem for Democrats concerning the environment is that although there is broad concern for the environment, it doesn't register as a main issue people cite when casting their vote. Year after year, exit polls show little support for the environment relative to issues like government, the economy, jobs, immigration, and wars as the reason people turn out to vote. I think there are a handful of reasons for this.

First, the Democrats have decided that based on the overwhelming concerns voters express when asked about the environment, they set about making it a political issue to be exploited rather than an issue to be solved. Compare recent judicial reform where a bipartisan solution ultimately corrected the injustices of the 1994 Violent Crime Control and Law Enforcement Act. Similarly, the immigration problem has been used by both sides for political gain rather than finding bipartisan solutions to the immigration problem, and so the suffering goes on. Likewise, the environment will also suffer until there is an effort to create bipartisan environmental solutions. But those solutions will take leadership, creativity, and compromise.

Second, the Henny Penny approach to building support for meaningful environmental legislation is not working. Continually proclaiming that the clock is ticking toward calamity unless we can solve the crisis within twelve years has not motivated voters to insist on the radical environmental legislative action the climate change religious adherents insist on. Like the dire warnings that a population explosion—raised by Professor Paul R. Ehrlich in his infamous 1968 book *The Population Bomb*—would cause worldwide famine, the "sky is falling" strategy will ultimately discredit the alarmists and their constant apocalyptic claims that the earth only has a few years until total destruction. People will simply begin to tune them out.

Third, the constant lecturing not only turns people off but it is also misguided.

If you are AOC, you live in New York City and represent the Bronx and Queens. You travel on a train to get to Washington. Known as the Acela corridor, the route takes you through New Jersey, Pennsylvania, Delaware, and Maryland. Outside the window of the train for most of the 226-mile trip you will see what looks like a toxic waste dump. I've made this trip hundreds of times myself, and I wonder how it came to be so polluted and why no one has done anything to clean it up. The route passes through fourteen congressional districts. Eleven are represented by Democrats and three by Republicans. Amtrak, which owns the track, is owned 100 percent by the federal government. Among the Democrats on the Environment and Climate Change Subcommittee, twelve of the fourteen members like AOC live in a city. Members of Congress who score best by groups who rate environmental votes live in urban areas. With some exceptions, Vermont being a significant outlier, the states and districts with the worst scores mostly represent rural areas. Yes, they also largely correspond with their party affiliations. Democrats largely score very high while Republicans mostly score low. Jerry Nadler, who represents parts of Manhattan and Brooklyn, has a perfect environmental score with the League of Conservation Voters, while Hal Rogers, who represents America's most rural district in Kentucky, has a lifetime score of 8 percent. Not uncoincidentally, Nadler represents one of the wealthiest districts in the United States, while Rogers represents one of the poorest. I offer this observation to point out that it may not be that more conservative members care little about the environment and more progressive members do. It may just be that in our congenital desire to connect with the natural world, urban dwellers are most wanting to make the connection. It's not a bad thing to live in a city but consider how urban dwellers would feel about people in the country constantly telling them how they should live. Worse, it's people who live in the noise-filled canyons of glass and steel skyscrapers towering above asphalt and concrete who are lecturing about an environmental crisis, which gets me to my next point.

Fourth, hypocrisy. Given his public persona was so inexorably tied to global warming and now climate change, you might think that Al Gore would do everything he could to limit his carbon footprint. I mean we're talking about the end of the world here—or, at least, *he's* talking about it. Yet, rather infamously, Gore seems to have an energy addiction. Gore owns at least three homes, one of which is a ten-thousand-square-foot house in Tennessee that uses *twenty times* more energy than the average house in America.[21] Gore routinely flies private jets and avails himself of gas-guzzling automobiles.[22] I once talked to an owner of a studio where they do remote television satellite interviews. Al Gore was scheduled to be at the studio, but before he arrived someone representing the former vice president called to insist that before Gore arrives the studio must be at sixty-eight degrees. Even before the incalculable demands for icebox studios, Al Gore has fifty times the carbon footprint of the average American. Even those who agree with his climate change stance have referred to him as a category 5 "hypocritical windbag."[23] Gore might speak like a true believer, but his actions go well beyond that of a skeptic; his utility bills are higher than most climate change deniers' annual income. But it's not just Al Gore whose climate change words don't seem to align with his actions. Microsoft founder Bill Gates also gives talks at climate change conferences while at the same time lives in a sixty-six-thousand-square-foot house, including, somewhat ironically for a guy who warns about the warming of the earth's surface, heated driveways.

One percent envy has never been my hang-up, but the aforementioned former vice president, Al Gore, according to *Forbes*, was worth a little less than $2 million in the year 2000, but by 2013 he was worth $200 million. Does the fact that the environmental movement has financially enriched Gore mean that his beliefs are insincere? Is he excused from the popular narrative that greedy corporate energy executives care only about money? I can't read hearts and souls and minds, so I wouldn't know. But if the logic is that money has a corrupting influence, that hardly relieves environmental executives and climate change celebrities of the same charge. Yet, you never hear Elizabeth Warren or Bernie Sanders complain about all the billions of dollars in the environmental protection sector or the greed of their executives. By all accounts, the environmental industry is one of the most financially lucrative industries in the world, raking in enormous sums of cash. If you look at just the top fourteen environmental groups in America, you discover that they have about $11 billion in combined assets with annual revenue of around $3 billion. The top executive pay in this group ranges between $190,000 and $960,000, with an average pay of more than $550,000. This group includes more than two hundred executives with an average annual pay of about $280,000. Of course, these numbers don't include speaking fees, which can be in the five- and even six-figure range. Plenty of executives have made plenty of money because of climate change—

man-made or otherwise. And the fact that mega-millionaires are the ones who dictate energy policy—who are the squeakiest wheels demanding the most government grease—sets the stage for a serious problem.

Fifth, with the introduction of the Green New Deal, climate change advocates ask us not only to fully accept their findings, contradictions and all, but to fork over hundreds of billions of dollars to the federal government to solve it. Giving an already massive, inefficient, and ineffective government more power and more money is a nonstarter with conservatives.

Here's why.

Overreaching governmental policies tend the hurt the poor the most. For instance, a policy that stifles immigration endangers the lives of the poor; a strict gun control policy leaves the mostly urban poor more susceptible to crime because they have the least ability to protect their homes and families; a tariff-laden trade policy makes the purchase of healthy fruits and vegetables a budgetary impossibility for poor families. And so it is with energy policy. Because manufacturing and shipping are energy dependent, higher energy costs immediately translate to higher prices on virtually anything you buy, including higher prices at the pump, higher utility bills, and higher grocery bills. If you're Al Gore or Bill Gates, that doesn't matter much. At their income levels, no matter the level of increase, the price of gasoline, utilities, and food will only ever account for tiny percentages of their overall income. If you are Bill Gates, you're not going to stop heating your pool (or your driveway) because your utility bill went up last month. Very likely, you never even see it, worry about it, or contemplate it; your bills are paid through an accounting firm. As far as food costs are concerned, your major expense in that category isn't meat and produce; it's your private pastry chef. But back in the real world, for the poor, energy and food expenses constitute a huge percentage of their income. If gas is $3.50 a gallon, Bill Gates and the single mom with two jobs both pay the same $3.50. Except for her, it's a crushing blow.

In a 2013 assessment of how a carbon tax would affect the American economy, the Congressional Budget Office (CBO) made the point that a carbon tax would economically devastate America's poor. After the report opens with a politically obligatory statement conceding climate change, it goes on to detail the negative repercussions of a carbon tax. Such a tax, it states, "would have a negative effect on the economy" for the reasons that it would increase inflation, decrease investment, and cause unemployment.[24] Though those are broad negatives, the poor and middle classes would suffer exponentially more. Regarding inflation, the report points out that sweeping increases in the prices of "goods and services throughout the economy" would occur.[25] That's not great news for those living paycheck to paycheck (or struggling to even do that). More specifically and more immediately, the prices at the pump would rise, and "low-income households generally spend a larger percentage of their income on emission-intensive goods."[26] Regarding unemployment, the report points out that the lower economic classes are disproportionately employed in "emission-intensive industries" such as the coal and manufacturing.[27] A carbon tax would devastate the economic futures of many of those employed in these industries. In economics, a tax that hurts the poor the most is called a "regressive" tax. And that is exactly how the CBO characterizes the carbon tax. Here's the logic of the carbon tax: the poor must suffer so the rich don't risk suffering.

We should learn from a lesson recently taught in the "land down under," which almost turned into the *economy* down under. It was then that the Australian government decided to impose a carbon tax, which is a monetary penalty for emitting carbon dioxide through the use of fuels such as natural gas, oil, or coal. Such a tax can be assessed on a person, persons, or a corporation. The world's first carbon taxes went into effect in Finland in 1990. Australia's carbon tax program went into effect in 2012, driving employment down, bureaucracy up, and increasing the average utility bill by 25 percent.[28] It proved such a disaster for the people of Australia that it was repealed only two years later. It proved unworkable for plenty of reasons, but ultimately because people simply couldn't afford higher energy bills.[29] Another oddity was that emissions dropped only marginally. Some countries have passed a carbon tax only to see their emissions *increase*. Australia has the distinction of being the first country to eliminate a carbon tax, but it has set the stage for others as it is a consistent losing issue when put to a vote. As *The Wall Street Journal* put it, "Climate alarmists have convinced elites. Their problem is democracy."[30]

The argument that people will use less energy is certainly part of the argument behind the carbon tax. Yet in Finland, since the carbon tax was implemented in 1990, its CO_2 emissions were lower in only eight out of twenty-four years from 1990-2014. Moreover, the government only recently announced its goal of becoming carbon neutral by 2035, forty-five years after the imposition of a carbon tax and will raise other taxes 730 euros to meet its "lofty" goal. But another argument behind the carbon tax is that it will force innovation; it will force the creation of better energy sources. But there's a problem with this argument: it's not possible to impose creativity, force innovation, or systematically plan genius as "settled history" tells us. These things are unpredictable. Alexander Graham Bell invented the telephone not because the government ordered him to invent one but because he had a flash of genius. The smartphone came about not because landline telephone rates were taxed but because Steve Jobs and his team had the unique intelligence to come up with the idea. It's the same reason two unknown bicycle mechanics invented the airplane and not the government-sponsored Smithsonian effort to do the same. At their finest moments, governments can *foster* creativity when there is political leadership and vision. The Apollo program, the original moonshot, was a good example where Americans rose to meet the threat of losing the space race to the Soviets. Still, the private sector has consistently and dramatically out-produced government-initiated innovations.

Governments more often stifle creativity with high taxes, which takes money from the creative private sector and hands it to the decidedly uncreative government sector. It leaves the government in the position of picking winners—of picking those companies they believe will be the most innovative. And the nice way of saying it is that the government's record of doing so is less than stellar.

Government can foster innovation in a few ways: The first is to offer a specific prize for solving a particular problem. It costs nothing if the problem can't be solved and paying an actual prize would be a very small price to pay for a breakthrough innovation that has a societal benefit. Second, the federal government does an enormous amount of basic scientific research for which there is no market incentive. From the benefit of this research, especially in health, the private sector has been able to advance new discoveries to produce breakthrough products. Third, the government can invest in private sector research by providing funding grants as in the air force's grant to GE that created Holonyak's LED. Nevertheless, the best hope for America's future—energy producing or otherwise—requires our continued faith in private sector entrepreneurs. Fourth, we can look to the market where recently beer producers have been inexpensively capturing carbon that would normally be released during the production process and selling it to cannabis growers.

LOOKING FORWARD

Progressive or conservative, we all want a healthy and clean environment. The questions are: How do we achieve it? How much is it going to cost?

The claim is sometimes made that climate change is not a political issue, but the truth is that the environment has become highly politicized. The environment, I believe, could be a winning issue for both Republicans and Democrats. Let's return to where we began this chapter: with Nick Holonyak, inventor of the LED. The now almost ubiquitous LED light became that way because it filled a market need. They last longer, don't produce heat, consume little power, and provide beautiful light. In 1997, the Department of Energy sponsored research and development of compact fluorescent lighting. Up until that time, CFLs sold poorly. While they consumed a third of the energy of the comparable incandescent lighting the government wanted to phase out, they had some serious flaws consumers hated. They were ugly, they had an audible buzz that got worse with usage, they contained mercury (making them toxic when they break), and they produced a very unattractive, eerie light. When LEDs were finally made widely available, consumers bought them up, leaving CFLs in the dark.

There is a way to talk about and campaign on the environment in an attractive and positive way that doesn't frighten people. The conservative approach would be to combine the desire most Americans have to connect with the natural world with technological market-driven solutions to preserve and protect the environment. Sadly, today's Republicans—instead of capitalizing on this popular political issue—have handed it to the Democrats, while being reflexively opposed to any ideas concerning the environment.

Democrats could also consolidate their gains on the issue by dropping the doomsday scenarios and replacing their static worldview. Historically, Democrats have built constituencies around the status quo, so when disruptive technologies threaten union jobs, Democrats end up protecting the past instead of embracing the future. Uber's ride-sharing service displacing taxis is just one example. Instead of trying to scare voters into consolidating power at the federal level, they would do well to promote a vision that combines good jobs created by a new green economy. To be fair, many Democrats are speaking this way already, but the dominant message of the party still emphasizes inescapable calamity. The focus should be on better jobs for a better future to alleviate the fears of the older non-college-educated working class who are naturally fearful of disruptive technologies and events that might eliminate their jobs, or worse, make their skill sets obsolete.

My solution is simple. And it has no price tag.

If you want to foster clean water and air and healthy ecosystems, you need to focus on one thing: prosperity. For some, that sounds crazy. It is true that emerging economies have higher rates of pollution, fewer established prosperous economies do. So it is no coincidence that the twenty-five most polluted cities on earth are also the poorest. By contrast, the most economically efficient societies are almost always the most environmentally responsible ones. And while it is true that prosperous societies consume the most energy, it is also true that nations where capitalism is allowed to flourish, people live longer, enjoy better health, and have a better quality of living. But perhaps equally as important is that market-based economies far outpace Socialist countries in inventing the future. The answer to replacing the fossil-fueled economy will likely come from free market innovation not a government bureaucracy. The history of free market capitalism coincides directly with the history of energy because the free market is essentially impossible without it.

Many see a hydrogen-based economy in our future. The idea excites me. The problem with renewable fuels like hydro, wind, and solar is that unless the sun is shining, the wind is blowing, or the water is flowing, you can't produce power. Storing that amount of power has so far proved unfeasible with battery technology. But what if we could store all the power renewables produce in the form of hydrogen? Excess nuclear power could be used to do the same by converting water into hydrogen gas.

The by-product of burning hydrogen is water. (I can hear the future alarmists' cries that all scientists agree that the water produced by hydrogen power is going to destroy the planet.)

Whatever the solution to a healthier, cleaner, and safer environment, I'm confident that it's not going to happen by government fiat—any more than the iPhone happened because a politician demanded it. What we must avoid is creating a command economy in which the government dictates *what* and *how* we produce. That's never worked anywhere—and it won't work in America. The solutions are going to come from the free market: whether it's a railroad worker or a coal miner, a homeschooler, a scholar, or a second-grade dropout, the next LED light is going to surprise us and yet again make the world a brighter place. The current energy debate in America risks losing sight of all this, but the story of capitalism is not a story about interest rates, borrowing, and marginal taxation; capitalism is the story of human creativity set free.

Juxtapose that vision with "settled science," which simply means there is nothing more to learn. And if there is settled science, I will be dealing with it in the chapter on life. In any case, I remain open to being convinced about the prescriptive solutions on climate change. I'm just not sure how I'll be convinced when I'm not supposed to even discuss the topic.

6

IMMIGRATION: AMERICA'S GREATEST STORY

One Sunday night in 2018, I'd just finished an appearance on MSNBC's *Kasie DC* show hosted by NBC News's Capitol Hill correspondent, Kasie Hunt. We'd been discussing the plight of the "caravan migrants" that had been amassing at the southern border. We focused mostly on the deplorable conditions the refugees were living in. After my segment, I went back to the greenroom where guests wait to go on. I recognized Senator Angus King (an Independent from Maine) sitting on the couch in front of the window that overlooked the Capitol. I had been the executive director of the Maine Republican Party when King was governor. Most notably during my tenure as ED, we had beaten King on a forestry referendum. He reminded me about his defeat when, subsequent to moving to Washington, I traveled back to Maine with Newt Gingrich to get a daylong briefing from then governor King on a variety of policy initiatives he'd been working on.

He didn't place me from either of those times, but he pointed to one of his staff members who accompanied him to the studio wanting her to repeat what she had apparently just said to the governor and people who were in the room. She reluctantly repeated her comment about being surprised I was a Republican and was taking a pro-immigration stand. I took a breath or two before responding. It was an "accusation" I'd heard a lot recently. I responded that being pro-immigration *was* a conservative position.

"Well, it used to be," King said, acknowledging my assertion.

For all the time and news stories that go into reporting the immigration issue in America, you would think that most of the American press was pretty well versed on the issue. But it's funny how little they really know and understand about it. A recent story provides an excellent case in point. In 2019, the Trump administration announced that Honduras, El Salvador, and Guatemala would cease to get any more funding because their governments were doing such a terrible job keeping their citizens within their respective borders. Fox News, in its hasty effort to congratulate the decision, ran in the chyron text at the bottom of the screen: "Trump Cuts U.S. Aid to Three Mexican Countries."

On a network that mercilessly mocks Alexandria Ocasio-Cortez and other progressives for their lack of knowledge, Fox failed a basic geography test.

Though later apologizing for the goof after someone in the control room apparently remembered the rather obvious fact that these were independent sovereignties, the slip had already been made—the slip being that all things south of Texas are both indistinguishable one from another and uniformly bad. With the mindset and viewpoint they've been fed for the past few years, many Fox viewers might be asking: So what if Honduras and Mexico are different nations? For some people, any discussion of Mexico and Honduras is largely a distinction without a difference—an irrelevant happenstance of geography that obscures the larger issue, that issue being this: illegal immigration is the biggest threat to the republic in our nation's history. In their telling, illegal immigration (and, increasingly, *legal* immigration) is demolishing our culture, devastating our economy, and drugging our children—and only a wall can provide an adequate defense. But is any of this true? And if so, when did it become true? When did Republicans start speaking like this?

WHY ARE PEOPLE IMMIGRATING?

What is so rarely addressed is why so many people are emigrating from their home nations in the first place. Future generations might be confused as to why today's discussion has focused so narrowly on whether to build—and on how high to build—a wall. *How* to halt immigration has obscured the focus on *why* people want or need to emigrate and immigrate at all. Let's look at the three countries (the "three Mexican countries") mentioned above.

With its high rates of crime—many of which are committed against the most defenseless citizens—including murders, home invasions, assaults, stabbings, extortions, and kidnappings, Guatemala is one of the most dangerous and violent countries in the world. A century and a half ago, America's Civil War lasted four years. A few decades ago, Guatemala's lasted closer to forty. Along with other factors, this has created a society steeped in violence that is largely governed by gangs that victimize the populace. Guatemala is a nation in which murder, abduction, rape, carjacking, and armed robbery occur in broad daylight. In a country where the ultraviolent Mara gang serves as the most powerful branch of government, Guatemala currently has the fourth-highest murder rate in the world. The Mara Salvatrucha (also called Mara or MS-13, it originated in prisons in Los Angeles, California) gang members have also adopted their own version of tax collection. Many citizens are forced to pay monthly dues to the gang; otherwise, the noncompliant will be systematically murdered along with their families. Guatemala's rule of law is almost nonexistent, and to the extent that it exists, it is largely corrupt. Some Guatemalans are more afraid of the police than the Maras. Even if the police were not corrupt, it would make little difference; Guatemalans know that filing a police report is more likely to get them murdered than to get them justice. Further—as the State Department suggests—as eye-popping as the crime statistics are, they are likely understated since many of the numbers are collected by the very people whose job is to enforce the law. Of course, the term "law enforcement" vastly overstates what goes on in the country, as many police are unable or unwilling to halt crime or are complicit in the commission of those crimes. It is sometimes difficult to catch the killers because so many of the murders are random acts of violence, perpetrated by gang members for whom murder has become a commonplace terror tactic. In Guatemala, nearly everyone seems to have known someone who has been murdered. The US State Department is less than eager to see Americans travel to the country, observing that even the comparatively wealthy sections of the country have seen violent crimes committed against tourists.

If you make a list of everything you would want in a country and then reverse it, you would have Honduras. For starters, the nation of Honduras has one of the highest murder rates of any country on earth. While gang violence is mostly perpetrated by males against males, so many Honduran women have been murdered—as many as one woman every thirteen hours—that a new term has been coined: femicide. This reality was thrust on the national scene in America when the winner of the 2014 Miss Honduras contest, María José Alvarado, was gunned down by a gang member at a birthday party at which Maria's sister was also murdered. Though Maria's whereabouts were unknown for a week after the killing, her bullet-riddled body was eventually found at the edge of a river in Santa Bárbara, Honduras. It was discovered that Maria had been shot a dozen times in the back while trying to escape the violence. What made Maria's case so significant was not that she was murdered but that the police even bothered to *investigate* the incident. Rape is much more common in Honduras than murder, yet it is almost never prosecuted even if reported to authorities. Transparency International considers Honduras to be one of the most politically corrupt regimes in the Western Hemisphere. The *The World Factbook* lists the Honduran form of government as a "democratic constitutional republic" but perhaps only because "gang" is not an official category. As with Guatemala, drug lords and gangs have significant overlap and influence with the ruling class. Of course, absent the rule of law, there is little chance to overcome the brutal poverty that has made Latin America infamous. Honduras's GDP per capita is about $5,500, making it one of the poorest nations in the world, yet the vast majority of Hondurans never even see this kind of money, as 60 percent of the people live under the poverty line with little chance to improve their condition.

It is a fact that El Salvador, a country named for the King of Peace (the Savior), is the most violent country in the world, and its capital of San Salvador—also so named—is the one of most murderous major cities on the planet. El Salvador is a nation so brutal that the trucks of local morgues randomly patrol the streets at night for bodies. Entire neighborhoods are controlled by gangs and their continuous threat of violence to a populace held hostage. In the year 2017, the nation saw about four thousand homicides, of which more than three hundred were children. This number does not count the number of children who "disappeared" from the country. Hundreds of rapes are reported to the authorities every year, although it is well established that these numbers represent a tiny fraction of the sexual assaults that occur for two main reasons: First, the chances of the police conducting any investigation are remote. Second, the reporting of such an incident leaves the victim much more likely to suffer a subsequent rape and/or murder. Because of the presence of gangs in police units, a rape victim might unknowingly be reporting her rape to a member of the same gang who raped her. The corruption and collusion among gangs and government runs so deep that it even influences how campaigns are conducted in the nation. Imagine that instead of having town hall meetings like we do in America, candidates meet in gang headquarters to curry favor with drug warlords. To various degrees, every political party in the country has pandered to gangs in hopes of their votes at the ballot box—a pragmatic view considering that there are an estimated sixty thousand Salvadorian gang members, and they constitute one of the nation's most powerful constituencies. [1]

To briefly summarize all this, the countries of Guatemala, Honduras, and El Salvador have three of the five-highest murder rates in the world. Sexual assault and forced disappearances are commonplace and are largely disregarded by corrupt officials, who sometimes terrorize populaces more than gang members. Economic conditions are disastrous except for the few people who have risen to the top, many of whom achieved that status through violence and corruption. The majority of the citizens of these nations live in squalor. Chances for any type of economic advancement among people are almost nil, largely through no fault of their own. Many parents see their children grow up mostly uneducated, literate only in the violent realities of street life. Conditions are so bad that they are willing to risk their lives to escape these hellish conditions.

And how do some people in the Western world respond to all this? By saying that the governments of these nations must do a better job of keeping them *within* their countries. For the record, the idea that a nation must legally prevent its citizens from leaving—in effect, to lock its citizens within the nation's borders—is the very definition of totalitarianism. We may not categorize these nations as totalitarian, but that is only because the word "totalitarian" implies organization—and these countries are adrift in a sea of chaos. But if a government can be judged solely by how well it keeps its citizens contained within its borders, these countries have done an excellent job, because they have created a poverty-stricken society in which the majority of the populace cannot afford to travel. For all intents and purposes, they are stuck within the borders of sovereign prisons.

Yet, that does not stop many people from trying or others from funding their efforts.

At the close of 2015, PBS highlighted the story of a teenage Honduran girl named Lillian Oliva Bardales who had been repeatedly raped and threatened with death at gunpoint by her former boyfriend (now a gang member), the father of her young child. Lillian had an uncle living in Texas who paid smugglers $4,000 to bring her to America, where she was detained upon arrival. Not understanding immigration law or how to plead her case for asylum, Lilian was sent back to Honduras by American government officials. Four months later, after undergoing repeated death threats by her former boyfriend, she again tried to escape to America. When she arrived, she presented herself and her four-year-old son to immigration officials, asking for asylum—this time explaining that she was trying to escape a homicidal maniac. This time, Lilian was let into America but was put in a detention center for eight months while her case was being decided. At the end of the eight months, she lost her case, and she was put on a plane with her young boy and sent back to Honduras.[2] Lilian's story is heartbreaking for lots of reasons, not the least of which is that she represents tens of thousands of others whose names the world will never know. And people like Lillian will not stop trying, because even considering the war-torn past of Central America, there has never been a more difficult time to live there. In the current political environment in America, however, it has rarely been more difficult to do so. The current American policy is akin to calling first responders because your home is on fire, but when help arrives they force you back into the burning house.

Of course, though they are geographically closer to the United States, it is not only people from Latin American countries who undergo difficulties in coming to America. Just a week into office, President Trump issued a "Muslim ban," the first in a series of executive orders that didn't recognize valid visas from nationals of countries with a Muslim majority. Although the lower courts struck down these executive orders, the Supreme Court upheld the constitutionality of rejecting valid visas from Iran, Libya, Syria, Somalia, and Yemen.[3] And while it is possible to obtain an exemption from the travel ban, exemptions are rarely made—even for spouses and children of American citizens.[4] This means that thousands of family members of US citizens are left waiting on foreign shores—with a dwindling hope of ever coming to America to reunite with their moms and dads and husbands and wives.

If that sounds heartbreaking, the reality is much, much worse. Each of these nations—Iran, Libya, Syria, Somalia, and Yemen—has been devastated by brutal civil wars that have caused millions of civilian casualties. Among them, the plight of civilians in Syria may be the worst. While most civil wars have two sides, Syria's conflict arguably has at least four—and this has turned the country into a devil's playground that seems to get only worse. According to widespread reports by various agencies, the Syrian government has repeatedly tortured, kidnapped, and executed children, and it conducts systematic and ongoing use of chemical weapons against civilians. So many Syrians have been injured or killed that the United Nations announced in 2014 that it could no longer keep reliable statistics. However the rough estimate is that since 2011, more than 10 percent of the country's population has been killed or injured, and more than 11 million Syrians have been displaced within their own country or fled to other nations.

Many more try to flee to other nations but never make it.

That fact became all too obvious in 2015, when a group of twenty-three people from Kobanî, a war-ravaged town on Syria's northern border, boarded two boats with hope of making it to a Greek island. After their boats capsized, twelve of the people drowned on the journey. One of the drowning victims was a three-year-old boy named Alan Kurdi, whose body washed ashore in Turkey. That story—one of countless such incidents—would never have been known to the Western world except for one thing: a photographer with Reuters had taken Alan's picture. With a member of the Turkish police standing over him, the jarring photo captured Alan's small and lifeless body. Still dressed in his traveling clothes of black shoes, red shirt, and blue shorts, his body lay facedown in the sand. Alan Kurdi was later buried in Kobanî, his hometown, which has become a mass grave for innocent victims and a monument to the desperation of immigrants. Alan's father later claimed that he had applied to the government of Canada for refugee status, but a response never arrived. For those children still trapped in Syria, including even the children of American citizens, the gates of America remain closed.

SWITCHING SIDES

Angus King had a point: prominent conservatives used to be pro-immigration. Conservatism recognizes that men and women and children have basic, natural human rights such as life and liberty, and if a government refuses to guarantee these rights (or worse, brutally violates them), people have a natural right to emigrate. And it stands to reason that if someone has the natural right to *exit* an oppressive country, there must also exist the right to *enter* a different country. And while a nation may justly have immigration laws—even relatively restrictive immigration laws—a person's right to life takes precedence over those laws. Conservatism desires "ordered liberty" and recognizes human rights not only for *some* people but for *all*—both foreign and domestic. In practice, that does not necessarily mean that America must accept all refugees from all corners of the world, but it stands to reason that geography plays a central role. Specifically, if one is suffering persecution in Mexico or Honduras or El Salvador, the geographically closest ordered liberty nation is America.

Of course, Angus King didn't mention the fact that political progressives used to be anti-immigration—and not all that long ago either. To be fair, the Republican pro-immigration stance was sometimes driven by business's interest for low-cost labor while the anti-immigrant position was sometimes driven by unions for the same reason. Barack Obama's presidency saw a wide-scale crackdown on undocumented workers in which apprehension, turnaround, detention, and deportation were business as usual. Though his defenders will point to the policy of Deferred Action for Childhood Arrivals (DACA), it is nevertheless the case that during Obama's two terms and two years with Democratic majorities, no significant legislative immigration reforms were passed. Obama even came to be known in some circles as the "deporter in chief." Moreover, the number of people granted refugee status was relatively low under Obama. While the administration of the senior George Bush granted asylum to more than a hundred thousand refugees in each of his four years in office, the Obama administration never reached that number in a single one of his eight years.

For his part, President Clinton greatly increased the number of border control agents, bragged about the increased number of deportations during his presidency, and presented a plan to decrease the numbers of *legal* immigrants. The Clinton administration also aggressively captured and detained the Cuban "boat people," who were desperately trying to escape Castro's murderous dictatorship—a marked change in policy from his predecessors dating back to President Lyndon Johnson.[5] Those Cubans picked up in the Straits of Florida were detained at Guantanamo Bay and given the option of returning to Communist Cuba or finding another country for asylum, but come hell or high water, they weren't coming to America.[6] Human Rights Watch pointed out that Clinton's policies "subjected hundreds of thousands of people to arbitrary detention, fast-track deportations, and family separation."[7] All in all, the sixteen years of the Obama and Clinton administrations often treated *legal* immigration as a necessary evil and *illegal* immigration as an unnecessary one.

Both Obama and Clinton jettisoned the immigration position of Ronald Reagan. In 1986, Ronald Reagan signed the Immigration Reform and Control Act (IRCA) into law. In response to the ongoing issue of illegal immigration, the law was designed to accomplish three things: first, to provide a greater security presence along the border of Mexico (along with providing funding to deport illegal immigrants who had committed crimes); second, to allow a temporary worker program for noncitizens; and third, to provide amnesty and a path to legal citizenship for those who had lived in America for the previous four years. With the exception of the temporary worker program, the law also made it illegal for employers to knowingly hire illegal immigrants; notably, however, many of those who were already working here legally were grandfathered in, allowing them to keep their jobs. After the bill's passage into law, roughly 3 million illegal immigrants applied for legal status, 90 percent of whom were granted that status. According to the Migration Policy Institute, "IRCA remains the largest immigrant legalization process conducted in history."[8] The IRCA law was pragmatic yet compassionate, respecting the human rights and dignity of illegal immigrants while simultaneously respecting law and order. Most of all, it recognized the value of immigrants and America's proud history of immigration—as did Reagan.

In the final days of his presidency, Reagan gave his farewell address to the American people that encapsulated his view on immigration:

> *I've spoken of the shining city all my political life, but I don't know if I ever quite communicated what I saw when I said it. But in my mind, it was a tall proud city built on rocks stronger than oceans, wind-swept, God blessed, and teeming with people of all kinds living in harmony and peace—a city with free ports that hummed with commerce and creativity, and if there had to be city walls, the walls had doors, and the doors were open to anyone with the will and the heart to get here.*

Reagan's words were illustrative of his belief that immigration is good for America—that immigrants built America and each new wave of immigrants make America better and stronger. Simply put, immigrants make America great. So when confronted with the "make America great again" chant, Reagan (who also ran on that slogan) might have observed that if America were to be made great *again*, it will require a recognition that America was made great in the first place by immigrants with the heart and will to build a shining city. That was once the Republican view.

And then it all changed.

THE ABOUT-FACE OF 2016

While the Republican immigration policy proposals have adjusted over time since Reagan, respect and compassion toward immigrants was a constant. Even Republicans who disagreed with one another agreed that immigrants and asylum seekers were coming to America for good and lawful reasons and that they should be treated with dignity. In 2004, for instance, the Republican Party platform called for a reform of immigration that was "legal, safe, orderly and humane." Senator John McCain's own views on immigration law greatly varied over the years—with ABC News even referring to him having a "near 180-degree flip" on his position—yet, McCain's compassion for immigrants was never in doubt, a fact evidenced in his rhetoric. And more than a simple expression of compassion, Republicans were unafraid to highlight a historical reality: America is a nation not only *of* immigrants but also built *by* immigrants.

This rhetoric completely changed in 2015.

In the Trump Tower speech in which he announced his candidacy— a speech that served as an appetizer for a smorgasbord of the xenophobia that was to come—Trump declared, "When Mexico sends its people, they're not sending the best . . . They're bringing drugs, they're bringing crime. They're rapists and some, I assume, are good people, but I speak to border guards and they're telling us what we're getting." In context, the concession that there might be a few "good people" among the horde of Mexico's denizens was a begrudging one, and it was a concession that was largely abandoned as the campaign wore on.

"They're rapists." That rhetoric found an audience.

Though it makes for cheering speeches, this is statistically false. Regarding the criminal activity of illegal immigrants, the data clearly indicates the opposite of the story Trump and the Republicans are now telling. In the quarter century from 1990 to 2013, illegal immigration tripled. If the rapist/drug lord/criminal narrative of the Republicans is correct, that period should have witnessed an uptick in crime, right? Yet, it didn't. In fact, the FBI reports that the incidents of violent crime were cut in half during this same period.[9] Numerous studies have shown that immigrants commit crimes at a much lower rate than those born in America. This makes sense. They are leaving to escape crime not to commit it. In Lilllian Bardales's example (mentioned earlier), she was trying to *escape*—not *commit*—crime.

Something else that should be part of this conversation is the question of how many American liberties should be sacrificed in the process of enforcing immigration law. Make no mistake: the ramifications of stepping up deportation has immediate repercussions for American citizens. In "red meat" speeches at Republican rallies, the talk of "cracking down on immigration" is met with wild applause and cheers. But if crowds realized what these crackdowns sometimes entail, they might not cheer as loudly. First off, the US Customs and Border Protection (CBP) is legally permitted to search any vehicle within one hundred miles of the US border perimeter without a warrant or even probable cause—a situation with plenty of immediacy considering that roughly two-thirds of Americans reside within that one-hundred-mile zone. When defined this way, consider that the "border" does not consist simply of a thin strip along the Rio Grande but extends to the northern metro area of Columbus, Ohio. In many parts of America, fourth-generation citizens of Latino descent dare not go out without proper identification, lest they be suspected of being illegal immigrants and having their electronic devices searched.[10] And with tax dollars being thrown at the "crackdown," all Americans can expect a heightened level of surveillance.

There were those political observers who thought that Trump's anti-immigration sentiment would be dialed down at the convention, but they were quickly proven wrong as anti-immigration speeches formed the centerpiece of the convention. Sheriff Joe Arpaio (who was later found guilty of criminal contempt of court and pardoned by President Trump) claimed there were "terrorists coming over our border, infiltrating our communities, and causing massive destruction and mayhem." Florida attorney general Pam Bondi assured the audience: "Donald Trump will take control of our borders, because we must stop the influx of cocaine and heroin coming into our country and my state, killing our kids." These sentiments culminated in Trump's acceptance speech, in which he unmasked the notion that it was not simply illegal immigration that was the problem: it was *legal* immigration. To a cheering audience, he stated, "Decades of record immigration have produced lower wages and higher unemployment for our citizens, especially for African American and Latino workers."

(This is incorrect or, at minimum, incomplete. While it is commonly argued that immigration naturally lowers wages, the Cato Institute's research indicates that though wages can be reduced by a few percentage points in the short term, the wages of native-born

Americans over the longer term have not been reduced at all with an increase in immigration.[11] In this debate, it's also important to remember that Americans act as both producers and consumers. If it is true that low-wage immigrants lower wages by a few percentage points, that may cost Americans as producers, but it helps them as consumers because of lower prices. Ultimately, what matters is what economists call buying power, and that has been consistently increasing.)

These sentiments were echoed—in some cases word for word—in the 2016 Republican platform. The platform itself wouldn't have made a dime's worth of difference except for the fact that it formally confirmed the party's new focus in writing. The Republican Party platform of 1988—Reagan's last full year in office—highlighted the fact that some immigrants needed to flee oppressive places and regimes and relocate in the free nations of the world. That is an admission largely absent in the 2016 Republican platform. Instead—and it doesn't take long, as the platform's *preamble* starts in with the rhetoric—it contains what amounts to a counterargument to 1988's platform, falsely criticizing outgoing president Obama for his staunch refusal "to control our borders." Later, bizarrely claiming to speak for every American, the document continues: "With all our fellow citizens, we have watched, in anger and disgust, the mocking of our immigration laws by a president who made himself superior to the will of the nation." That's an interesting charge considering that Obama's immigration policy was equal to if not tougher than most of his predecessors. The document goes on to make the case that illegal immigration was damaging the American economy and driving down wages. The platform further argues that while America should allow some refugees, the overall policy to admit refugees should have "major changes" that would allow only those refugees suffering from "political, ethnic or religious persecution." In other words, there's no room for people like Lilian and her young child. Lest one miss the point of the new platform, it boldly proclaims the urgent need for a wall along the entire southern border with Mexico, stating: "Our highest priority, therefore, must be to secure our borders and all ports of entry and to enforce our immigration laws." One wonders if the first draft of the 2016 party platform contained a formal denunciation of Ronald Reagan.

Again, although Republicans have certainly disagreed over the years on the particulars of immigration and reform, they were never an anti-immigrant party. Sadly, today's Republican Party is relentlessly negative toward foreign refugees seeking entry into America, asylees (those on American soil seeking legal asylum), and immigrants. And it's only gotten worse. In his 2020 State of the Union address, President Trump spent a great deal of time painting immigrants as violent criminals to be feared. For Republicans today, it is not just *illegal* immigration that needs to be halted but *legal* immigration as well.[12] Beginning in the Trump campaign and continuing in current Republican rhetoric is the notion that immigrants are to be viewed suspiciously, and "guilty until proven innocent." They decry "illegal immigration" and speak about America being "a nation of laws," but if you listen closely, Republican references to legal and illegal immigration are used in a back-and-forth, interchangeable way to shape an overall anti-immigrant narrative. Republicans are heard routinely making the claim that Democrats are for open borders and illegal immigration, yet there is not one Democrat in Congress who has stated that position. In April of 2019, meeting near California's southern border with Mexico, President Trump announced, "We can't take you anymore. Whether it's asylum, whether it's anything you want, it's illegal immigration, we can't take you anymore. Our country is full, our area's full, the sector is full. We can't take you anymore. I'm sorry, can't happen. So turn around, that's the way it is."[13]

The "sector" is full? Sounds like a sci-fi movie.

For the record, the idea that America does not have room for any more people is absurd. Anyone who makes the drive from central Kansas to Las Vegas can let you in on a little secret: there's no one there. That overstates things a bit but not by much. Driving that route is reminiscent of the "Where Is Everybody?" episode of *The Twilight Zone*. I've driven in every one of the lower forty-eight states and across the country three times in a car and once on a motorcycle. We are largely an unoccupied country. Critics have countered by saying that much of our country is inhospitable to life. I countered that Las Vegas is not livable, yet more than six hundred thousand people live there. But don't take my word for it. Just look at a population heat map on Google. Notwithstanding the metro regions of Salt Lake City and Denver, there is a massive swath of land (Trump might call it a sector) in America including the Dakotas, Arizona, Idaho, Nebraska, Montana, Wyoming, and New Mexico that is downright lonely. There is a further argument made that while this may be true, the lands are not developable. That's absurd. America's pioneers took largely forested land with no machinery, cars, trucks, railroads, airplanes, or steam engines and built these areas into towns and cities while the rest of the world marveled. Despite enormous mountains that could have been blamed for impeding the development of cities, Denver and Salt Lake City have been booming since the mid 1800s. Despite being in a desert in the middle of nowhere, the city of Las Vegas was built in 1911. I'm not advocating that we develop our national parks into cities, but the idea that states like Wyoming and New Mexico and Montana have no room for people and no potential industry is not just shortsighted, it's indefensible. John F. Kennedy had the vision to send people to the moon; President Trump doesn't even have the vision to imagine a vibrant New Mexico, and so he sends immigrants back to old Mexico.

Moreover, there are currently more Americans moving to Mexico, mostly to retire, than there are Mexicans illegally entering the United States.

Curiously, there does seem to be room for immigrants from countries other than Mexico, El Salvador, and Haiti—in other words, those places famously deemed "shithole countries" by the president. The country that has the most illegal aliens (the legal term for people in the country illegally) is not Mexico or any of the Central American countries. It's Canada. Yet, there is no clamoring to stop illegal Canadians. Notwithstanding the fact that America is "full," Trump has publicly lamented the fact that America cannot attract more immigrants from Norway. (This comment later came up in a public congressional hearing in which the new secretary of Homeland Security, Kirstjen Nielsen, was asked about it. At that hearing, Vermont senator Patrick Leahy asked, "Norway is a predominantly white country, isn't it?" Nielsen, who is ancestrally Scandinavian, claimed to be unaware, answering, "I actually do not know that, sir, but I imagine that is the case.") The short answer to Trump's question is that not too many people seek asylum from Norway, but the comment itself illustrates an indifference to the plight of immigrants and an intentional callousness among some in the administration toward the families of immigrants. Just as he has picked winners among certain industries in America over others (like the steel industry), Trump's comments illustrate the fact that he wants to pick the winners in the immigration lottery as well. But his preferred country for immigrants has no need to emigrate. America does not have room for someone seeking asylum to escape brutality in neighboring nations, yet it does have room for an immigrant from the Kingdom of Norway? In essence, the administration's immigration policy can be summed up in five words: only white people need apply.

This is the new Republican Party.

The architect of this house of cards is a man named Stephen Miller, who serves as senior adviser to the president. Born into extreme wealth, the main trait that seems to keep putting Miller on the map is his flagrant and smug contempt for the poor and downtrodden. In high school, Miller delivered a campaign speech for class president in which he angrily yelled, "Am I the only one who is sick and tired of being told to pick up my trash when we have plenty of janitors who are paid to do it for us?!"[14] As a junior, he wrote a letter to Santa Monica's *Lookout* newspaper, in which he lamented that "all announcements are written in both Spanish and English" and observed that there were "very few, if any, Hispanic students in my honors classes, despite the large number of Hispanic students that attend our school."[15] (It apparently had not dawned on young Miller that not every student had been born into a family blessed with a seven- or eight-figure net worth that made it possible to afford tutors, educational aids, SAT prep, or even the time left in the day to study.)

Following high school, Miller went on to Duke University, where he wrote a column ridiculing Duke's home city of Durham (in which the majority of citizens are black or Hispanic), claiming, in effect, that the school was the city's only redeeming quality. He wrote: "Durham is not a hub of civilization overflowing with people, commerce and activity. It's not even a hubcap."[16] Though Duke did not even admit black students until the 1960s, Miller makes a comment that was unintentionally ironic and self-defeating, writing that "Duke has about as many racists as Durham has museums." Continuing to express his bizarre disaffection for janitors, Miller lamented that at Duke he "was told to make a birthday card for one of the janitors that serviced my dorm." He writes that while he "had struck up a few conversations with this janitor, she would not have expected a birthday card from me any more than I would from her." (On that point, he may be correct. It is highly unlikely that Miller is on his high school or college janitor's Christmas card list.) In response to the idea that Duke students should be more involved in the town of Durham, Miller seems offended by the very prospect, writing: "Durham isn't a petting zoo. The residents won't get lonely or irritable if we don't play with them." In Miller's view, America is not a melting pot—it's *us versus them.*

Two years after graduation, Miller began working for Senator Jeff Sessions and quickly ascended to the role of communications director; in this capacity, his work for Sessions was pivotal in blocking the immigration reform of Marco Rubio. Making a name for himself by quashing immigration, he was hired by the Trump campaign and later as an adviser to the president. There, he has been the architect of the family separation policy at the border—an intentional policy that has the express goal of frightening asylum seekers from coming to the border.[17] Miller has an ideal number of legal immigrants in mind for America: zero. Along with Peter Navarro, Miller has certainly proven to be one of Trump's favorite policy makers—a fact with which many Republicans are less than thrilled. As Lindsey Graham once upon a time put it, "As long as Stephen Miller is in charge of negotiating immigration, we are going nowhere. He's been an outlier for years."[18]

To maintain his positions, you would think that Miller relies heavily on serious research done by serious people; however, he either backs into a few handpicked numbers or just—how shall we put this?—makes shit up. A good case in point occurred in 2016. One of the principal arguments made by anti-immigrant Republicans is that refugees cause a huge tax burden on Americans—that refugees take advantage of social services in America thereby victimizing American taxpayers. President Trump had instructed the Department of Health and Human Services to research this point and prepare a report, presumably with the idea that the report would confirm his assertions. In September of 2017, however, *The New York Times* reported that it had obtained an initial draft of an internal study prepared by HHS that concluded otherwise. The research indicated that in the decade following 2005, counting federal, state, and local taxes, "refugees brought in $63 billion more in government revenues over the past decade than they cost."[19] Predictably, the administration scoffed at the findings, claiming that the fifty-five-page report was faulty and unreliable. It was then that Stephen Miller got on the phone and provided clear instructions to the researchers at HHS. That instruction was not: please recheck your figures, folks. Rather, it was blunt: produce a new study that supports the president's numbers.[20] In the final report, reduced to three pages, they couldn't do it—or, at least, didn't do it. The report claimed only that refugees were more expensive than native-born Americans with no mention of their contributions. That's classic Stephen Miller.

LOOKING FORWARD

For conservatives, any and every discussion of immigration must begin by reaffirming the dignity, sanctity, potential, and right to life of every person above, below, or at the border. Current Republican rhetoric and America's recent immigration policies have obscured these truths, if not rejected them altogether. But the basic human rights of every person must be recognized and promoted regardless of country of origin.

Not only does man have God-given rights, but he also has God-given genius—and that genius develops economies. Man is productive by nature, taking raw materials and adapting them to his own wants and needs as well as those of his fellow man. It is through the intelligence, creativity, and perseverance of men and women that economies develop and flourish. It is certainly true that "supply creates demand," but it is genius that creates supply. As Pope John Paul II once put it, "Man's principal resource is man himself."[21] And man himself is America's principal resource. Conservatism has always recognized all this, but the current anti-immigrant talking points deny or ignore this reality.

Today's anti-immigration rhetoric argues that immigrants amount to one giant drain on the American economy. That's provably incorrect. Steve Jobs, cofounder of Apple Computer, is the son of a Syrian father who immigrated to the United States; the father of the other Apple Computer cofounder, Steve Wozniak, emigrated from an area of Poland that's now a part of Ukraine; Sergey Brin, cofounder of Google, came to America as a Russian refugee; Pierre Omidyar, founder of eBay, is an American immigrant with Iranian parents. Imagine life without your iPhone or Google or eBay. But it's not just the occasional outlier: *Forbes* magazine recently noted that more than 10 percent of their famous Forbes 400 were immigrants. Nor is it just the billionaires who have made a difference; it's all the entrepreneurs who seek to answer the needs and wants of America. Immigration has meant the importation of innovation and creativity. That's not a theory. That's American economic history.

If population growth hurts an economy, how do you explain America? And not just the current economy, but how do you explain the entire economic history of America? Since colonial days, a funny thing has happened: immigrants came to America to seek a better life and bettered the lives of so many people around them. With innovation and drive, they turned America into an economic powerhouse.

Keeping in mind the dignity of man as well as his economic contribution, conservatives should push for a threefold policy that addresses those attempting asylum, those attempting to immigrate by traditional means, and those already in America illegally.

First: asylum seekers. While the IRCA sought to provide a greater security presence on the border, we should seek to provide not more security but more adjudication of asylum seekers. Though Republicans equate a border wall with border security, that is an odd claim that must come as a surprise to the thousands of people at the border.

The current budget for border security is now more than $4 billion per year. By contrast, the Executive Office for Immigration Review (the agency of the Justice Department that adjudicates asylum cases) has an annual budget of about $300 million. Thus, we are spending more than ten times the money to keep people out than we are spending to help asylum seekers come in. Although some undergo "catch and release" programs that allow them entry into America to await their hearings, sometimes asylum applicants wait two years to have their cases heard. That process can be improved simply by expanding the Executive Office for Immigration Review. We must put more social workers, healthcare personnel, and asylum advocates on the border with Mexico.

We must also be a country that seeks to keep families together. This must be a hallmark of our policy. One particular incident in America's history perhaps best illustrates this point. In the early 1960s, as Fidel Castro came to power and began to establish a totalitarian regime in Cuba, it became clear that Castro's regime was going to be worse than the previous dictatorship of Batista. It was not long before Castro seized private businesses, executed or imprisoned political opponents, criminalized Catholic newspapers, and shut down every Catholic school in the country. Cuban troops loyal to the revolution marched into Catholic schools and announced that they were taking over. For many parents, it became clear that if their children remained on the island nation, they would be undergoing forced indoctrination into Marxism and forced military conscription. So they frantically tried to find a way to help their children flee. Around Thanksgiving of 1960, one of the children, fifteen-year-old Pedro Menéndez, made it to America to live with relatives, but they could not sufficiently care for him. So Pedro went to Father Bryan Walsh with his story. Father Walsh, himself an immigrant from Ireland and the head of the Catholic Welfare Bureau, listened to Pedro's story and quickly realized that tens of thousands of other Cuban children were in trouble. So Father Walsh contacted American government immigration officials in the Eisenhower administration for assistance in helping these children immigrate. Walsh also met with the principal of a school in Havana named James Baker, who was willing to coordinate their escape from Cuba.

In addition to being a compassionate man, Walsh must have proven quite a salesman: not only was he able to arrange this broad mission with plenty of moving parts, but he also was able to finance it through American funds and a vast network. For the plan to work, it also had to be largely kept secret, which was no easy task. Amazingly—Father Walsh might say "miraculously"—the entire operation was so clandestine in both Cuba and America that almost no one knew much about it until years later. Walsh probably anticipated the daring nature of the plan, but he likely underestimated its magnitude. Between 1960 and 1962, Walsh's plan, dubbed Operation Peter Pan, brought more than fourteen thousand Cuban children to America. About half of the children were reunited with family members upon arrival; most of the rest were cared for by the Catholic Welfare Bureau. We can only speculate how many of the parents of these children that didn't get out were later executed by Castro. Today, years later, the "Pedro Pans" (the term for which the children involved have come to be known) still speak of Father Walsh with grateful affection. Though he is virtually unknown outside Florida's Cuban community, Father Bryan Walsh was a hero of the Cold War—as are many of the American officials and families who participated in its success. As Father Walsh later wrote, "The real heroes of Pedro Pan were the parents who made the hardest decision that any parent can make."[22]

But for all its success, Operation Peter Pan had one significant downside: it didn't bring the parents. The parents had various reasons for staying in Cuba: Many had elderly parents or other family members who needed care, not to mention the fact that they were under the watchful eye of a Marxist regime. Some may have been worried about leaving all of their material wealth and possessions behind to start fresh in America. Almost all of them, it appears, thought the operation was temporary. They believed and certainly hoped that Castro would be quickly overthrown. These children were not sent to America for the purpose of permanently finding new lives and new families; rather, it was hoped to amount to a political game of hide-and-seek until Castro was removed from power. As Father Walsh wrote, "No children were placed for adoption, since the whole purpose of the program was to safeguard parental rights."[23] Of course, to the detriment of not only Cuban families but also to the world, Castro held power for decades. While half of the children were reunited with family, many never saw their parents again, a reality lamented by Father Walsh.[24]

Father Walsh wrote that "the Cuban parents who sent their children to the US were exercising a fundamental human right which antecedes any human constitution or law."[25] His statement should shape American immigration policy. The fundamental right of parents to raise their children should not be denied to immigrants and should be recognized in law and in practice.

Second: those seeking to immigrate. Much of the anti-immigration rhetoric contains some version of the claim that "they're coming here to take our jobs" or "they're coming here to disrupt our culture." We've already discussed these points in some detail, but a few more points need to be made about both economics and culture.

Regarding economics, let's be blunt: Americans are not reproducing at a maintenance rate, so America needs immigrants to advance the economy. And since a large part of a country's GDP is achieved through the production and consumption of real-life people, America's greatest economic risk is not that immigrants will take jobs but that there is an *excess* of jobs that need to be done and *not enough* people to fill them. If Americans want economic growth, we need people to grow the economy. The numbers don't lie: if America were to severely limit or cut off immigration for a number of years, it would be almost impossible to avoid a recession. Though politicians harp on their perceived economic downsides of immigration, American businesspeople see the upsides on their balance sheets. As economist and author Bryan Caplan puts it, "Millions of Haitians want to move here. Millions of American landlords, employers, and stores would be happy to house, hire, and feed them. For the U.S. government to criminalize these transactions for no good reason is not merely uncharitable. It is unjust."[26] To illustrate this point, ask any retail store owner in America if he or she would rather double the population or reduce it by half. It's not even close. For that matter, what if you were allowed to work only in your own home state: if you're born in Virginia, you could only work in Virginia. That might be the single fastest way to gum up an economy. And the economic effects of a policy like this are worse than many people realize. As Caplan points out, it is a principle of economics that the freer immigration and emigration, the better it is for an economy.

The fact is that even limited immigration in America is already helping the economy more than most people realize. If it is true that illegal immigration is epidemic, as the Trump administration insists that it is, how can it be that the economy is simultaneously doing so well? If illegal immigration sinks an economy, how is the American economy still afloat? Even more specifically, if illegal immigrants are taking American jobs and destroying the economy, how is America at full employment with stock market records? How does America keep setting employment records month after month? The reason is that immigrants help grow our economy. According to the Economic Policy Institute, the share of immigrants' total output was almost 15 percent from 2009–2011 and larger than their 13 percent share of the population. If we are ever once again able to achieve GDP growth of more than 3 percent, someone is going to have to do all that work. Moreover, the three largest expenditures in the federal budget are Social Security, Medicare, and Medicaid. All are funded by payroll taxes. If you are at or near retirement and you expect to collect your benefits from Social Security and Medicare, you are going to need an expanded workforce to keep them funded through your retirement.

The fears of cultural decay caused by immigration are unfounded, bizarre, and unfortunate but, sadly, common. These basic arguments have been used for literally hundreds of years and yet the same old cultural and economic nativist claims never come to fruition. In the 1840s, a panic was spread that the Irish immigrants were not only bringing disease but also a "strange religion" (Catholicism!) that would corrupt the youth. And there were plenty of them coming to America—more than 1.25 million in fact. A pro-slavery political faction called the Know-Nothings routinely terrorized Irish Catholics. In the 1870s, specific legislation was enacted against Chinese immigrants, while President Grant seemed eager to crack down on Chinese for the crime of being Chinese. The literature at the time, including from major newspapers, warned that keeping Chinese in America could turn America into a country like China. An official congressional report of 1877 concluded that "there is no Aryan or European race which is not far superior to the Chinese."[27] Five years later, Congress passed the Chinese Exclusion Act, which prohibited, as the name implied, immigrants from China. In the late 1910s, there was a significant backlash against Germans because of Germany's involvement in the First World War; during this period, German Americans were deported or put in internment camps. In the 1930s, many German Jews were not allowed to immigrate to America because they were from Germany.[28] In the 1940s, in the days following Pearl Harbor, more than 120,000 Americans of Japanese ancestry—many of whom had never set foot on Japanese soil—were sent to internment camps. The stories of crackdowns on various ethnicities were usually made with the idea that this particular ethnicity would change America. America would be germanized, italianized, irishized, or spanishized. Yet, after wave upon wave of immigrants, we did not become a Catholic nation or a Jewish nation; nor do we speak Italian, German, or Chinese. Each time, whether the argument was made in 1840, 1910, 1950, or 2019, the argument has been that we must keep America the way it is *right then*.

It's time we realize that whether it was Germans, Chinese, Japanese, Jews, Irish, or Latinos from various nations south of the American border who settled in America, the United States of America was still America. Xenophobia stems from a fear that a nation will lose its identity to foreign influences. Yet, no group of immigrants have overwhelmed the American culture; they instead have assimilated into it, and we are better for it. We are not a multicultural nation; rather we are a multiethnic and multitradition country, and America has benefitted immeasurably from immigration.

Our history of *not* welcoming immigrants has been shameful. Latinos and Muslims are getting that disgraceful treatment now. Many of the recent Latino immigrants you see working in low-wage jobs like landscaping, construction, or in hotels and restaurants today are raising children who will become doctors, lawyers, CEOs, and congresspeople tomorrow. They will speak English as well as Spanish. But like the immigrants who came before them, they bring their traditions, foods, and customs. The wave of Latino and Muslim immigrants, like the waves that came before them, does not mean we will become a Spanish-speaking or Muslim country as some want us to believe. This current wave of immigrants, like all the others, will assimilate into American culture, and we will hardly notice them, because they will be our friends and neighbors. They will just be Americans.

On that point, I often ask people to name three things Rudy Giuliani and Nancy Pelosi have in common. Though their last names give them away, most people don't point out that they are both Italian Americans. This point, however, would not have been missed several decades ago. Why don't they think of it today? They don't think of it because they think of them as Americans like anyone else. A day will come soon when I can substitute the names Rodriguez and Hernandez or two Arabic names and ask the same question, but their ethnic heritage will not come immediately to mind; like the Germans, the Irish, the Jews, and the Italians, we will first think of them as Americans.

Third: illegal immigrants. It is up to Congress and the president to fix our irrational immigration laws into ones that are rational, compassionate, and better for America. But our Washington politicians have punted their responsibility at the cost of great human suffering to keep a political issue alive for the benefit of one party or the other. Until that solution arrives, there is something that can be done.

Similar to the IRCA, we should seek to grant amnesty and a path to citizenship for those who have lived in America for a certain number of years. Some will be infuriated and argue that amnesty constitutes and encourages contempt for the law. Yet, amnesty has not only a precedent in law but in the Constitution itself. In *The Federalist Papers*, Alexander Hamilton argued that not only should the president have the power to pardon, but that his power to pardon also should not be impeded; otherwise the letter of the law would result in cruelty. Thus, the power to pardon is a constitutional one. And there is a specific legal precedent that applies. It happened under the presidency of Gerald Ford.

During the Vietnam War, thousands of young men were drafted to serve in the military. Some chose honest and legal means to avoid service; others used fraud, claiming various phony medical ailments, like getting a diagnosis for bone spurs. Others simply refused to respond to the orders—opting instead to burn their draft cards and, in some cases, to move to Canada to escape prosecution. What this meant was that thousands of Americans were guilty of the felony of draft dodging. There was another group of Americans who had gone to serve in Vietnam but deserted their military platoons, some of whom came back to America. The presence of deserters and draft dodgers in America (along with some still abroad) presented a problem for Republican president Ford. It would be impractical to prosecute thousands of Americans. Yet he if offered them a full pardon, he could be accused of illustrating a contempt for the law as well as those who had followed the law. But he came up with another idea.

Ford said that both draft evasion and desertion were things of "serious offense" and cannot be "condoned," but "reconciliation calls for an act of mercy to bind the nation's wounds and to heal the scars of divisiveness."[29] Ford announced that all draft dodgers and deserters would receive conditional amnesty, which in effect granted them a pardon provided that they serve two years in some form of public service. Calling it an earned reentry program, Ford announced his hope that the program of clemency showed an appreciation for everyone involved and a "common purpose as a nation whose future is always more important than its past."

This provides a blueprint for how illegal immigrants might be addressed. The president could offer an amnesty program for those who presented themselves to immigration officials and offered some form of public service for a period of time. During that time, they can work toward gaining full citizenship. That plan would potentially put 11 million illegal immigrants into the system, allowing them to pay taxes and participate in the rights and duties of citizenship.

All in all, the way we treat those seeking immigration by standard means, those seeking asylum, and those in America illegally defines who we are as a country. Reagan liked to say that "the United States remains the last best hope for a mankind plagued by tyranny and deprivation." The world is still plagued by tyranny and deprivation. The question is whether we still want to be that last best hope.

7

COST-DRIVEN HEALTHCARE
MAY PUT YOUR HEALTH AT RISK

In April of 2016, HBO's show *Real Time with Bill Maher,* flew me to Los Angeles to appear on the program. I had an appearance on MSNBC the same afternoon I arrived. The network sent a car and after my appearance I asked the driver for his recommendation on a good place to get sushi. He dropped me off, and I went inside for lunch. The waiter explained that during lunch sushi was "all you can eat." This was very exciting news and not for the restaurant because I can eat an inordinate amount of sushi. Sushi can be very expensive, but I've always argued that it was cheaper than a heart attack. So with abandon, I ordered as much sushi off the menu as I thought I could reasonably eat. What I didn't, however, pay attention to was that each order contained two pieces of sushi and not one. When the waiter delivered the order, it was nearly twice as much as I thought I could eat. Luckily the rolls were just one order each. Then the waiter pointed out the disclaimer on the menu. "You must consume everything you ordered or pay full price. Taking food to go is not allowed." I heroically ate it all.

Here is an example of the second-party payer phenomenon. Second-party payer is when you are a consumer of a product that someone else is paying for. In this case, the restaurant substantially subsidized my love of raw fish. I didn't care about the price because it was fixed and for the amount I got, it was a bargain. No matter how much I consumed the price wasn't going to change. I did, however, care about the quality because I was eating it. The first-party payer is when you are the consumer of the same product you are paying for. In the first-party payer scenario, you care about both the quality and the price. Then there is the third-party payer phenomenon. That is when you make a purchase with someone else's money for a product that you will not consume. I take it you have deduced already that in the third-payer scenario, the price is of little concern because you are not paying and less about the quality because the product is not for you.

Here's the lesson: every government purchase is made by a third-party payer who cares little about the cost and less about the quality. The government purchases an enormous amount of things with other people's money that will not be used by the people purchasing them. If you were ever astonished about the amount of waste, fraud, and abuse the government is capable of, this is the reason.

Although there are advocates to make it so, the American health-care system is not one seamless system. It is a series of complex systems like the original landline phone system. Even technical experts had a difficult time explaining how its multitude of systems were integrated, but for the most part it worked. Similarly, today, our healthcare systems are comprised of thousands of doctors, clinics, and hospitals in both the public and private sectors that provide care for millions of patients every day. Most patients are part of one of the following payment coverage systems: Medicare for the elderly and disabled; Medicaid for the chronically poor, mostly single mothers, and for the blind; the ACA exchange known as Obamacare for the individual market; a temporary insurance market open to those without preexisting conditions; and finally, the employer- and union-based insurance market. In addition, there are government-run systems that provide both care and payment coverage: Tricare, which is a worldwide healthcare program for 9.4 million people who are members of the military, military retirees, and their families. They run fifty-five hospitals and hundreds of health and dental clinics. The US Department of Veterans Affairs, a cabinet-level department, also runs a network of regional hospitals for active and retired veterans that are uniquely competent in prosthetics and mental health services; under the Department of Health and Human Services, another cabinet-level department, falls the Indian Health Service, which provides culturally appropriate healthcare to Native Americans and Alaska Natives.

In general, it helps to think of each part of the healthcare system as being comprised of two separate parts. There is the delivery of care and there is how the care is paid for.

On the care side, life expectancy in America has never been higher. Cancer—once a dread diagnosis that meant nearly certain death—is often treatable. And in just the last generation, pharmaceutical companies have produced a variety of drugs that treat hypertension and prevent clogged arteries, substantially reducing the chance of coronary disease. But despite recent breakthroughs and advances in medical technology, many Americans feel like they're being sucker punched by the healthcare system. Why? What's broken? And is there a conservative prescription for a sick healthcare system?

As I write this in the middle of the Coronavirus pandemic, there have been many calls by public official and others for a national government-run healthcare system similar to those that exist in Europe where people are guaranteed health services to one degree or the other and at the very least, will not loose their health coverage in the event that they loose their job.

I have routinely pointed out the horrendous failures of our government to respond to the pandemic as a caution against a one-payer system. Progressives would point out that if Donald Trump were not president, we would not have been so far behind on testing and protecting Americans and particularly the people in our healthcare system. I take this point believing that there is no doubt another president could have done a much better job, but Trump is president and there is no guarantee he won't be again or that someone equally incompetent wouldn't be in the future.

The fact is getting large bureaucratic systems to respond quickly is difficult. It's not that there are not good people that work in government bureaucracies, there are. In fact, very skilled, competent, and knowledgeable people throughout our government. But government performance is a function of political considerations and priorities. We can easily point to the fact that Trump disbanded the group on the National Security Council responsible for preparing and responding to pandemics as an example. Having done so was clearly a short-sighted decision by the president that cost money and lives. But the failures don't end there. State after state was not technologically prepared for so many unemployment payments. There really was no adequate stockpile of ventilator and personal protection equipment. The ability for the CDC to produce and distribute tests was a colossal failure. All of which was indefensible and should not have happened. But let's step back and look more closely at the current system.

There is a broad consensus that the existing healthcare system needs serious repair. But those on Medicare seem generally happier with the healthcare system than those who have insurance, and those who pay their insurance premiums out-of-pocket without the benefit of discounted group insurance seem to be the least happy. Yet, all three groups see the exact same doctors who take Medicare, individual, and union-and employer-based insurance. Could it be that the most subsidized are the happiest and the least subsidized are the least happy?

When people say the system is broken, they are almost never referring to the care they actually receive. They are almost exclusively expressing frustration about affording or having access to the care they need. I often hear the refrain from the right that everyone has access to care because the law prevents emergency rooms from denying care to patients who don't have the ability to pay. While this is true, it's a wholly inadequate response. When you show up to the emergency room because you had a heart attack, were in a car accident, or sliced your finger cutting your breakfast bagel, you will not be denied emergency care based on your ability to pay. But 65 percent of Americans suffer from chronic conditions like diabetes, hypertension, heart disease, alcohol-related issues, Alzheimer's, cancer, or arthritis. For the poor, those chronic conditions are often left untreated. The lack of access to affordable care to treat chronic diseases leads ultimately to the condition becoming so acute or life-threatening it requires an emergency room visit. In the ER, the patient is stabilized enough to send him home, at which point the cycle be-gins again. The underlying chronic condition goes untreated until the next emergency room visit or death. For the poor with chronic conditions, emergency care due to lack of access to routine or preven-tative care is not only the most expensive way to provide care, it is the most ineffective.

Americans are divided about how to fix the affordability problem, which is a function of the payment system. Some believe healthcare should be fully privatized to allow market forces to bring about inno-vation and competition to improve the quality of care and its afford-ability. And there are those who equally believe the system should be socialized to ensure that everyone has access to the care they deserve without the additional worry of losing their life savings, going into medical debt, or becoming a financial burden to their family. Oth-ers think the best solution is to fix what is broken but not radically change the system one way or the other.

The payment conundrum has become an emotionally volatile political issue. And why shouldn't it? Our health and the health of our loved ones and friends is the most important aspect of our lives. There can be no more sense of injustice than to be denied access to the care you or someone you love needs.

IS HEALTHCARE A BASIC RIGHT?

In the early 1900s, the average American spent $5 annually for healthcare—about $100 in today's dollars. There was no insurance. You simply paid cash or paid when you could. Hospitals were a place you went to die. Cancer treatment cost $0 because there was no treatment for cancer other than to cut it out and hope for the best. Most medicines were more like potions. They weren't expensive and they didn't work. Around 1920, hospitals began marketing them-selves as places to give birth. Over time, as treatment and surgical procedures improved, hospitals slowly became places where patients went to get well. Today, there are thousands of drugs that do work—

many lifesaving and many that help people live more normal lives. Advancements in technology help doctors diagnose conditions and offer treatment options that were not available to your parents and grandparents. Healthcare was once cheap but not very good. Today it's expensive, but the capabilities are nothing less than extraordinary.

Despite its seemingly ever-increasing costs, I absolutely recognize healthcare as a basic human right. The reason is simple: the right to life is the most basic and most foundational human right. Thomas Jefferson and the founders agreed that life is the primary right in the Declaration because all the other rights we talk about—free speech, freedom of religion, freedom to keep and bear arms—presuppose life. Liberty is wonderful, unless you're dead. Then it is fairly meaningless. Pursuing happiness is similarly without purpose, unless you are free to pursue. But life must come first, or all other rights are pointless. And the right to life extends far beyond the right to be born; it is the right to maintain life. And to the extent that essential healthcare is necessary to maintain life, healthcare is therefore an inarguable basic human right. If there exists a right to life, there also exists a right to maintain it. In the profession of that right, surely conservatives and liberals can find a large measure of agreement. But conservatism also professes—and this is where we part company with progressives— that there is a huge difference between *protecting* the human right of healthcare and government *providing* a system of healthcare.

Before we get into the meat of the issue, let's agree to dispense with some misguided notions. The first is that conservatives don't care about people or their health. You can accept my conclusions or reject them. Either is fine. But don't reject my prescriptions based on the idea that you don't think I care about people. I care deeply. Second, lack of a full-blown government-controlled healthcare coverage plan does not constitute not having a plan. It is possible to support a plan that remains largely in the private sector and still have a plan. Having said that, during the debate leading to the passage of Obamacare, the Republicans didn't seem to have any plan—public or private—at least not one that was articulated with any coherence. Although, I think it is important to point out an inherent advantage progressives have over conservatives. When convincing the public and the media about the seriousness of solving a problem, progressives will most often point to a government plan. Conservatives have to show that their solutions are better without the benefit of pointing to a new government-expanding program which leads to the criticism of not caring about the problem and doing nothing.

In that united spirit, I don't believe I'd get much of an argument with progressives that the individual is in a better position than a government bureaucrat interpreting a policy to make healthcare decisions for themselves and their families. But I'm sure to get a disagreement when I propose that the market remains the best way to ensure the most treatment options and the highest quality care at the lowest costs to the patient. Progressives make sound arguments that private institutions and the free market have proven incapable of providing the right to basic healthcare. They observe that the free market is not working in the field of healthcare. Even for some of those people predisposed to favor the market economy, they argue that the free market has proven itself incapable of such a large project as providing healthcare to a nation currently in excess of 330 million people. They may observe that while the free market might work in theory, it has proven both disastrous and deadly in practice. Many reject as immoral the profit motive having a place in decisions as important as healthcare. The government, therefore, must be more involved; in fact, that government should run the show. This is the essential argument behind the Affordable Care Act (ACA). It's worth noting that it was Republicans who branded the ACA as "Obamacare." It's particularly galling given that mandating health insurance—a prominent feature of Obamacare—was originally an idea floated by the conservative Heritage Foundation. Moreover, the existing model for Obamacare was the brainchild of Massachusetts Republican governor Mitt Romney.

When I worked for Newt Gingrich, he and I paid a visit to Governor Romney at the state capitol in Boston, where in his office for nearly three hours we sat and discussed his "Romneycare" plan. In another historical irony, the success of that plan was going to be a key selling point for his policy chops as he was then considering his run for president.

The branding of Romneycare's twin, the ACA, as Obamacare was supposed to be a pejorative moniker, but President Obama deftly accepted the name and over time support for "Obamacare" grew, especially among Democrats and non-party-affiliated voters. So much so, that governors began renaming the ACA exchanges their states administered to be able to accrue its successes to their administrations, notably allowing people with preexisting conditions to purchase coverage.

Signed into law in 2010, Obamacare was debated for many months and invited superlatives from its opponents. In particular, Republican presidential candidates engaged in a rhetorical sparring match, competing to explain just how horrifyingly bad Obamacare really was. For instance, Representative Michele Bachmann claimed that Obamacare was "a crime against democracy."[1] Rick Santorum concluded that Obamacare was "the most ambitious power grab I've ever witnessed."[2] But Dr. Ben Carson won the battle of one-upmanship, preposterously claiming that "Obamacare is really I think the worst thing that has happened in this nation since slavery."[3] The Republican messaging strategy was to equate Obamacare with Socialism, arguing that if Medicare amounted to flirting with Socialism, Obamacare was a torrid affair. If the debate were about how to defeat Socialism, the Republicans would have won—but that's not what the debate was ultimately about. It was about providing uninsured poor and middle-class Americans with health insurance coverage. The problem was that the Republicans failed to overcome the central argument made by Obamacare's advocates: tens of millions of Americans were uninsured. In failing to address that fact in a meaningful and practical way, they often came across as unfeeling and uninformed. While Democratic strategists went on TV and explained the desperate plight of Americans who had lost their coverage, Republicans would counter with the "this is Socialism" argument.

Listening to the arguments about Obamacare then and today, you might conclude that it was either a sine qua non or as Dr. Carson said,

the worst thing since slavery. Of course, it was neither. Obamacare—
or the Affordable Care Act—makes up a relatively small part of the
insurance market, about 7 percent. By contrast, the employer- and
union-based insurance market makes up almost half the total market.
Medicaid and Medicare together make up around 32 percent. Although
Obamacare did lead to 16 million more people getting insurance largely
because it made it unlawful to deny people with preexisting conditions
from getting coverage, there are still more voluntarily uninsured people
than people actually on Obamacare, 27 million—around 12 percent. Of
the Americans that remain uninsured even with subsidies to help low-
income Americans make coverage more affordable, 45 percent of those
living without insurance say the main reason they remain uninsured is
the high cost of coverage offered on the ACA-created exchanges. The
costs have stabilized but have remained high partly because even under threat of penalty which has now been removed, too many people
who were not eligible for a subsidy and therefore would themselves be
subsidizing others didn't sign up. Some decided to self-fund their care,
some bought inexpensive renewable short-term policies, while millions
of others joined one of the Christian and other medical expense sharing
associations allowed under the law.

Republicans should have made an entirely different argument in
opposing the ACA, and that argument revolves around the free market. Many of the Republicans who argued against Obamacare maintained that the proper solution for the healthcare system was to keep
the free market in place. Of course, this overlooked a rather glaring
reality, and this is the main premise of my argument: our healthcare
system does not operate in a free market or anything close to a free
market. To state it again more plainly, there was then and is now no
free market in healthcare. Healthcare has been and remains stuck
somewhere between a government-controlled and a market-based
system. But it is neither, and that is what is not working. It neither
responds to market forces because the government has so distorted
the market, nor responds to government because so much of it is
outside the control of government bureaucratic decision makers. The
debate we are having now is between moving toward a bureaucratic-

controlled system—the side that is currently gaining ground—or moving more toward the free market, the side that is currently losing ground. If you haven't guessed by now, I believe that more free market is needed not less.

When I talk about a free market system, I am not describing an unregulated market with no government guardrails. Free markets do need a set of rules by which to operate, not only to keep bad actors out but also to keep people safe. Contrary to today's conventional wisdom about capitalism and free markets, the free market is not driven by greed and selfishness as it has often been characterized. Markets are mostly incompatible with greed once you understand what greed is. Greed is the hoarding of assets to oneself. But because markets require investments in capital and people, which is actually pushing money away from you as opposed to keeping the money close, greed really has no place in a functioning free market. Markets also work best when sellers spend their days thinking about the needs and wants of their customers and meeting them before someone else does. It's hard to be selfish and successful in business when success comes from fulfilling the needs and desires of other people. Are there greedy and selfish people in a free market? Count on it. But I would counter with asking where this utopian government with its altruistic angels exists? Of course it doesn't, it never has, and at the risk of sounding cynical, never will. Not because there are not good people in government; again, there are. They care about their families and friends, but they operate on an impersonally grand scale that makes it impossible to respond to their clients' needs the way the market does. Greed and selfishness are simply antithetical to a free market and if government really worked on keeping the market truly free, the greedy and the selfish wouldn't really be able to compete. A true free market is millions of voluntary transactions that take place between buyers and sellers. There is nothing coercive about a free market transaction; it is completely voluntary. It's all about the freedom to choose the best products and services at the best price.

Like millions of others, I take a statin to control high cholesterol levels. The first drug I was prescribed was Lipitor. With my insurance,

I had a co-pay of $15. It didn't matter what that drug actually cost, with my plan it was a fixed cost. Later, after the introduction of Health Savings Accounts (HSA), I no longer had a co-pay or even a discount for prescription drugs. I remember the pharmacist telling me the cash price for Lipitor was $130 for a thirty-day supply. I had gone from $15 a month to $130 a month, an 867 percent increase. I immediately began thinking that the free market sucks. So I went home and got online and learned that there are actually three classes of statin drugs; each worked differently to reduce cholesterol. I made a list and found out the cash prices for each and took the list to my doctor. He asked me why I was learning so much about these drugs and seemed impressed with what I now knew. I told him about the change in my insurance and he prescribed Zocor, which cost about $40 per month. Since then, I was able to switch to a generic statin, which then cost $4 but today is about $16—nearly the same as my original co-pay without the higher insurance premium.

For a market to work, the consumer, in this case a healthcare consumer, must have access to information about both quality and price. Those are the two most important factors in making a buying decision. With the $15 co-pay, I frankly did not care about the price of the drug because under the second-party payer scenario, someone else was absorbing the bulk of the actual cost. I did care about the quality because I was consuming the product and wanted it to work. When I became a first-party payer and the price did become a factor, I sought out information to see if there were other options that would work equally well for less money. For me, there was, and I actually saved money for a time when a similar generic was available at $4 per month, a 375 percent decrease in cost. Not every less-expensive drug will work for everyone, but the point still holds. Millions of people making informed healthcare choices will cause the market to respond. If no one chooses a drug based on cost, then the drug manufacturers are free to arbitrarily set the price of drugs much higher than a free market with informed consumers who cared about the cost would allow. Today, there are almost no downward cost pressures on drugs because not only does the consumer has no idea what the real cost is, worse, like most healthcare costs, it's a trade secret.

When I talk about how a free market could work in healthcare, I get some typical objections. This recent one on Twitter: "So let me understand, I break my arm and go to the doctor and she presents me with a pricing menu, if I determine that the cost is more than I can afford, what am I supposed to do?"

I want you to think about the last time you had to make any sort of healthcare choice like making an appointment, finding a specialist, or where to fill a prescription. OK? Got it? Now that you remember when you made your last healthcare choice, were you in the back of an ambulance? No? Good.

Or if you were, it would definitely not be the time to educate yourself about your choices in healthcare or to decide if you can afford it. That time has passed, and you need immediate care.

But back to my friend with the broken arm. Should he have to worry if he is going to get quality care and how much it costs? He wouldn't, if he had done a little homework before he broke his arm. If he had done some basic research, he might have been assured that he was at the best quality facility available to him at reasonable market prices. If everyone did similar research, they could pick the best providers for them. Similarly, if consumers had variable out-of-pocket costs for prescription drugs instead of a flat co-pay, the price of the drug would be a determining factor in deciding among other appropriate drugs. When consumers consider price in making their choices, the market will respond, in this case by pricing competing drugs more competitively.

While it should be readily acknowledged that there are often limited choices or even only one choice of hospital and not realistic for most people to fly across the country for treatment at the best-in-class hospital for their condition, the same market principles hold true when there is a choice of hospitals closer to home. If you needed to have a surgical procedure, wouldn't you want to know that the doctor and the hospital you choose are going to keep you safe? I had a colonoscopy last year. Before choosing a provider, I did a couple of hours of research for the fifteen-minute procedure. I chose Johns Hopkins out of the many hospitals near where I live because in colorectal care, they are far and away the best hospital system for that type of care.

While it is impossible to definitively know your prognosis after a medical procedure, you can make informed choices by looking at some of the hospital's measurable outcomes. How many procedures do they routinely perform? What is the mortality rate? What is the post-op infection rate? What has the patient experience been? Do they have access to the latest equipment relative to your procedure? What is the readmission rate? What is the average recovery time? And finally, what is the cost?

Sometimes it is hard to get answers to these questions, but if a facility is reluctant to offer them, consider another hospital. If enough consumers demanded them, the market would respond. Hospitals with too many post-op infections would work harder to ensure and prioritize patient safety so they could get their rate down. The bottom line is if you don't know the quality of what you're buying and you don't know how much you're paying until long after you buy it, you don't have a free market. Now, let's consider how the distortions in the market keep the free market from working in healthcare as it does almost everywhere else.

MARKET DISTORTION IN HEALTHCARE

Often, when the topic of American healthcare comes up, politicians and economists look at the similarities between healthcare and other industries. They should be looking at what is different. One thing that is different—and what makes healthcare unique among America's industries—is the susceptibility of Americans to be victimized by healthcare. Steven Brill, author of *America's Bitter Pill*, lays out part of the problem, and that problem can be expressed like this. When you go shop for a new 8K television—or just about any other product in America—the process is pretty simple: once you decide which model you want, its then a matter of finding the best price. If Amazon has it cheaper than Best Buy, they win. If you have to wait a week to buy it for $80 less at Best Buy's Black Friday sale, you might wait. Unless they're independently wealthy, this is how most consumers shop for electronics, cars, computers, and virtually everything else. But when it comes to healthcare, the process is completely different. The consumer's process of deliberation hardly takes place. Not only do consumers fail to price shop, they don't even *ask* about prices. As Brill puts it, "When you're staring up at someone from the gurney, you have no inclination to be a savvy consumer."[4] But it goes well beyond trips to the ER. In the cryptic world of health and medicine, we don't know what a "good deal" is, and, further, we trust our physician, who may or may not be acting in our best interest without outside bias. Of course, he or she might be biased, as we'll see. This system—the impracticality of price shopping under duress—opens the floodgates to fraud, monopoly, and collusion; three things antithetical to the free market.

FRAUD

There are many instances of fraud we could cite here: medical over-billing, hospital price gouging, and so forth, yet the most ubiquitous example of fraud occurs in the pharmaceutical field. We've all been there. You're watching a baseball or football game and an ad comes on for some drug that claims to make your life better. Though I'm sure the ad execs on Madison Avenue get paid plenty for producing these ads, they're more formulaic than a random episode of *The Love Boat*. Seemingly every drug ad begins with a slightly older, attractive couple walking on an empty white-sand beach where the sun is always setting. A few frames in, suddenly she is dancing with her husband. They circle around and around holding hands, leaning back, smiling and laughing. The voice-over is calm and reassuring and like *The Love Boat*, promises something for everyone. Much of the time, you don't even really know what illness the particular drug seeks to alleviate, though it does list a rapid-fire litany of side effects, most of which are frightening—something like: "If you have strange dreams or a terrifying death-like experience or feel the urge to make paper dolls out of tinfoil, stop taking Reallyitsallinyourhead and immediately seek medical attention." Bizarre disclaimers notwithstanding, these ads end the same: "Ask your doctor if Crapola is right for you!"

This direct-to-consumer advertising for pharmaceuticals is relatively recent. In fact, besides New Zealand, the United States is the only country to allow it. Prior to the 1980s, drug companies would market their drugs directly to physicians,[5] yet direct-to-consumer marketing proved wildly successful as patients began calling their doctors and asking, as the ad suggests: "Doctor, is Crapola right for me?" In 2016, the pharmaceutical industry ran more than seven hundred thousand television commercials for their drugs.[6] The big drug companies realized that marketing to doctors was just screwing around. The real profits were made by encouraging patients to market drugs to their own doctors. Medical organizations such as the American Medical Association and the occasional politician will point out that this is inherently deceptive. Defenders of the practice might cynically claim that all advertising is deceptive—that women will not *necessarily* throw themselves at you if you eliminate dandruff, or that not all cats *actually* ask for Meow Mix by name, or that sometimes M&Ms actually *do* melt in your hands but even if they do, there is no real harm done. The same cannot be said for pharmaceutical drugs like Chantix, OxyContin, Ritalin, Prozac, and Prednisone. Never mind the drugs that have been recalled.

But here's the thing: the drug companies went a step further to complete the marketing circle. If you ask your doctor if Crapola is right for you, it turns out that he or she has a pretty good chance of saying yes. Why? It might be because he or she is paid serious money to write the prescription. Every year, doctors across America receive billions of dollars in cash for "consulting fees," food and beverages, and travel junkets. In fact, you can look up any company (as well as your own physician) on OpenPaymentsData.CMS.gov to see who is paying what to whom. In 2017, for instance, Pfizer Inc. (the company that makes Lipitor) made $47.7 million in "general payments" to a total of 587,081 physicians.[7] Some physicians have very meager payments, while others receive more than ten times the average American salary. Is your doctor writing a prescription because he needs the money or because you need the drug? Certainly, there are ethical physicians out there who would never prescribe an unnecessary drug. Surely, your own physician wouldn't, right?

A free market presumes that professionals in the field are not being biased and influenced by outside forces. A free market presumes that consumers are aware of the relevant facts in making a purchasing decision rather than being lied to. As previously established, in order for a free market to work, consumers must have accurate information to make informed choices. They also have a right to know if their doctor is prescribing medicine for the benefit of the patient or the doctor.

MONOPOLY AND COLLUSION

One of the defining characteristics of free market capitalism is competition. Though the subject of competition takes up a full chapter or more in most economics textbooks, competition can be briefly summarized simply as "the freedom to enter a market to buy and sell." The ability to enter a market to compete against existing companies constitutes the "free" in free market. The opposite of competition is a "monopoly," a word that comes to us from a Greek word meaning "one seller." And one seller might be the best way of explaining the entire health industry. (In America, laws against illegal monopolies are often referred to as "antitrust" laws.) From pharmaceuticals to hospitals to medical device companies to insurance companies, monopolies are flagrant—and the direct effect is higher prices for almost everything.

As much as prescriptions cost Americans, they spend more than triple that amount on hospital care, largely because of monopoly-inflated prices.[8] Hospitals and health systems tend to be monopolistic within cities and metro areas. Rather than compete with each other, they merge together, followed by price increases.[9] In the healthcare industry, this is called a "network"; in the oil industry, this is called a "cartel." A good example of near-monopolistic control of a market is ironically in the industry that benefits the most when healthcare fails—the death industry. The average funeral today costs nearly $9,000 as a few companies have consolidated ownership of funeral homes where the name is often preserved to appear local but is now owned by a conglomerate. The same is true in the headstone and casket businesses as well as in the cemetery business.

Medical device companies often have a monopolistic stranglehold in their particular areas as well. To illustrate this point, Open Markets Institute cites Becton Dickinson, which has a nearly two-thirds market share on syringes.[10] Why is that? How can a company have a two-thirds market share on a seemingly generic product? In 2015, a class action lawsuit filed in US district court claims Becton Dickinson had been "suppressing competition and maintaining a monopoly in the syringe market through exclusionary bundled rebates, penalty contracts, and sole-source contracts meant to penalize acute care providers that switch to lower cost competitors."[11] The prior year, a jury found that Becton Dickinson had violated false advertising rules and awarded $340 million in damages to a competitor.[12] The award was later reversed but at the time the initial decision was made, Zacks Equity Research issued a statement telling investors not to worry, writing: "Although the adverse ruling is a setback for Becton Dickinson, we believe that it will not have any material impact on the company's overall results."[13] And that's just the point: even a $340 million fine has a comparatively small impact on the Becton Dickinson empire. It's simply attributed to the cost of doing business. As Steven Brill notes, the medical device field "is the only industry where technology advances have increased costs instead of lowering them."[14]

While hospitals and device companies use monopolistic tactics, it is the pharmaceutical companies that have the most famous monopolies. As of this writing, there are around four thousand new drugs in development in America. Most will fail and never come to market, but for each one that does, it takes around $2 billion in investment. Drug companies are generally granted patents on their FDA-approved drugs for twenty years, during which the companies enjoy the profits that come from their relatively few big breakthroughs. Of course, no one would risk that amount of capital and time if competitors were legally permitted to take a new discovery and make their own generic versions. Granting patents encourages the necessary investments to keep developing new drugs. While it's understood that monopolies and patents drive drug prices up, companies should have the ability to recoup their research and development (R&D) investment. Without patent protection, there is no doubt that innovation would cease. This argument has plenty of merit, yet it fails to tell the whole story.

As physician and author Dr. Robert Pearl phrased it, "Prices should bear a reasonable and logical relationship to the cost of development in return for protection against competition," but, sadly, "we are nowhere near that optimal point today."[15] Looking at the numbers, it's hard to disagree. As of 2019, Luxturna (a gene therapy that treats a hereditary retinal problem in children) was the most expensive medicine made in the United States at $850,000. It's not the most expensive drug in the world, however; that distinction belongs to Zolgensma, which is produced by Switzerland's Novartis. At more than $2 million per patient, Zolgensma is a one-time treatment for a children's disease called spinal muscular atrophy—a veritable death sentence to children left untreated.[16] Whenever people raise the issue of limiting profits by drug companies, Big Pharma execs respond by telling horror stories about what the world would be like without such drug discoveries. To be sure, new drug discoveries have bettered and saved countless lives, but the drug companies are not exactly teetering on the edge of bankruptcy. Quite the contrary: large pharmaceutical companies are consistently the highest profit margin sector in the S&P stock universe, and they are not going out of business anytime soon.[17] For instance, in 2018, the operating profit margin of Big Pharma giant Pfizer was more than 49 percent and is expected by Wall Street analysts to move higher in coming years.[18]

Though companies charge astronomic amounts for their drugs, pharma execs attempt to justify these prices by saying that most of the money goes right back into research and development. But the reality is that the large pharmaceutical companies have relatively small R&D budgets when you compare them to their marketing budgets.

Big Pharma, as the companies are collectively called, are largely sales and marketing firms—less so R&D firms. The comprehensive financial statements of major drug companies confirm this fact. Then where do they get their new drugs? Answer: from smaller pharmaceutical companies that actually develop drugs. Often, these drugs are the result of research done in taxpayer-funded entities like the National Institutes of Health or publicly funded state universities. In other words, these drugs are often the result of public money not the corporation's money.[19] Many drugs are also developed with tax subsidies and preferential tax treatment—that is to say, some of their drugs are developed with your tax dollars.[20] But even though your money goes toward the development of a drug, monopolistic pricing is used against you.

But it gets worse. There's no more depressing day in the life of a drug than its twentieth birthday—the day when the monopoly ends and most of the company profits dry up because rival companies can produce generic forms of it. At least, that's how it is supposed to work. But as the authors of *Drug Wars: How Big Pharma Raises Prices and Keeps Generics Off the Market* point out, it often doesn't work that way at all. They document the fact that drug companies engage in "schemes, strategies, and tactics . . . to keep prices high and generic drugs off the market, denying consumers billions in cost savings and health benefits every year."[21] Referring to it as a system of "pay-for-delay," the authors describe "a darkly ingenious approach in which the brand-name drug company shares a portion of its monopoly profits with the generic company in exchange for the generic company's agreement to stay out of the market."[22] Sometimes it's legal; sometimes it's not. But the system is common. And even when pharma companies are slapped with antitrust fines, the basic formula of "profits minus fines" is often far greater than meekly surrendering the patent.

Consider Cephalon, the maker of Provigil. That drug maker was charged by the Federal Trade Commission (FTC) for paying $300 million to several other manufacturers to effectively pay them for not producing a generic version of Provigil. Frank Baldino, the CEO of Cephalon provides a compelling explanation, "We were able to get six more years of patent protection. That's $4 billion in sales that no one expected." In 2015, Teva, a pharmaceutical manufacturer based in Israel, which had purchased Cephalon in 2011, settled the FTC case for $1.2 billion in 2015.[23]

That's not even the cost of doing business. That's a huge return on investment for violating the law! The fines for pay-for-delay are common, but the truth is that most incidents of the practice don't ever get to that stage, and the pharma companies are finding better ways to maintain their monopolies. It's a sad irony that some of the most significant innovations in the drug industry have taken place not in research labs but in courtrooms.

Moreover, the drug purchasing system is corrupt and arcane. Middlemen called pharmacy benefit managers (PBM)—who are supposed to negotiate discounts for the end user—are actually paid a portion of the size of the discount they negotiate so it is in both the interests of the PBMs and the drug manufacturers to keep drug prices artificially high while the consumer gets screwed.

When the game is rigged, it's hard to know exactly where a healthy profit ends and price gouging begins, but when drugs are priced in the seven-figure range, it's time we start asking questions about whether we're even close to the perfect model. And for that matter, we should question whether twenty-year monopolies encourage innovation as much as some think. What if Apple had a twenty-year patent on the smartphone and no one else could make them? You might still be using the iPhone 2G or more likely, a less-capable but much more expensive iPhone. Why would you innovate when it would be financially counterproductive to do so? The same question might be asked of pharmaceutical companies. Regarding the treatment of an illness, why would you innovate when you already own an existing drug with patent protection, even if that new drug might be better or save more lives? The data increasingly suggests that these long-term pharmaceutical monopolies betray the public interest. Patent protection for drugs needs revisiting. While protecting intellectual property is paramount to our economy, a shorter window of five years for drug patents seems reasonable.

Returning to the debate that was raging about Obamacare before and after its passage and implementation, the argument should not have been about keeping the free market but restoring the free market. The main reason that Obamacare is a mess is that rather than *overcoming* the institutional problems of fraud, monopoly, and overcharging, it *ingrains* these problems. Worse, it increases one more problem: collusion. Simply put, collusion involves two or more people (or entities) coming together in an effort to defraud or deprive a third person. Under that definition, there is plenty of collusion in the healthcare world—the two entities being healthcare companies and government. Private corporations—hospitals, insurance companies, and Big Pharma—come together with the federal and state governments in such a way, whether intentional or not, to deprive "third persons." Over the years, but particularly in the lead-up to Obamacare, the relationship between government and the healthcare industry has grown increasingly incestuous. In this case, the third persons are you and me, because collusion drives up prices. And yet, some people envision the solution is to get the government even more involved in healthcare, as we're about to see.

MEDICARE FOR ALL?

Brought to greater national attention in the Democratic debates of 2019, Bernie Sanders has insisted that Obamacare doesn't go far enough to socialize healthcare; rather, America needs a Medicare for All program. (In 1987, Sanders said offering Medicare for everyone would "bankrupt the nation" but I'll let that alone. Bernie isn't the first politician to contradict himself.) To make sense of all this—or to realize why the Sanders plan makes no sense—here's a quick refresher. The Medicare program signed into law by President Johnson in 1965 was a promise to America's seniors. Since then, it has grown more expansive over time. Today, nearly every American over age sixty-five is covered (along with younger Americans suffering from a few particular illnesses such as ALS). Medicare has four abecedarian parts—A, B, C, and D. Parts A and B include hospital, nursing, and hospice care, as well as "medically necessary services" defined as needed to diagnose or treat your medical condition. Medicare Part C, sometimes called Medigap, is supplemental private insurance that is meant to cover some things not covered by Medicare A and B.

Medicare Part D was signed into law by President Bush in 2003 with the Medicare Modernization Act, and it amounted to a massive expansion in the system by subsidized private insurance covering prescription drugs for seniors (at present, 45 million Americans have Part D insurance). You might naturally think that since the Medicare Modernization Act (MMA) would make the federal government the largest bulk buyer of drugs in world history, MMA would allow for some serious bargaining power with drug companies. It didn't. Shockingly, the act disallowed the government to negotiate prices with pharmaceutical companies. By some remarkable coincidence, the pharmaceutical industry had made more donations to politicians in the previous election cycle than ever before. In the year 2000, the pharmaceutical/healthcare industry contributed more than twice as much as it had in any preceding election in history. The 2002 election cycle saw an even higher number of political contributions.[24] By 2004, even though it was a huge election year, pharmaceutical companies felt much less of an urge to donate money to politicians, and donations fell by more than 30 percent. A cynic might call that collusion, because there was certainly someone deprived: American taxpayers. Market prices of pharmaceuticals skyrocketed.

Overlooking the massive internal problems with the current Medicare system (which we might call Medicare for some), Sanders and some others on the Democratic side of the aisle advance Medicare for All. Medicare for All is a galactically awful idea for a host of reasons.

First, it eliminates Medicare. You read that correctly. Medicare is a promise to seniors. Medicare for All puts everyone in a one-size-fits-all system, therefore the program intended for seniors no longer exists. Moreover, Medicare for All doesn't work like Medicare; it simply borrows on its good name. Most seniors like Medicare, but Medicare for All is not Medicare at all.

Second, it eliminates private insurance. One of the ways in which Medicare for All is not like Medicare is it does not allow people to purchase private insurance or even supplemental insurance, thus eliminating millions of private policies people now hold, including insurance negotiated by unions. Even some countries that have socialized medicine, like Sweden, allow for private insurance.

Third (although it may be considered a minor point by someone like Sanders, who believes that the government has endlessly deep pockets), the present form of Medicare is predicted to be insolvent by 2026.[25] The combination of a growing percentage of older Americans coupled with a smaller percentage of younger Americans to fund Medicare with payroll taxes has created a fiscally untenable house of cards. Medicare for *some* is going bankrupt; now, Sanders wants Medicare for *All*?

Fourth, devoid of competition, overall healthcare prices would skyrocket under such a system. Sanders's plan is to eliminate the free market altogether. As *The Wall Street Journal* points out, "The Sanders Medicare for All bill would *ban* private coverage that competes with government."[26] It is competitive forces, however, that drive prices lower. That might not be a popular admission in the minds of Sanders and his followers, but it's a law of economics. Universal Medicare would create the largest monopoly in history.

Fifth, Medicare for All would drive up pharmaceutical prices drastically, even more than Medicare for some has already done. So says Seema Verna, the administrator of the Centers for Medicare and Medicaid Services. Verna points out that Medicare B's policy of paying the average drug price plus a 6 percent fee "creates a perverse incentive for manufacturers to arbitrarily set higher prices, and for providers to pick drugs that are more expensive."[27] At least the list of drugs that are driven up is somewhat limited because some of these drugs are for geriatric conditions like osteoporosis. But universal Medicare would drive up the prices on everything from prenatal drugs onward.

One of the main economic arguments for a Medicare for All system is the savings from consolidating healthcare administrative tasks into one massive bureaucracy. But there is little evidence to support any projected savings given that the government has never proven it can be more efficient than the private sector. Moreover, both the conservative Mercatus Center and the liberal Urban Institute agree that the

Medicare for All scheme would cost at least $32 trillion over ten years; that's more than double what is collected by the IRS in individual and corporate taxes combined over the same period.[28] To be fair to Senator Sanders, who has addressed how he would pay for his Medicare for All plan in a straightforward way: he would raise taxes. But he believes the increase in taxes would be offset by savings from the elimination of premiums, co-pays, and deductible payments. In addition, he states the consolidated administrative tasks of a government payment system provide substantial savings from the currently aggregated system.

But what Sanders is describing is a cost-based system where the priority is cost and not care, which can lead to rationing of care, denied care, waiting lists, and denied access to expensive but life-changing and lifesaving treatments.

The list of problems goes on and on, but there's one more issue that fails to get enough attention: because of the massive administrative size of Medicare, a Medicare for All system would encourage even more wide-scale cheating and overbilling than it currently witnesses. How much is that? Plenty. Multimillion-dollar Medicare fraud cases are commonplace and widespread across the healthcare universe. Not content with the money that can be made from monopolistic tactics and government overpays, nearly all the large pharmaceutical companies have repeatedly engaged in illegal practices involving Medicare. Aventis, a subsidiary of French pharmaceutical maker Sanofi, has paid nearly $200 million in violations of Medicare overbilling for one drug alone.[29] Because the Medicare system as it is today is so massive, it is impossible to monitor it carefully enough.

This point could be illustrated with thousands of cases, but perhaps never quite so vividly as with the case of a Michigan pharmacist named Babubhai "Bob" Patel. In 2011, Patel was indicted for a massive Medicare fraud scheme. Patel was the veritable godfather of Michigan drugs. Through a vast network of more than two dozen pharmacies that he owned or controlled, Patel offered "kickbacks, bribes, and other inducements"[30] to doctors in exchange for their bogus prescriptions. And it wasn't just a few dozen prescriptions; nor were they harmless drugs for treating acid reflux. According to the DEA, Patel and his accomplices conspired to write "more than 6 million doses of opiate painkillers and depressants" including OxyContin, Vicodin, and Xanax.[31] Though many of these prescriptions simply went unfilled, many of the drugs were sold on the streets of Michigan. It is estimated that between 2006 and 2011, Patel billed Medicare for around $40 million in his scheme. The federal grand jury's indictment against Patel also named numerous physicians and pharmacists, an accountant, and several others listed simply as "business associate." [32] There were also some indicted under the heading of "patient recruiters," who talked patients into becoming part of the conspiracy by accepting cash for their Medicare numbers.[33] Patel and many of his cohorts were eventually convicted and sent to jail in 2013.

It would be nice to think that Patel's case is a significant outlier, but it is not; many other cases—larger cases—have surfaced. And it's not just prescriptions for drugs. In 2019, government officials threw a net over a scheme that allegedly bilked Medicare out of more than $1 billion. Similar in some ways to Patel's scheme, this case involved physicians prescribing "medically unnecessary orders" to "patients."[34] And also like Patel's scheme, seemingly everyone was in on it: two dozen defendants were named in six states, including doctors, business owners, and telemarketers.

Regarding the case, the IRS Criminal Investigation Division chief said the case "details broad corruption, massive amounts of greed and systemic flaws in our healthcare system that were exploited by the defendants."[35]

But that's just the point: "greed and systemic flaws." The two schemes mentioned above illustrate not only the ease with which fraudulent schemes can be done but also the willingness with which they are done. Patel's conspiracy lasted five years and had dozens of players (hundreds if you include the patients who sold their Medicare and Medicaid numbers). Yet, it's likely to have continued for much longer except for the fact that some irregularity at Medicare was finally noticed. How many more "Patels" are out there who will never be caught? How many pharmacists are billing Medicare for opioid drug-running operations? Medicare is called a "system," but that understates its broad scope.

There are 60 million people with Medicare; those 60 million are cared for by millions of others who are—by extension—also part of Medicare. Those millions are serviced by millions of others: accountants, attorneys, and healthcare professionals who are part of Medicare, too. Because of its sheer size, cheating Medicare is common. And that's in its current version.

Medicare for All would create the largest monopolistic bureaucracy in the history of the world, creating open season for wide-scale fraud and abuse. Medicare is not a system; it's an impossible-to-police universe. And now Sanders wants to create a Medicare *multiverse* by multiplying the current universe by five. Despite all the available data that proves his claims wrong, Sanders and his followers have an unshakable belief that the government can provide universally successful solutions. But in real life, the best policy is to allow the free market to operate: to allow companies to enter markets and compete on a level playing field with government regulation but without government interference or collusion. Then ensure every consumer has access to quality and cost information and allow them to set the standards for quality, convenience, and cost by giving them choice. Such a system would deliver more choice and higher-quality care at greater convenience for the lowest price.

SOCIALIZED MEDICINE

A great many comparisons are made between the healthcare in the United States and other countries around the world, and that's good. But some comparisons lack context. While it is true Americans spend roughly twice what other first-world countries spend on healthcare, there are good and bad reasons for that. First, healthy people are cheap and sick people are very, very expensive. Some people live in so-called food deserts where healthy food choices are scarce. More often though, it's a choice. Americans have not always been the most health conscious, making the wrong food choices and living sedentary lives instead of active ones. We could all do better at staying healthy, but the cost of being unhealthy is not a function of the care delivery system; it's a lifestyle choice of too many Americans that we pay for with our dollars and with our health.

Second, if you are living in a country with socialized care and you are healthy and rarely need to see the doctor, chances are you are happy with socialized healthcare because although you might pay higher taxes, you feel the reassurance that you are covered in case you do get sick and that is worth something. But for too many who do get sick, their satisfaction with the system can be quite negative. In the United Kingdom today, the average wait time just to begin cancer treatments is sixty-two days. That's after you've gotten to see your doctor who has given you a referral. By comparison, in the United States, time to treatment initiation (TTI) is twenty-seven days but getting longer.

Third, there is a reason our healthcare is more expensive than other countries. Socialized medicine is a cost-driven system whereas our system, while far from perfect, is more of a care-driven system. It's just a fact of life under socialized care, there is less access to the best and latest treatments based on a policy of the cost benefit to the taxpayer where actuaries are used to consider a patient's life expectancy, young or old and likely outcome. In general, the United States doesn't have a one-size-fits-all cost-benefit analysis treatment option, and while insurance companies do deny some treatment options, it is based on the treatment data and not the demographic data of the patient. Of course it's much less expensive to deny grandma a hip replacement or grandad a pacemaker or a newborn a very expensive drug, but is that the cheaper healthcare system we want?

Fourth, Americans have access to much more advanced and expensive treatments that other governments don't offer because they are cost focused and not care focused. For example, Orkambi—a lifesaving drug that was created to treat the underlying cause of cystic fibrosis and is available in the United States—is not available in the United Kingdom for purely cost reasons. Similarly, the United States leads or is near the top in cancer treatment outcomes where Americans have access to 95 percent of all cancer-treatment drugs. In the United Kingdom, only about 76 percent of cancer-treatment drugs are available. In Japan, it's 50 percent, and in Greece only 8 percent.

There is plenty to be said about insurance company treatment denials but giving the government control over your life-and-death health decisions with the force of law is not the answer.

LOOKING FORWARD

Markets work when the consumer knows what the choices are, knows the quality of each choice, and knows the real price they will pay. Armed with information to make informed healthcare choices, knowledgeable consumers can set in motion the powerful forces of market dynamics that create more choices, improve the quality of care, and provide better outcomes, all at the greatest convenience to the patient at the lowest cost.

Contrast the free market model with a government-controlled model where there is no incentive to improve care, generate competition, foster innovation, cater to the patient, create efficiencies, or drive down costs. Indeed, a government-run healthcare payment system would lead to cycle after cycle of political promises to make the system work, then throw good money after bad trying to get the system to move. When that inevitably fails, politicize the issue, blame the other party, and run on making the system better, promising even more money. Repeat as necessary.

The free market is not a panacea for healthcare. It won't solve every problem, but no approach is going to bring us to a perfect healthcare system. My argument is that markets are a superior choice in getting the most people the greatest access to care including advanced treatments which lead to better health outcomes. Moreover, markets best spur innovation and competition to drive down costs. But it will only work when innovators and entrepreneurs are allowed to compete on a level playing field, without government conspiring against Americans by colluding with corporations to create monopolies and where fraud is severely punished.

Healthcare now represents nearly 20 percent of overall GDP—a twentyfold increase from a century ago, when it was a mere 1 percent.

Clearly, some of this is due to advances in medical technology, drug discoveries, and the better ways that patients are treated. But these positives do not negate the fact that we can do healthcare better in America. We need to do it better. And it's not only about saving money; it's about saving lives. Having better policies is how we save lives. If we truly believe that healthcare is a basic human right, we need to eliminate fraud, monopoly, and collusion. We need to adopt a system that works better and cheaper. That should be our overriding concern. And it just so happens the free market best answers the call of providing this basic right. It is not that the free market has failed; it is that it hasn't been tried, at least lately. The free market—the truly free market—is the best treatment for our failing healthcare system.

If you're a progressive and still skeptical about a market-based healthcare system, let me offer a couple of observations. First, Medicare, which covers seniors and represents about 14 percent of the total insurance market as it is today is going broke. Second, Social Security is also going broke as it pays out monthly more money than it takes in. From an economic historical perspective, government has no record of driving down costs or saving taxpayers money. None.

But perhaps your main concern is not economic but rather treating the sick with the compassion and dignity they deserve. Or you're worried that a market system would be unjust to the poor. Consider this: as I write this, along our southern border today, there are men, women, and children, some who are infants, in cages whose only crime is to seek a better life, who are being detained in the most unimaginably inhumane conditions. How can you look at the shameful way our government is treating those human beings on the one hand and believe that the same government would treat the poor with any justice and compassion in a government healthcare system?

I am convinced that we can create a fair and just healthcare system that works for all Americans, but I don't believe a government one-size-fits-all system administered by a massive bureaucracy will work. I believe we can have better health and healthcare when millions of people engage in a free market system.

8

EVENING OUT THE SUPREME COURT

Chief Justice John Roberts began his confirmation hearing by drawing a comparison between the Supreme Court and baseball.[1] While most baseball fans center on pitchers and hitters, Roberts spoke about a less-appreciated team on the field without whom professional baseball would not be possible: umpires. In Major League Baseball, four men dressed in black officiate the game. Specifically, their job is to call balls and strikes, safe or out, fouls, interference with a batter or runner, and whether a manager should be ejected. There are times when the calls are easy, but there are also times when the umpires need to huddle together to discuss a particular call in question. But what they will *not* do is change the rules. They will not decide that games go on too long and therefore change a few of the rules that both shorten their work hours and make the game more exciting for the fans. For instance, making the pitcher pitch the ball within thirty seconds of the last pitch. Or calling a strike on a batter who steps out of the batting box once he's stepped in. Or maybe two strikes and you're out if the game runs longer than three hours. Nor will they huddle together during the game and decide that players on one team may no longer wear batting gloves. Their job is to take the given rules and apply them to each pitch and to each play. But what also goes without saying is that no fan of any team would ever accept that they would actually play in the game. As Roberts put it, "I will remember that it's my job to call balls and strikes and not to pitch or bat."[2]

Although the founders of America didn't have baseball in mind when they wrote the Constitution, they nevertheless viewed the Supreme Court as more of an umpire than a player. Familiar with the power and abuses of the British courts, the founders wanted to ensure that the judiciary's power did not replicate the Crown's unchecked courts. As Alexander Hamilton phrased it in *The Federalist Papers,* the judiciary is the "least dangerous" branch of government, "because it will be least in a capacity to annoy or injure" the political rights of Americans. Hamilton writes: "The Executive not only dispenses the honors but holds the sword of the community. The legislature not only commands the purse but prescribes the rules by which the duties and rights of every citizen are to be regulated. The judiciary, on the contrary, has no influence over either the sword or the purse . . . It may truly be said to have neither FORCE nor WILL, but merely judgment." Hamilton viewed the judiciary as the least dangerous branch because it was, by constitutional design, the branch with the least power by far.

If there's any doubt about that designation as the branch with the least power, consider the following. The judicial branch is listed in the Constitution as Article III—after the legislative and executive. And while the Constitution lays out substantial specifics about the powers and authority of the first two branches, the judicial branch is much less detailed; in fact, the part of Article III that references the Supreme Court consists of a mere five sentences. Simply put, the first two branches receive much more detailed focus. There's another point that might surprise even those who consider themselves well versed on the Constitution. The Constitution takes great pains to detail the requirements of the president, senators, and congresspeople. For instance, to be president, a person must be a natural-born citizen, must have been a resident of the United States for a minimum of fourteen years, and be at least thirty-five years old. Similarly, a senator must have been a citizen for at least nine years, be a resident of the state on election day, and be at least thirty years old. A congressperson must have been a citizen for seven years, a resident of the state on election day, and be twenty-five years old. In other words, both the executive and legislative branches have specific requirements, without which the office cannot be held. And then we come to Article III.

What are the requirements to be a Supreme Court justice? The answer is: none. No age requirement, no citizenship requirement, no residence requirement. Nothing. It is constitutionally permissible that an infant from Singapore be nominated and serve as the chief justice of the Supreme Court. The framers were confident that the powers of the court were so limited by the Constitution that the individual qualifications were secondary. Not only was it seen as the least dangerous branch but its duties were also viewed as the easiest to fulfill. Of course, the one worry might be that the Supreme Court justices would be susceptible to public opinion—that their judgments might be more influenced by public opinion than by the Constitution. So the framers had a solution that should quell that temptation: the judge had a lifetime appointment. A Supreme Court justice never had to face reelection. While congresspeople, senators, and first-term presidents always seem to be running to stay in power, Supreme Court justices never are; in that regard, their job is strictly legal rather than political. Lifetime appointments were designed to direct judges to rule according to the Constitution rather than public opinion or political influence. At least, that's how it was drawn up.

So what happened? If the judicial is the "least dangerous" branch, why do both parties talk about the Supreme Court as if it were the most important branch? If the Supreme Court lacks the "capacity to annoy," why does everyone eventually get aggravated by it? If the justices are simply supposed to be umpires, why the temptation to both manage and play? Has it always been that way? If not, when did it all change?

If we had to locate one particular answer to all these questions, we can look to Woodrow Wilson.[3] In 1908, future president Woodrow Wilson wrote a book titled *Constitutional Government in the United States*, in which he turned Alexander Hamilton's arguments upside down, arguing that the Supreme Court should free itself from the

Constitution's mortal coil and take it upon itself to write decisions
that reflect American society rather than the Constitution and its
limitations. In baseball terminology, it was time for the justices to
come out from behind the plate and step into the batter's box. In
that book, Wilson coined the term "living political constitution." As
president, Wilson appointed Louis Brandeis to the Supreme Court.
Brandeis made a national name for himself by representing private individuals against large corporations, and Wilson hoped that Brandeis
would bring that same approach to the Supreme Court. Wilson did
not hope in vain, as Brandeis proved eager to advance a progressive legislative agenda from the bench. (Even those sympathetic to
Brandeis's political and legal views admit as much.[4] In some of his
decisions, the Constitution is almost incidental; for instance, in the
case of *Muller v. Oregon*, the decision is more than one hundred pages,
but a mere two pages could be recognized as legal analysis. *The Oxford
Companion to the Supreme Court of the United States* is ebullient in its
praise of Brandeis, yet it admits that his contact and consultation
with the Roosevelt administration in its New Deal programs "violated both his own professed rules of judicial restraint."[5])

Looking back at Brandeis's decisions, we might celebrate the outcome in an individual case or cases, but the problem is that the power
of the court—in taking on the role of legislator—was expanded far
beyond the imaginations of the founders. Some Americans, both
then and now, might be willing to accept the fact that judges commonly overstep constitutional boundaries—as written—in order to
obtain a greater good. That is essentially the argument in favor of judicial activism—that Supreme Court justices must treat the Constitution as a malleable and reshapeable document in order to advance
the will of the people. Of course, beyond the fact that they are acting
in violation of America's founding document, judicial activism is not
without significant problems.

The most obvious of these problems is that the highest court in
the land is today regarded as the final word on the law. That wasn't
supposed to happen in a democratic republic. The final word on the
law rests with the people who elect their representatives to Congress,

the legislative branch that makes the law. The Supreme Court is not to make the law but to decide cases by interpreting the meaning and intention of the law where possible without rewriting the law or to determine whether the law violates the Constitution or not. By virtue of its lifetime appointments, the Supreme Court is the least democratic federal branch of government—by design. In stark contrast to the offices of president, representative, and senator (the Senate was originally designed to be responsive to the respective state legislatures who chose their senators until 1913 when the Seventeenth Amendment was ratified), the Supreme Court is crafted specifically to *not* be answerable to the people—but only to the Constitution, which is a document that limits power.[6] That was no oversight. The Constitution established two other branches that were answerable to the people. Their idea was that legislation should be left to the legislative branch. Unlike in a monarchy where law was not a reflection of the people's will, law in a democracy has the consent of the governed through a representative legislature. Do we really want the least democratic branch to make laws for the people? Do we really want the people to have no input? If a House member, senator, or president pushes through unpopular legislation, the electorate can vote them out. Obviously, there is no recourse if a Supreme Court justice pushes through legislation that is at odds with the minds and hearts of Americans. And let's not forget that by taking on legislative power, the Supreme Court is not simply usurping power from Congress; it is usurping power from the people. Once you grant lawmaking power to justices, there's no wonder that the nomination contests are so hotly debated. Under that arrangement, the chief justice of the Supreme Court is the closest thing America has seen to a king since George III.

Also inherent in judicial activism is the notion that the founders were pretty damn uninformed about the inner workings of government. As conservative author and commentator Jonah Goldberg put it, "It is difficult to exaggerate Wilson's arrogant and sovereign contempt for the system set up by the founders."[7] Wilson might have been an early adopter of judicial activism, but he wasn't alone.

Whether Republican or Democrat, when faced with the frustration of trying to advance a political agenda through the cumbersome legislative process, it is a great temptation to attempt to use the courts to further your cause—to go beyond calling balls and strikes and to play the game. Of course, not all agree that judges should legislate from the bench. And that brings us to Robert Bork.

BORKED

On July 1, 1987, President Reagan's announcement of the nomination of Robert Bork came as little surprise. Just a year before, Reagan's attorney general had recommended a total of two names for potential nomination after the resignation of Warren Burger; those names were Antonin Scalia and Robert Bork. Both men had been serving on the DC Circuit Court of Appeals, which has been a veritable farm system for the Supreme Court. Both men had enviable résumés and were strikingly similar in judicial philosophy, so if these were the only factors, it would have come down to a coin toss. But the prevailing factor in Scalia's favor may have been his age: Scalia was almost a decade younger than Robert Bork, which meant that—all things being equal—Scalia was in a position to serve for ten years longer than Bork. In the end, youth won out, and Scalia went on to be confirmed by the Senate 98–0.

Only about nine months afterward, when Justice Lewis Powell announced his resignation, the nomination of Robert Bork by President Reagan seemed predetermined. Moreover, Bork's confirmation seemed assured, as there was not a dime's worth of difference between Scalia, who sailed through the process, and Bork. To Bork's detriment, however, those nine months had given birth to a much different political environment from the one Scalia experienced. Between the two nominations, a scandal in the Reagan administration had come to light. The Iran–Contra affair (as it came to be called) saw administration officials unlawfully direct the sale of arms to Iran and hide it from Congress. While the scandal played out in the press, it obfuscated a simultaneous political plot that was brewing to take advantage of Reagan's weakening public support, which was to have a major impact on the Bork confirmation process.

After President Reagan nominated Judge Bork to be an associate justice, Democratic senators didn't wait until Bork's confirmation hearings to attack him. In fact, they didn't even wait an hour. Literally within minutes of Reagan's announcement of Bork's nomination, Senator Ted Kennedy rose in the Senate chamber and announced: "Robert Bork's America is a land in which women would be forced into back-alley abortions, blacks would sit at segregated lunch counters, rogue police could break down citizens' doors in midnight raids, and schoolchildren could not be taught about evolution."[8] This was the same Ted Kennedy who just a year earlier voted to confirm Bork's judicial twin, Antonin Scalia, both in the Senate Judiciary Committee and in Scalia's final confirmation.[9]

From there, it got worse. When the bell rang on July 1, the Democrats' first action was to take off their gloves. This wasn't going to be a confirmation process; it was going to be a bare-knuckle barroom brawl.

The chairman of the Senate Judiciary Committee was then Delaware senator Joseph R. Biden, Jr. He, like Kennedy, initially slammed the Bork nomination but then walked it back, apologizing for prejudging Bork. The move seemed like an attempt to appear evenhanded, knowing that as chairman he would have a significant influence in the confirmation hearings and perhaps a political opportunity.

Meanwhile, Democratic senators were already weeks into the public hearings on the Iran–Contra affair that were taking a toll on the Reagan administration when a strange thing happened: the Democrats on the joint select committee suffered a major embarrassment. The main character behind Iran–Contra was a previously obscure marine lieutenant colonel named Oliver North. As congressional hearings involving North began in early July of 1987, there would have been every reason to believe that North would be excoriated by Congress and condemned by the American people. Yet, something unexpected happened: North turned the tables on his prosecutors. The Democrats had perhaps failed to consider how it would appear for a (literally) highly decorated marine who had repeatedly risked his life for his country to (again, literally) sit in judgment of out-of-touch senators and congressmen—many of whose only military experience was in sending men like North into battle. That scene might have worked inside the beltway, but as the saying goes, it didn't play well in Peoria. Handsome, charismatic, and sincere, many of the American people rallied to Oliver North. (By the second day of his testimony, he was no longer Colonel Oliver North to the American people; he was affectionately called "Ollie.") In fact, the more the American people saw the North hearings, the more they liked him—and the less they liked his senatorial accusers. At one point, Democratic senator Daniel Inouye was browbeating North, telling him that the American people disapproved of his rogue actions. Brendan Sullivan, North's attorney, interrupted Inouye by saying they didn't need Inouye to tell them what the American people thought; he pointed out that the American people had sent them twenty thousand telegrams in support of North. The credibility of the Reagan administration had taken a bad hit, but Democrats were unable to take the victory lap they wanted. Though they might deny the fact or spin it to this day, the episode proved extremely embarrassing for the Democrats in Congress.

The timing of the Bork nomination couldn't have been better for Democrats but especially for Joe Biden. Still stinging from the mortification of Colonel North turning the tables on them in the Iran–Contra hearings just weeks earlier, Democrats were looking for a way to put it behind them but still capitalize on a weakened Ronald Reagan. They found their opportunity to vicariously stand up to the president in the person of Robert Bork, and Joe Biden would be center stage.

For the first time, Americans outside the Northeast would get to know Joe Biden, and he knew that. To make matters even more interesting, three weeks prior to Bork's nomination, Biden had begun his presidential campaign in an effort to gain the Democratic nomination and to challenge the presumptive Republican nominee, George H. W. Bush. In that regard, Biden's nationally televised role in the upcoming hearings was not simply a process that would break what was seen as a 4–4 tie between conservative and progressive justices; it was the most important campaign stop of his nascent presidential campaign.

After making several TV appearances expressing his reservations about Bork, Biden was criticized by various media like *The Wall Street Journal*, who accused him of using the hearings as a campaign springboard.[10] The criticism is simultaneously fair and unfair. It was fair because it was true but unfair because it was unavoidable. Further, there was no guarantee that the process would benefit Biden, largely because the hearings presented Biden with a significant problem. On one hand, if he appeared deferential to Bork (or even fair-minded), he might be seen as weak to his own party members and potential donors. On the other hand, if he came off like his woefully ignorant colleagues had going up against Oliver North, it could easily have backfired on him in much the same way.

Through a series of conversations with staffers and liberal activists, a brilliant strategy was devised. It was to demonize the hell out of Robert Bork. That was essentially the missing ingredient in the Oliver North hearings; the senators had failed to do the opposition research that might have presented him as an unsavory character. But if Biden's team could research everything Bork had ever done, said, or written, they might be able to convince Americans that Robert Bork really was the devil—even before the hearings began. And if Bork were the devil, Biden could castigate Bork and still appear fair. After all, no one thinks less of a person because he tells the devil he's bad. The basic argument against Bork's judicial philosophy was that he did not believe in the same body of civil rights that were broadly held by most Americans and that he would use the highest court in the land to roll back these rights.

There were a number of reasons why this demonization effort might not prove easy. First, Bork was unanimously approved for the circuit court a few years prior and was unanimously endorsed by the American Bar Association, which might have prompted questions about exactly when Bork's metamorphosis from mild-mannered man to lunatic might have occurred.[11] Second, just the year before, Scalia had been unanimously approved by the same Senate. You might conclude then, that Scalia and Bork held widely divergent views on constitutional law (and plenty of other things, for that matter). Yet, while on the DC Circuit Court, Scalia and Bork agreed on 98 percent of their case decisions. How can two jurists agree on nearly every case, yet one is universally admired and the other is thoroughly disdained? Why is one ideological twin considered acceptable while the other is not? That's difficult to just explain away.

The other main problem was that building the case for someone's idiocy takes time. But Biden had an answer for this problem. He would slowly drag it out (though he had promised he would not do so) in order to allow the process to ferment.[12] For Supreme Court nominees, the average time between the day of presidential nomination and the first day of hearings was fourteen days. In Robert Bork's case, it was seventy-seven days. All the while, his staffers worked feverishly to build a case against Bork, which resulted in a document known as the "Biden report," an internal manuscript that was researched and written by two of Biden's staffers.

But objections to Bork during this time were not only made by liberal senators like Kennedy and Biden; between his nomination and hearing, broad accusations were also hurled against Bork by special interest groups, news networks, and even Hollywood stars and starlets. Seemingly everybody wanted to get in on the smear. Political activists from the National Abortion Rights Action League (NARAL Pro-Choice America), the National Organization for Women (NOW), the People for the American Way (PFAW), and plenty of others lined up to denounce Bork, spending as much as $15 million in the process.[13] Media research indicated that almost 90 percent of the stories and comments about Robert Bork on CBS were negative.[14] The most notable Hollywood star to come out against Bork was actor Gregory Peck, whose most famous movie role was that of Atticus Finch, the courageous attorney from *To Kill a Mockingbird* whose personage had come to represent civil rights in America. In an ad commissioned by People for the American Way, Peck (still symbolically viewed as Atticus Finch) states, "He [Bork] defended poll taxes and literacy tests." Bork had done neither, but the goal was to destroy a reputation not check facts.

During this same time, Biden recruited the help of editorial boards of major newspapers to advance the anti-Bork narrative. Mark Gitenstein, the chief counsel to the Senate Judiciary Committee, worked very closely with Biden and later penned a book about it titled *Matters of Principle*. Not only is Gitenstein sympathetic toward Biden in his book, but Gitenstein also even admitted that he cried when Biden suspended his presidential campaign. In that book, Gitenstein notes that Biden had meetings with "eight editorial boards during August and early September."[15] And these weren't casual encounters. These were "full-dress dinners or luncheon meetings with the whole editorial board and key reporters" with "the *Los Angeles Times, Time, New York Times*, and *U.S. News and World Report*."[16] Apparently, the *Newsweek* dinner didn't go as well as Biden had hoped or expected, as Biden was pointedly asked, "Haven't you prejudged Bork?"[17]

"Prejudged" is gentle euphemism for Biden's actions. Imagine for a moment that you are indicted for robbery. The judge immediately appears on television expressing his doubt that you may be innocent. The judge also immediately commissions two of his staffers to write a go-to playbook for the jury to ask you tricky questions that might trip you up during the trial. The trial is set to begin in two weeks, but the judge intentionally delays the trial so he can stir up public opinion against you. In the meantime, the judge wines and dines the press corps to encourage them to write negative articles about you. Unsatisfied that this might be enough to throw the book at you, he helps line up witnesses against you. Seventy-seven days after your indictment, he sits down and explains to you and the rest of the world that he is going to be as fair as possible toward you. In the political house of cards, Biden stacked the deck against Bork from start to finish in the constitutional process known as "advice and consent."

By the time the hearing began, it was largely anticlimactic: most senators, perhaps all senators, had already made up their minds. To be fair, Robert Bork was not a great witness for himself. To put it charitably, he lacked the photogenic quality of an Oliver North. At the age of fifty, largely due to his chain-smoking habit, Bork easily could have passed for sixty. Even his unkept beard became a focus of the hearings. In short, he looked like the law professor whose class you'd try to avoid. Though even his detractors admitted his genius, that intelligence served to work against him, because it made him appear aloof to his national audience. When asked why he wanted to be a Supreme Court justice, Bork responded that the position would be an "intellectual feast." Considering the office he was applying for, Bork paradoxically came across as overly legalistic. At times, he seems to have thought that his viewing audience was composed of third-year law students in torts class rather than people who were just pissed off that *The Price Is Right* had been preempted for the hearings. This is all a shame because privately Bork was said to be very personable—a conservative intellectual with a great sense of humor who was liked even by liberals. But this did not translate to the TV screen. In a surprise to exactly no one, on October 23, 1987, Robert Bork was rejected by the Senate by a vote of 58–42.

But it's important to recognize that ultimately it was never really Robert Bork who was on trial in the first place. Despite all the time and money spent on opposition research to vilify him (even a record of his videotape rentals were obtained),[18] nothing was found to indict Bork's personal character. Few people could face that level of scrutiny; in fact, as a footnote to the Bork nomination story, it turns out that Joseph Biden couldn't face it either. While this confirmation/rejection process was taking place, Biden, who had often cited Neil Kinnock's quotes in the past, delivered a plagiarized speech from the British politician in September. This started a domino effect in which it was discovered that Biden had also plagiarized the public addresses of Hubert Humphrey and Bobby Kennedy, and a lengthy section in a law school term paper.[19] Biden also claimed that he had participated in civil rights marches, which he hadn't. He further claimed that he had graduated near the top of his law school class, though he actually finished near the bottom.[20] Faced with all this, Biden dropped out of the race on September 23, 1987—one month to the day that Bork was rejected.

ORIGINALISM ON TRIAL

But if Bork was not on trial, who or what was? Today, even progressive commentators often admit that Bork was treated unfairly. While that's true, it misses the point that it was neither the real Robert Bork nor even a caricature of Robert Bork that was on trial. It was a senatorial referendum on constitutional originalism.

Most famously championed in modern times by Antonin Scalia, originalism is the belief that the Constitution should be viewed in light of the original meaning of the Constitution at the time of ratification. To achieve this goal of determining original meaning, Scalia put significant value on historical research. An originalist like Scalia, for instance, would treasure *The Federalist Papers* as well as other writings from the colonial period because they could provide some insight into these words and meanings. For instance, in order to understand the meaning of the Second Amendment, an originalist would try to determine the late 1700s meaning of words like "militia," "bear," "arms," and "infringed." (This notion also applies to the amendments and when they were each ratified.) Though originalism is often equated with conservatism, originalism does not automatically make someone a conservative; originalism and liberalism are not necessarily at odds.[21] Originalism is not a cookie-cutter approach to legal interpretation, and even Bork and Scalia disagreed occasionally about how to decide a particular case. But it is a solid starting point.

Of course, not everybody feels this way. There are those who believe it is patently absurd to constantly apply the meaning of old words to modern cases. They argue that this approach deadens the Constitution and that instead we need a "living Constitution." As Scalia put it, however, "The Constitution that I interpret and apply is not living but dead, or as I prefer to call it, enduring. It means today not what current society, much less the court, thinks it ought to mean, but what it meant when it was adopted."[22] To an originalist, the Constitution is an enduring document *because* it applies these concepts to modern difficulties and legal questions. Picking up the baseball analogy, the Constitution is the rule book. And just as the official rules of Major League Baseball can change, so can the Constitution. While baseball has rule changes, the Constitution has amendments. No originalist makes the argument that the Constitution should not be amended; they merely make the argument that the amendments should be interpreted according to original meaning at the time of ratification. And one other thing: that the judicial branch should not invent their own amendments.

Again, not everyone agrees. Some argue that a Constitution written almost 250 years ago (along with the subsequent amendments over the years) cannot possibly apply to modern day. Yet, an originalist sees little difficulty in doing so. Though there was no internet or electronic publishing at the time of James Madison, the principle of freedom of speech applies, nevertheless. At the time of ratification of the Bill of Rights, the religion of Mormonism did not yet exist, and yet the freedom of religion would still apply. Originalism generally professes that America's founders hit upon some of the most important political freedoms in history. We might say that the truths of the Constitution are not dead simply because they were given to the American people a quarter millennia ago, any more than the truths of the Ten Commandments are dead because they were given to the Jewish people five millennia ago. In either case, one often violates them because he distrusts or disagrees with the author.

Admittedly, the original meaning of each and every element of the Constitution is not always perfectly clear or understood. For instance (as will be further illustrated in chapter 10), the original intent of the Second Amendment somehow escaped an in-depth examination until recent decades. Further, it is a fair criticism of originalism that not even the framers agreed with each other when they ratified the Constitution. That's a fair critique as far as it goes, but Scalia pointed out that neither originalism nor any legal system can be condemned because it is imperfect; our goal is not to find perfection but to find the least imperfect system. In an imperfect world, the question is: what system is the best? In the field of economics, Scalia uses free market capitalism as a comparison. One could easily say that free market capitalism is imperfect, but as a creator of wealth, it is clearly the best.[23]

Originalism also accomplishes something else: it seeks to keep the Supreme Court in the role originally intended—and this might be its most appealing characteristic. There are those who find the logic of originalism backward and stupid. They might wonder why the people of today should be handcuffed by the people of yesterday. But there's an answer: we're not. The Constitution allows for amendments. In fact, amendments become part of the body of the Constitution; the Fourth Amendment has no greater weight than the Fourteenth. And if the legislators of America ratify a constitutional amendment, the Supreme Court must take that new amendment into account in its decisions. That was another genius of the framers: the Supreme Court could not amend the Constitution; only the legislative branch could along with three-fourths of the states as passed by their legislatures. In this sense, conservatives believe that the Constitution is not only living but alive and well. Bork's interrogators made it appear as though it was the Supreme Court's job to interpret *not* the Constitution but the will of the people—to make laws that the Congress did not want to make for itself. Bork's refusal to do so—his insistence on originalism—is what was on trial.

One last observation about the Bork nomination and what we should have learned from it. The Supreme Court nomination and approval process has become a national nightmare. Much of this problem would be solved by simply refusing to televise Supreme Court nomination hearings. As the Bork hearings illustrated—not to mention the Clarence Thomas hearings and the Kavanaugh hearings—televising these events does no favors to the Senate or to the nominee. The Constitution calls for "advice and consent" from the senators, but what we get instead is political grandstanding. We get absurd speeches, wacky comparisons, and self-congratulatory remarks that make the senators, frankly more often than not, look stupid.

In the Kavanaugh hearings, for instance, New Jersey senator Cory Booker produced a diatribe that fell under all of these categories. In the course of the hearings, Booker claimed that emails from 2002 illustrating Kavanaugh's acceptance of "racial profiling" were classified. So, at the Senate bench, he gave a speech in which he insisted that he would break the Senate rules and publicly release them. (In a series of television interviews following, Booker didn't just *admit* that he had broken Senate rules in doing so; he vehemently *insisted* that he had broken the rules.) Booker considered himself a hero for this—and not just a hero generally but specifically. Perhaps Booker had recently seen the movie *Spartacus*, in which the title character (played by Kirk Douglas) leads a slave rebellion against the Roman authorities. At one point in the film, the Roman centurions announce to hundreds of rebels that they would be spared crucifixion only if Spartacus turned himself in. As Spartacus rises to admit "I am Spartacus," all the men rise with him and announce: "*I* am Spartacus!" In the course of Booker's statement, appearing to be defiant of Senate rules, Booker claimed his actions were "the closest I'll get to an 'I am Spartacus' moment."

The Spartacus reference would have been embarrassing even if Booker's allegations were true—after all, one of the marks of heroism is that it does not ascribe valor to itself. But more to the point, his allegations were simply wrong. The documents in question had already been released by the time Booker made his "defiant" speech. The documents in question were no more classified than the score from the previous night's Washington Nationals game. Beyond that, the documents in question did not illustrate an endorsement of racial profiling.

While Booker's comment was accidentally hilarious, it was by no means unique. Kirk Douglas references notwithstanding, many senators make equally bizarre claims and comments; they know the camera is rolling and often give in to the temptation to self-aggrandize. Supreme Court confirmation hearings should take place just as Supreme Court cases are heard—privately, apart from the TV cameras.

LOOKING FORWARD

Conservatism dictates that the recent preeminence of the Supreme Court be tempered and returned to its previously held place as the least dangerous of the three branches of government. Two reasons account for the court's amassing of power: first, its appropriating legislative powers to itself, and second, Congress's unwillingness to check it. The most obvious solution to this is to find originalist judges who understand that it is not their job to make law and to find congresspeople and senators who understand that it *is* theirs. Clearly, that has proven difficult. Say what you want about activist judges, but at least the judges have some guts, which is more than I can say for Congress. As you may remember from high school civics class (and as the Congress seems to have forgotten), Congress is the legislative branch. But Congress has become cowardly. Anytime a congressperson passes a law, he or she risks being voted out because of it. Supreme Court justices have no such concern. There is a simple remedy for rebalancing power between the Supreme Court and the Congress. It is to add a justice to the court bringing the number to ten.

It might surprise many Americans to discover that the Constitution establishes no fixed number of Supreme Court justices; rather, it is Congress that determines the number. And the number wasn't always nine. In fact, the original number of Supreme Court justices was six, where it remained for eighteen years.[24] Again, in 1863, the number was fixed at ten. Over the years, the change in the number of justices has sometimes been the result of Congress trying to limit the president's power to make appointments in his term. Famously, FDR failed in his attempt to "pack the court" with additional judges in order to push through more New Deal legislation. Notwithstanding attempts at change, the Judiciary Act of 1869 set the number of justices at nine, where it has remained ever since.

It's time to go back to ten.

This might seem like an odd thing for a conservative to advocate, because in recent days it has been progressives that have argued in favor of such a proposal. Their logic has been that adding justices constitutes the most efficient way of furthering their legislative agenda. They're not wrong—at least in their pragmatic assessment: the Supreme Court since Earl Warren has been furthering the progressive agenda. In response, conservatives have argued that the idea is terrible.[25] If the number were eleven or thirteen or fifteen, I might agree. But an *even* number of judges would have the opposite effect: it would be more difficult to legislate from the bench. In a government founded on a system of checks and balances, an even number of justices would produce a Supreme Court check on itself. Maybe that was the logic behind the even number of justices that served on the very first Supreme Court.

This prompts the obvious question: what happens in the case of a tie? Remember that the Supreme Court always acts as an appellate (appeals) court; that is it hears cases that are appealed from lower courts. If the justices have a tie vote, they issue a statement about the tie and the lower court's opinion is upheld. Other than as appellate, the only other capacity the Supreme Court can act in is as a court of original jurisdiction, that is, the case *begins* in the Supreme Court. Original jurisdiction cases are extremely rare, constituting perhaps fewer than 1 percent of all cases. The vast majority of these cases regard disputes between the states—and generate less dissention than cases involving individual rights. If the justices cannot come to a decision in an original jurisdiction case, they would be forced to do something that the other branches do quite regularly: sway others as to the merits of their position.[26] One need not wholeheartedly agree with a position to vote a certain way—a point that Supreme Court justices have made since the dawn of America.[27]

There might be those who would say that this does more than provide a check, but rather it renders the court useless. They might think that if you have to wait for a majority of two votes (a majority of 6–4 or greater) you'd wait forever—that the Supreme Court may never come to a decision again. But for those who think this would remove all power from the court, consider this: between 2000 and 2016, only 19 percent of the cases were decided by a single vote; in fact, 45 percent of the cases were unanimous.[28] During the vacancy of 2016, when the Republicans refused to even hold confirmation hearings for any Supreme Court nominee of President Obama, the court operated with eight justices, and a funny thing happened: the world didn't end. The American republic went on as usual. But Americans did stop doing something that they had done for many years: wait with bated breath to see whether Anthony Kennedy felt conservative or liberal on that particular day. Kennedy, the most famous swing vote of the modern era, became one of the most important people in America, making major decisions of policy—in effect—all on his own. But as law professor Eric Segall put it, "Do you want to live in Justice Kennedy's America?"[29] More broadly, should the swing-voting justice wield this amount of power?

Having ten justices does not remove the court's power and/or authority; it simply limits it by returning power to lower courts and by making Congress, the legislative branch, do its job. Something that the framers seem to have envisioned and desired from the beginning.

9

THE RIGHT TO KEEP
AND BEAR CHILDREN

"I sent her to school yesterday, and she was supposed to be safe. My job is to protect my children, and I sent my kid to school." These heartbreaking and chilling words were uttered by a father devastated by grief whose daughter was killed in a school shooting. Even speaking as the father of a daughter, I can't comprehend the depth of his misery and sadness. All this father did was send his child to school with a reasonable expectation that she would be safe. But he was unable to protect his daughter as she, along with thirteen other Parkland, Florida, students and three staff members at Marjory Stoneman Douglas High School were killed by a former student with an AR-15 on Saint Valentine's Day 2018.

Is it unusual to begin a chapter on the defense of the Second Amendment with a horrific story that would seem to undermine my case? I think so. But if I am going to be intellectually honest about a conservative view of the right to keep and bear arms and what that means, I need to start with the hardest questions on the most difficult issues. Why did I choose to begin with Parkland? Because it was the first mass shooting? Hardly. Because it was the latest? Far from it. Because it was the worst? Sadly, not even close. I chose to start with Parkland because I met Fred Guttenberg, the father quoted above.

In the early spring of that same year, a little more than a month after Parkland, I traveled to New York City to appear on MSNBC's *Morning Joe*. Typically, we are seated on the set at around 5:45 a.m. Among the newspapers strewn across the table, I look for the list of guests for that day and the hour they will appear. I don't remember seeing Fred's name. After the first two hours of the show, I returned to the greenroom. From 8:00 to 8:30 a.m., MSNBC usually replays the top stories of the day previously aired in the 6:00 to 6:30 a.m. half hour before going live again from 8:30 to 9:00 a.m.

In the greenroom, I sat on the couch across from a kindly look-ing man who was sitting just below the famous chalkboard familiar to *Morning Joe* fans. Even though he had been on television many times, I didn't recognize him. I seldom ever watch cable news, so I don't see the faces that appear on the screen. Instead, I listen on TuneIn or on SiriusXM in the car. I find without the visual, I can focus much more intently on what is being said without being distracted by what appears on the screen. The man started our conversation with an enthusiasm that seemed in rebellion to his impassive body lan-guage. He was generous with praise about the show, how he loved to watch and enjoyed the discussions. He was even complimentary about me. I felt as though he already knew me.

Before my political career, I worked in the hospitality business both in hotels and restaurants. To be successful, you have to anticipate the needs and desires of your guests. They have high expectations—not in the demanding sense but in a romantic sense. They are seeking an experience they have been daydreaming about, and they are full of hope that it can be fulfilled whether they are with a loved one, family, on business, or even alone. Your job as a hospitality profes-sional is not just to meet their expectations but to exceed them. More than that, you have to want it for them as much as they want it for themselves. It is truly satisfying to help someone find what they are looking for. To do this, you must be sensitive and a keen observer of human behavior, tactfully but quickly discerning what it is they need.

But on this morning, I forgot all that and just blundered ahead asking, "What are you here to talk about?"

He didn't hesitate in his answer. He said he was there to talk about gun violence and about his daughter, Jaime, who was killed in the Parkland shooting. "I'm Fred Guttenberg."

Wow, did I feel dumb! I knew his name but not his face. *This is Fred Guttenberg.* What could I say? Trying mentally to regain my composure, I thought here was another opportunity to do something I needed to do more of: shut up and listen. Sensing my discomfort, it was Fred who put me at ease. He readily acknowledged that we disagreed in our views about gun control. He spoke openly and honestly about his goals and the abrupt redirection his life had taken. He was traveling nonstop around the country speaking, making media appearances, and meeting with other families whose loved ones had been killed in mass shootings. As he spoke, his voice never cracked. He was fully in command of his emotions, almost as if he were carrying his burden but apart from it. He was so consumed with activity I got the sense that if he were to stop, his sadness would consume him. We talked about when he might slow down.

"Maybe after the election," he said. He told me how his wife and his son were struggling, even more so during his prolonged absences. We talked about Jaime. She was fourteen. She was so strong and full of life that her presence changed the atmosphere whenever she was in the room. She was gone and it was never going to be the same again.

"In my head, it's always there. Even talking with you now. It's there—how she died," he told me. Fred knew exactly how Jaime died because it had been recorded on video surveillance. She was running away from the shooter toward the stairs. She ran down the stairs to a landing and was turning the corner when she was shot. She was less than a second to safety. She died on the stairs. While the intensity of grief may slowly fade, Fred carries the moment of his child's death with him constantly while moving through the demands of his self-punishing schedule. As horrific as losing his child was, endlessly calculating how that day might have been altered by even a fraction of a second to have spared Jaime, Fred at least had this: he knew what happened in the final moments before Jaime died. He was not left to spend countless hours like so many others, imagining how their child spent their last terrifying moments. He knows.

I have wept many times listening to the stories about the lives of the victims of senseless mass shootings. That doesn't make me a "snowflake." It makes me human. If you are thinking that Fred used our brief time together to manipulate me, you are wrong. But there is no question that our brief conversation profoundly affected me.

I was moved by the respect Fred showed me for having a different perspective. The very least I can do is return that respect. That is not to say that Fred won't avoid confrontation. He was thrown out of a Trump State of the Union address for being disorderly in the House Chamber. He has on numerous occasions confronted people in power when they engage in repeating canards. I also don't think Fred has a hidden agenda. Nothing about him is hidden. He stands out in the open willingly—making himself vulnerable.

MY OWN STORY

I first learned to shoot in 1974 at a YMCA summer camp in Kingston, New Hampshire. I was nine years old. We shot .22 long rifles at fifty yards on an outdoor range. Over the next four summers, I would learn gun safety and marksmanship in a program designed in partnership with the NRA. At the end of the program, I qualified for my Marksman First Class and could assemble a .22 rifle from its parts and then fire it within a few minutes. Those years gave me a respect for weapons that I still carry with me today. I have, however, been in situations where a gun owner did not share my respect. In one instance, I was living with a group of males who shared a house. One of our roommates ate a steak from the refrigerator that wasn't his. The owner of the stolen meat came home from work, produced a gun, and set it on the kitchen table.

"What are you planning to do with that?" I asked.

"I'm going to shoot Paul," he said.

"Why are you going to shoot Paul?"

"Because he ate my steak."

Looking at my expression, he confessed, "OK, I'm not really going to shoot him. I just want to put the fear of God in him."

"That will do it," I agreed.

Over the next several minutes, I convinced him that this was a very bad idea (threatening someone with a deadly weapon is a crime) and that I was the one who ate his steak and had already replaced it. It was in the refrigerator. He put the gun away.

Paul never knew what happened.

Attitudes about guns range widely not only by individual but also by region. Today, forty-three states are "shall issue" states, meaning that the state by law must issue an applicant a concealed carry license unless that applicant is not qualified. Disqualifications vary by state but include alcohol and substance addiction, mental health issues, drunk driving convictions, domestic abuse, and prior conviction for a felony offense. Seven states—California, New York, New Jersey, Massachusetts, Connecticut, Delaware, and Rhode Island—are "may issue" states, meaning, in most cases, you must prove that you need a gun for self-protection, usually from a known threat. Proving that threat would include a police report in which you have reported already being threatened or worse are already a victim of a violent attack.

I am a gun owner. I own many types of firearms. I routinely carry. I hold a license to carry a concealed weapon (CCW) in my home state of Virginia and nonresident permits to carry in Pennsylvania and the District of Columbia. My permits allow me to carry legally in thirty-nine states. I train. In 2019 alone, I logged forty-two hours of training with different instructors. My shooting partner is my brother-in-law Michael. His on-target draw time is less than a second. We are constantly challenging and encouraging each other to improve our marksmanship skills. We have a great time training together and learning about weapons, shooting techniques, and defensive gun tactics.

He and I are like most gun owners we know. We show respect. We do it safely and we care about the lives of other people.

One day in 2015, at the Houston headquarters for the presidential campaign of Senator Ted Cruz, I was working at my desk when one of the campaign staff came over to show me the new Glock 19 he had recently purchased. I examined it and compared its features to my own Glock 17. Others joined the conversation and started talking about the guns they owned and also brought some of them to my desk. Soon the desktop was filled with many types of handguns. Then one of the staff who worked with me in communications took out an AR-15. I said, "You keep an AR-15 under your desk?" "Yes, you never know who's coming through the front door" was the reply. At that moment our security guard walked by but stopped to see what was going on. His name was Tiny. He was armed and worked at the front door to keep out unwanted threats. Looking at the firepower now amassed on my desk I said, "Tiny, if someone ever does come through the door with a gun, you might just want to get out of the way."

In 2012, I went to Missouri to try to help put Congressman Todd Akin's campaign to unseat Senator Claire McCaskill back on track after he made his "legitimate rape" blunder. Akin had a solid conservative voting record in Congress, and I just didn't think it right that the party would abandon him for one thoughtless remark. They did worse. The RNC and NRSC put out the word, which was more of an implied threat to campaign professionals, not to help Akin as a tactic to pressure him out of the race. I knew enough about Akin—his father, who was still alive, served under General Patton, and his son was a marine who served in Iraq—to know that he was never going to quit. So the best we could do was help him win.

For the first few days I—being "from Washington and all"—was treated with suspicion bordering on contempt. The staff had been through hell, and they weren't sure if I was there to help or hurt the campaign. On about the third day, two of the staff stopped me in the hallway outside the headquarters. They said they wanted me to know that they both carried firearms. I said, "What do you carry?" Both produced .45-caliber weapons. One was safely handed to me. After examining it, I commented that it was a fine weapon and reached down and took out a .380-caliber, fifteen-round pistol I was carrying on my ankle and showed it to them. My loyalty was never questioned after that. I was accepted as part of the team.

Now those stories really did happen. I know that some reading them might find them shocking. But I can tell you that no one who was there in either case did. Readers who own guns most likely won't either. It is just natural that people who are experienced and knowledgeable about firearms are more comfortable around them than people who aren't.

ONE-SIDED NARRATIVES

To understand the gun control / gun rights debate in America, we can look at two separate diatribes that occurred on television within a month of each other; taken together, they serve as a microcosm of the current debate. The first occurred on the night of Sunday, December 2, 2012, when millions of NFL fans around the country were watching the lackluster three-and-eight Philadelphia Eagles take on the five-and-six Dallas Cowboys in Arlington, Texas. At halftime, while the Cowboy players were in the locker room trying to assess how they were down seven points to a team that had lost its previous seven games, NBC sportscaster Bob Costas appeared on-screen. Viewers might have suspected that the boyish-looking sixty-year-old was going to prognosticate about how Tony Romo could overcome the complexities of the Eagles secondary, but Costas went in an entirely different direction. Costas thought the time was ripe to launch into a jeremiad against guns.

The prior day had witnessed a terrible tragedy when twenty-five-year-old Kansas City linebacker Jovan Belcher had murdered his estranged girlfriend, Kasandra Perkins, by shooting her ten times. Then he climbed into his Bentley and drove five miles to a parking lot near Arrowhead Stadium. When Belcher arrived, he got out of his car and—in front of his head coach and several other coaches who were all pleading with him not to do it—shot himself in the head.

That night, Fox sportswriter Jason Whitlock penned an article about the incident in which he claimed that handguns were the primary culprit in this incident, and it was Whitlock's column that Costas felt compelled to quote in his halftime speech.[1] Though Whitlock had briefly mentioned the possibility that mental problems had played a role in Belcher's murder/suicide, Costas did not feel the need to make such reference. Instead, Costas launched right into the meat of Whitlock's gun control argument. "Handguns do not enhance our safety," Costas quoted. He continued: "They exacerbate our flaws, tempt us to escalate arguments and bait us into embracing confrontation rather than avoiding it."[2]

Costas maintains that if not for the gun Belcher and Perkins would still be alive; of course, it is impossible to know whether that is true. But Costas's observation prompts other questions and possible culprits. The consumption of alcohol—a depressant—has been scientifically proven to "exacerbate flaws" when consumed in large quantities, and Belcher's autopsy showed that Belcher had twice the legal limit in his body at the time of death, meaning that he was heavily intoxicated during the murder and his suicide. As one study showed, "About one third of homicide and suicide victims test positive for alcohol, and at least 60% of those meet legal criteria for intoxication."[3] Why didn't Costas, whose broadcast was heavily subsidized by beer companies, speak about the dangers of alcohol?

Regarding Whitlock's point about Belcher's possible mental problems, it was later discovered that Belcher had suffered from chronic traumatic encephalopathy (CTE), which has been found to adversely affect emotional response in its victims, up to and including the point of suicide. First brought into the public's wide attention in the 2015 movie *Concussion,* CTE is a common problem among NFL players who have suffered multiple brain injuries. Why not use the bully pulpit of the broadcast booth to further highlight the health risks of football and speak out against the NFL's reticence in addressing the widespread problem of brain injury? All this is to say that if you are going to lay the problem solely with handguns, you have to ignore a host of other factors that deserve to be addressed—both in the Belcher case and for the good of society.

Rather than address those and other possible contributing factors,

Costas simply reiterated the statement that Belcher and Perkins—absent the gun—would still be alive. Their entire narrative against guns rests on this point; after all, if it could be illustrated that a murder/suicide were likely to occur regardless of the weapon used, the argument against guns (at least in this case) would be largely moot. But to accept the Whitlock/Costas thesis requires us to believe that Belcher—a heavily intoxicated, extraordinarily angry, brain-damaged, and depressed 230-pound NFL linebacker whose highly paid profession required him to regularly apply blunt-force trauma to slam some of the best athletes in the world to the ground—could have peacefully resolved an argument with his girlfriend. That's a difficult thesis to accept. Nevertheless, Costas's solution is to simply outlaw handguns.

While Costas was making arguments to make handguns *illegal*, one of his political counterparts was making arguments to make all guns *legal*. Just one month after Costas's speech, Larry Pratt, the executive director of Gun Owners of America (GOA) appeared on CNN opposite host Piers Morgan. At the date of that interview, Larry Pratt, who has since been replaced by his son Erich, had served as the head of GOA for more than thirty-five years[4] and had spent much of his time desperately trying to outjockey the mighty NRA for the role of gun rights polemicist. His many off-the-wall statements make his message more satirical than serious. Combining a mixture of a few vague Old Testament quotes, some major leaps in logic, historical oversights, slippery slope arguments, and a heavy dose of paranoia about the federal government, Pratt produced a philosophy of gun rights that views *any* form of gun control as the defining act of totalitarianism.

From his perspective, a view of the Second Amendment that allows for any restriction is a faulty interpretation. He believes that "the right to keep and bear arms" is an unlimited right, granting people the right to buy any kind of gun they want without any background check whatsoever. He believes that the background check is a back-door way for the government to create a gun registry, which could—and, in his mind, *would*—then be used to conduct a door-to-door gun confiscation program. Larry is nodding his head yes when he's asked if he also regards waiting periods for gun purchases as an infringement of rights. Congressman Ron Paul once commented that GOA was "the only no-compromise gun lobby in Washington." This quote which now headlines GOA's website and promotional materials, serves as the organization's motto. Paul wasn't kidding. Pratt was once asked if he was in favor of allowing a minor teenager to buy a "belt-fed .30-caliber machine gun" (think *Rambo*) without any identification or background check, to which Pratt answered that this transaction should be allowed.[5]

In his book *Armed People Victorious*, Pratt not only recommends but also *insists* that Americans again restore "well-regulated" militias—part of the Second Amendment—to their former days of glory. Whether explicit or implicit, his unwavering distrust in the federal government colors many of his statements about guns and militias and has encouraged local sheriffs to arrest federal officers who are deemed to overstep their jurisdictional and constitutional bounds. In his view, any attempt to impose gun regulation is not only immoral but renders the government imposing them illegitimate.[6]

Pratt's views reinforce his marketing claim that the GOA is the only organization to uncompromisingly represent the constitutional intent of the Second Amendment and therefore the interests of gun owners in America.

To bolster its political clout, the GOA website claims that it "represents over 2 million members and activists."[7] That statement might reasonably lead one to believe that it has 2 million members. However, an annual membership in GOA costs $20 per year, although a member could sign up for multiple years at a time, and members could make an outright contribution to GOA, since it is a tax-exempt organization. Even so, assuming that *no one* donated any money beyond membership dues and that *no one* signed up for more than one year's membership, GOA's 2 million members should account for $40 million in annual revenue. Curiously, however, GOA's federal 1099 form for the year 2016 lists its total revenue at less than $2.5 million (along with a net loss after expenses).[8] That leaves one of two possibilities: either GOA is radically overstating its current membership numbers—perhaps by including people who were once members but didn't renew—or it is radically understating its income. Why does this matter? Because it leaves open the question of how strong Pratt and GOA's political clout actually is. If their revenue numbers are correct—even giving them every possible numerical benefit of doubt—GOA has no more than about a hundred thousand members: a tiny fraction of their membership claims. This from an organization that commonly references its own statistics to influence politicians in making life-and-death legislative decisions.

In the course of a month, American viewers were treated to the statements by both Costas and Pratt, each of whom was convinced that his view—in addition to being unshakably correct—represented a wide swath of Americans. In truth, however, each one's view represented only a tiny percentage of the population. What Costas and Pratt's comments do accomplish is to serve as a microcosm of the gun rights / gun control debate in America, which is often argued at the extreme ends of the spectrum. In fact, they serve as an even broader illustration of the false dilemma taking place in America that there are only two possible positions on a subject.

Conservatism suggests neither extreme.

THE SECOND AMENDMENT'S DOUBLE STANDARD

In 2008, a Supreme Court decision well explained the conservative position on gun rights—the now-famous *District of Columbia v. Heller* case. Heller challenged the District's ban on handguns particularly the right of an individual to own a handgun for self-protection. Writing for the majority in that case, Justice Scalia determined that the Second Amendment's right to keep and bear arms applied as an *individual* right rather than a merely *collective* right. That was the decision that gun rights advocates essentially wanted and it led to the district becoming "shall issue" for concealed carry permits. However, that was not the end of the decision, as Scalia was quick to point out that while the individual right exists, the right was not unlimited. Scalia pointed out that the rights of the First Amendment are not unlimited either. The First Amendment, for instance, protects free speech, but it does not guarantee the right of slander; nor does it allow belligerent shouting in public places.

Needless to say, people sympathetic to Larry Pratt and some gun rights organizations were less than thrilled with Scalia's decision. Instead, they made claims expressing that the founders of America would never have allowed this kind of rights-limiting intrusion. That argument—that early America was a land absent of gun control restrictions—is dismissed as irrelevant but is rarely challenged. It should be. Because there is one essential problem with wanting to go back to a time in America when guns had no restrictions: it never existed.

In an attempt to explain the logic and background of the famous *Heller* case, UCLA constitutional law professor Adam Winkler has produced a history of gun control and gun rights that is rarely told. In the course of doing so in his book *Gunfight*, Winkler provides a fascinating look at the attitude toward guns and gun rights during the time of America's founding and makes a startling conclusion that seems like a contradiction: namely, that early America was *both* more pro-gun *and* more pro-regulation than America today.[9] Winkler notes that George Washington owned more than fifty guns and that Thomas Jefferson owned plenty himself; beyond raw numbers, any cursory examination of the founding fathers would illustrate that it would not be much of an exaggeration to say that the founding fathers' attitude toward guns bordered on affection. Moreover, their belief in the necessity of a gun for protection found its way into local ordinances. Winkler explains that in some colonies "all free men between the ages of eighteen and forty-five" were legally required "to outfit themselves with a musket, rifle, or other firearm suitable for military service."[10] And based on historical records, these guns were not simply for show; rather, they were fired—a lot. Clayton Cramer, author of *Armed America*, notes that in the early 1800s, there were "208 gunpowder mills in the US," producing "at least 1,397,111 pounds of gunpowder in 1810."[11] All in all, the founders of America seemed about as pro-gun as you can get. That part of the story—that the colonists liked to own plenty of guns—is pretty well-known to most Americans.

But both Winkler and Clayton note a simultaneous and lesser-known reality: the founders were in favor of strict gun control measures and ordinances. Winkler writes: "The founding fathers instituted gun control laws so intrusive that no self-respecting member of to-day's NRA board of directors would support them."[12] He backs up that statement by pointing out that people could be denied the right to own firearms if they "failed a political test of loyalty to the Revolution" and that the governmental registration of guns was required of citizens.[13] "In some states, like New Hampshire and Rhode Island," Winkler writes, "government officials conducted door-to-door surveys of gun ownership in the community."[14] Moreover, local governments reserved the right to seize guns if these weapons were deemed necessary to defend the community. In a symbiotic hybrid of wealth distribution and gun rights, Virginia passed a law in 1673 that required owners of numerous guns to turn some of them over to the less fortunate colonists.[15] Winkler concludes: "The founding generation had many forms of gun control. They might not have termed it 'gun control,' but the founders understood that gun rights had to be balanced with public safety needs."[16] This is in line with conservatism. (although admittedly, reappropriating private property isn't).

I've tried to avoid citing scholarly studies in making my case in support of the Second Amendment because I've found that for every study proving one point, there is another equally compelling study making the counterpoint, and so not much is accomplished. Because, in the gun control debate—as with other socioeconomic and political issues—there are the usual lies, damned lies, and statistics. But in this issue, there is also the thing that's never mentioned at all. It is undeniable that gun control in America has terribly racist origins.[17] Though this fact should be central to the understanding of America's gun history, the historical influence of racism on this issue has either been missed entirely, vastly understated, or simply ignored. It would be fallacious to ascribe malice to those who never mention it; rather, it evidences the general lack of scholarly research that has generally plagued the gun issue in America.

The "right of the people to keep and bear arms" was not broadly intended to include blacks. (It was not just blacks who were disallowed gun ownership—though blacks suffered the most severe persecution and injustice by far—but extended to "nonwhites," which most notably included Native Americans and Mexicans.)[18] In early America, the natural-law right to self-defense was commonly infringed in law—and that infringement went far beyond guns. In 1811, for instance, lawmakers in New Orleans prohibited slaves from even carrying a "stick."[19] Cramer notes that several states restricted the slave's right to own a dog, ostensibly because his dog could be weaponized. Clearly, the human rights of slaves were broadly and violently trampled on in the antebellum South, but even free blacks were often legally prohibited from having arms.[20] The reality that they were not even allowed to defend themselves is a fact not often considered in history books—nor is it often considered that in the entire history of America, no group of people was more in need of defending themselves.

It was not until the Reconstruction amendments that many blacks in America could even hope to own a gun. And when they did try to own guns, white supremacists were none too happy about that fact. As Winkler observes, "Few people realize it, but the Ku Klux Klan began as a gun control organization; after the Civil War, the Klan and other violent racist groups sought to reaffirm white supremacy, which required confiscating the guns blacks had obtained for the first time during the conflict. To prevent blacks from fighting back, the night riders set out to achieve complete black disarmament."[21] To accomplish that goal of disarmament, they had the wind at their backs. As historian Allen Trelease notes, in many Southern areas, it was clear that many police forces, political offices, judges, juries, and newspapers were composed of—and staffed by—white supremacists.[22] Somewhat amazing, in retrospect, was the brutal bluntness of their white supremacy, which is to say they were very open in their bloodthirsty hostility. In 1868, for instance, *The Fayetteville Observer* condoned the lynching a black man who was accused of raping a white woman, defending the lynch party as "instruments of Divine vengeance."[23] Broadly, this type of comment was more the rule than the exception, and mobs who lynched thousands of blacks with impunity could look forward to reading about their exploits in the following days, complete with editorial endorsement.

Though the topic has received scant attention, volumes could be devoted to the issue of the relationship between racism and gun control laws in America. As we move forward on guns as a right of self-defense in America, we should remember that there was a time in America when legislators felt justified in outlawing entire groups of people the right to defend themselves. We must also recognize that racism, still prevalent in America today, manifests itself under cover of various gun control laws, especially with discretionary concealed carry laws.[24]

And we might make a related observation about the poor in America: poor people in America are not afforded the same ability to defend themselves, their families, or complete strangers as the wealthy. The wealthy can deter crime with gated communities and burglar alarms; while the very wealthy have these options as well as employing armed bodyguards. One recent ad for a bodyguard included this description: "Driver who will also provide personal protection to professional client and juvenile. Must possess a firearm and permit, be physically fit and willing to engage in hand-to-hand combat." Yes, it's good to be rich. The poor have few avenues available, and they are the class most likely to have their right to self-defense denied—or, in the framers' words—infringed.

MISLEADING STATISTICS

In many books and media outlets in America, there is an insistent narrative that guns are used almost exclusively in incidents like Columbine or Sandy Hook. For instance, horror novelist writes: "Semi-automatics have only two purposes. One is so owners can take them to the shooting range once in a while, yell yeehaw, and get all horny at the rapid fire and the burning vapor spurting from the end of the barrel. Their other use—their only other use—is to kill people."[25] Piers Morgan comments, "More guns doesn't mean less crime . . . It means more gun violence, death and profits for the gun manufacturers."[26]

I'm not sure Stephen King has ever been to a firing range, but I've never encountered that kind of behavior at any range or even on private property while shooting. It's tempting to dismiss his comment as a worthless pejorative against gun owners, yet it's worth answering because it likely represents the attitude of many people who don't own firearms. If what King says is true—that some guns have only two possible purposes—then guns have zero deterrent effect; in other words, King's proposition that no potential crime has ever failed to be carried out for fear that the potential victim was armed. But using King's own logic, the second use "to kill people" has absolutely no deterrent effect. I think the effect is self-evident.

But here's another thing, except for single-shot, bolt-action rifles, single-shot shotguns, and single-action revolvers (meaning you have to cock the hammer back in order for the trigger to release the hammer, thus firing the weapon), nearly every weapon is effectively a semiautomatic weapon. Whether an automatic pistol or a revolver, one trigger pull fires the weapon and reloads another round in the chamber ready to be fired until the ammunition is exhausted.

Piers Morgan's essential claim that "guns are bad, and more guns are worse" is also contradicted by facts—and right-leaning individuals and organizations aren't the only ones who profess that fact. In a 2016 piece in *The New York Times*, for instance, Nicholas Kristof writes, "We liberals are sometimes glib about equating guns and danger. In fact, it's complicated: The number of guns in America has increased by more than 50 percent since 1993, and in that same period the gun homicide rate in the United States has dropped by half."[27] Another oddity that Kristof mentions is that with all the talk about assault weapons—a politically charged term that has no precise definition—it's perhaps surprising that they are so rarely used in crimes. In fact, the early

1990s study he references admits the "relative rarity" of such occurrences, even though such guns as the AR-15 had been introduced decades prior. How rare? The study examines serious gun crimes committed in six cities: Baltimore, Miami, Milwaukee, Boston, St. Louis, and Anchorage. The city with the highest percentage of carbine weapons (generally rifles less than twenty inches in length) used in such crimes was Milwaukee, with 6 percent. The lowest was St. Louis, with 1 percent. In other words, crimes involving guns were of the *non*-assault-weapon variety 99 percent of the time. The reason is obvious: a carbine is very hard to conceal.

In his book *Rampage Nation,* Louis Klarevas paints America as a dystopic society in which we are all constantly under threat of attack. However, citing the fact that in Los Angeles County "half of all homicides each year are tied to gang violence," Adam Winkler concludes that the statistics indicate that "the gun problem in America . . . is largely a suicide problem and a gang problem."[28] That is not to say that America is a completely peaceful society. It's not by any means, and mass shootings have become a cause for urgent action.

Nevertheless, even considering mass shootings, the disproportionate number of crimes committed with guns occur mostly in relatively small geographical, mostly urban areas like Chicago (but not all of Chicago, again only a relatively small area of the city experiences gun violence) or Los Angeles (but there, too, only in a tiny part of that megaplex), places that already have the strictest gun control laws. Second, those crimes are disproportionately associated with gang activity and drug trafficking. But the legislative proposals always seem to target the guns the rest of us (99.9 percent) law-abiding citizens own, knowing their solutions will not have the slightest impact on criminals who use firearms to commit a crime.

But there is a larger problem with Klarevas's claim that regards guns as the root cause of a much deeper societal problem that much of the talk about gun control seems to ignore. Wherever one finds himself or herself on this issue, one thing we should all be able to agree on is this one observation: something has gone wrong in American society.

Something has gone terribly wrong.

So instead of talking about what has gone wrong, we want to talk instead about the demerits of the AR-15 and why it is regarded as the primordial evil. And in the interest of having an actual discussion, rather than engaging in an exercise of finger-pointing, let me just make a few quick observations. The AR-15 was first developed in the late 1950s by Armalite, which is where the letters AR originate. It does not stand for "assault weapon" or "automatic rifle." Colt bought the AR platform in 1959. Today, hundreds of manufacturers make an AR-type carbine. Since the 1950s, millions of ARs have been sold. The AR platform is a favorite among competition shooters, amateur shooters like me, hunters, and particularly well suited for home defense. While the weapon has been improved over the decades by many makers and the quality of ARs vary greatly by manufacturer, the basic underlying technology of the weapon is the same. The point is that the weapon and access to the weapon over the last sixty years has not substantially changed. So what has changed?

When I was in high school in New Hampshire, students brought their guns to school. That's right. If you walked down to the student parking lot during hunting season, you would see pickup trucks with one or more rifles in the gun rack of the back window. Students were bringing guns to school, but as far as I know, no student would ever have thought to point their weapon at another student and take their life.

Something has gone terribly wrong. Yet, we don't want to talk about that. We're too afraid to talk about it.

The problem, it seems to me, does not lie with which of my guns should be categorized as an "assault weapon" and which of my magazines should be categorized as "high capacity." Neither of those addresses the underlying problem.

Similarly, there are other gun-related issues that are rarely talked about. One of them is suicide. Judging by how relatively little attention the topic receives, there is an odd reluctance of gun control advocates to talk about suicide. Stephen King's short book *Guns* does not even mention suicide, while the topic gets short shrift in lots of other books. Why should that strike us as surprising? Because about 60 percent of firearm fatalities—year after year—are suicides. How does someone get to the suicidal stage? If we want to get to the heart of the matter—that is, why do so many young people commit suicide—we need to address the root causes of that lonely unhappiness. Broadly, that is not the focus of this book, but we might make the observation that high school and college students have become increasingly isolated by the very thing that is said to unite them: social media. Plenty of studies have illustrated that social media can lead to depression. Further, although it has become politically incorrect to speak of such things, it has become clear that the breakdown of the family does little to help children with self-esteem or overall happiness. Abuse of alcohol, by all accounts, is also a growing problem in high schools and universities. We can certainly argue about what brings teenagers and young adults to such a desperate state—and maybe that is exactly what we ought to be discussing. But if compassion dictates that we reexamine gun control laws, it also dictates that we investigate the causes for such depression and unhappiness that leads to suicide.

LOOKING FORWARD

This chapter began with my meeting Fred Guttenberg and how to answer his implied question of what he did wrong. He didn't do anything wrong. It's wasn't his fault. He did everything right. He was a good father to Jaime. He had every reasonable expectation that she would be safe and would come home from school that day like any other day. While his views on gun control and the views of conservatism might be deemed irreconcilable, I don't believe that they are. I don't believe Fred thinks they are either. In fact, some of his arguments should appeal to conservatives. That statement will shock some readers—and that's part of the problem. It is unfortunate that conservatives in America are often portrayed as "gun nuts." As this chapter illustrated, though there are some loud voices associated with conservatism who give cause for that accusation, the truth is that the vast majority of gun owners in America do not ascribe to their positions; quite the contrary, they feel betrayed by some of those leaders. Though it is not universally agreed upon by conservatives what the perfect set of regulations would look like, conservatism must be in favor of some gun regulations. Echoing the philosophy and practice of the founders of America, we should seek those regulations that protect innocent life and allow the defense of innocent life, while least encroaching on individual liberty. In short, we should seek to find an equitable balance between the extremes of Costas and Pratt.

In terms of our national discussion, we need to move past the idea that one is either in favor of the universal right to guns or is in favor of outlawing guns altogether; that is a false binary that is intellectually lazy. For his part, Fred Guttenberg has stated his support for the Second Amendment and for some gun control measures. Some people respond that this position is untenable. Of course, the same was said about Justice Scalia, who pointed out that the right to guns was intended to be a limited right.

Guttenberg has promoted a number of wide-ranging gun control positions, including raising the minimum age to buy guns from eighteen to twenty-one, universal background checks, and imposing a waiting period to buy guns. Those restrictions may not all be acceptable to everyone. And I disagree with some, but he is opening the conversation for a compromise acceptable to both sides.

Universal background checks for gun purchasers are criticized as a terrible violation of America's liberties, yet such a law may be consistent with the actual gun control practices of the founding fathers. Moreover, we should be consistent with our rights. For instance, though conservatism professes the right to travel, every state does some form of a background check before allowing licensees to drive on public roads. All things being equal, we don't want a sociopath in the lane coming toward us. Mandatory background checks for both dealers and private sales seem very reasonable to me. Having purchased many guns, I find them to be a very minor inconvenience. Once you've selected a purchase, you fill out a federal and—depending on the state—state questionnaire. My last purchase was at Dick's Sporting Goods for a shotgun, and I answered the questions on a terminal. In case you are wondering, yes, some Dick's stores still sell long guns for hunting. After about fifteen minutes, I was cleared to complete the purchase. I support universal background checks, but I would caution people to understand that background checks will not keep someone from illegally getting a firearm. It is, however, reasonable to expect legal purchases be made only by people legally qualified to own a firearm.

Depending on how it is structured, a waiting period for gun purchases may be a reasonable idea as well. While organizations like the Gun Owners of America are adamantly opposed to this measure, the overall good of such a regulation at the state level might save many lives in its prevention of suicide. Gun stores could do their part by helping to promote suicide prevention efforts by handing out material to people wanting to purchase a gun. Reliable and extensive studies have shown that a waiting period would prevent suicides. Since the majority of firearm fatalities are suicides, this is surely among the most reasonable and compassionate measures. I would actually take it a step further, which would negate the need for a waiting period, and that is to establish a standard of firearms use and safety training and be able to demonstrate proficiency to a qualified instructor before being able to own your first firearm. Much like getting a license to drive a car. The DC training requirement was sixteen hours of class time and two hours on the range. That seems reasonable to me, because owning a firearm is a big responsibility. Carrying a firearm is an even heavier responsibility.

Next, I am skeptical about severely limiting magazine capacities. My Glock 17 9mm standard capacity magazine holds seventeen rounds. I also have aftermarket magazines for the Glock that hold only ten rounds for states that have that restriction. My .380 has a standard capacity magazine that holds fifteen rounds. These are typical round capacities for many handguns. While I would agree that there is no reason to have a hundred-round capacity magazine, I think ten rounds is too restrictive. First, there is the practical problem of millions and millions of what I'll call larger-capacity magazines (more than ten rounds) already legally owned by millions of gun owners. I own dozens of them myself. Second, changing a magazine in what is called an emergency reload takes only two seconds or less. As I mentioned earlier, the AR-15 is used by many as a home defense weapon and it is a good choice (a shotgun is better for less-experienced shooters). Its standard capacity magazine is thirty rounds. The problem arises where the homeowner defending his or her family is limited where the guy breaking into your house is not. I have heard many people who are unfamiliar with guns say that if you can't "take care of business" in thirty rounds, then you probably shouldn't own a gun to begin with. That's a nice-sounding talking point, but it has no relationship to the reality of a gunfight. I've trained with handguns and an AR-15 with military special forces instructors. In several drills, they are shooting at you (with Sirts pistols that shoot lasers or CO_2 guns). Suffice it to say, thirty rounds in a real-world situation may not be enough to survive.

Needless to say, I would not support a so-called assault weapons ban. Mostly because it makes little logical sense, unless you want to ban all long guns or ban any gun that can accept a larger capacity magazine. Fully automatic guns (machine guns) like the military uses have been outlawed since 1934. (Although it is possible to own one with the required permit from ATF.) Most AR-15s fire a .223 round as well as a 5.56 round. Some only fire the .223. There are hundreds of guns that shoot the exact same round. While there are many differences between long guns, an AR-15 doesn't shoot harder or faster than other firearms that shoot the same caliber cartridge. I've been asked why do I need to own an AR. The answer is I don't, I could own an inferior weapon. Like driving a Chevy instead of a Ferrari. The AR platform is light and therefore easier to handle, it efficiently disperses heat, and it's highly reliable. People buy them because they have these highly desired features, but does that make it an "assault rifle"? I don't think so.

Will arbitrarily banning this and other models like it keep someone from getting one? No. Could they get another gun that fires the same round that is not banned? Yes.

Next, red-flag laws are needed cases where a person demonstrates that they are a threat either to themselves or someone else. If they have access to a gun, that gun should be taken by law enforcement. We also need to educate people on how to identify potential shooters and report them. I remember listening to live coverage of the Parkland shooting, and people were speculating about who they thought did it before the shooter was identified. They were right. It's sad to think that with the right tools law enforcement might have prevented this horrific event. But that kind of law would need to be accompanied by due process to allow for a speedy appeal where the gun owner can get back his weapon if falsely accused.

Finally, we need to rebalance the Justice Department's antiterrorism capability. After 9/11, the Justice Department reorganized and created a team to investigate terrorist threats originating outside the United States. There is no such unit specifically assigned to prevent domestic acts of terrorism nor is there a federal law applicable to domestic terrorism specifically. Only in cases where there is a provable link to al Qaeda or ISIS can an investigation be initiated inside the United States. That needs to change. Without violating the First Amendment with regard to speech and associations, Congress should specifically create a domestic terrorism unit within the Justice Department dedicated to preventing domestic terrorism by giving it the tools to investigate potential domestic terrorist threats.

The 2019 El Paso shooter was reading online material that essentially convinced him that shooting innocent people was justifiable, even laudable. He was in a real sense recruited and encouraged to kill as many innocent people as possible—in his case, Latinos. The young men who are susceptible to this type of recruitment are not entirely dissimilar to the targets of and the recruitment techniques used by gangs. Although it's not clear if those in the radical online forum who encouraged him to carry out the killing actually cared who he killed; perhaps they just wanted to radicalize him in any way they could so he would act. Why would anyone do that? There are a lot of hateful and disturbed people in the world, but there are also state actors like Iran and other hostile nations who could and probably are doing the same, which would make domestic terrorism an extension of international terrorism. In either case, a dedicated domestic counterterroism unit would likely have similar success as that of the international effort.

I think nearly all gun owners would agree that there are people who should not have access to guns. I think most would also like to see Congress take reasonable actions to prohibit them from buying or owning guns without targeting lawful gun owners' rights to keep and bear arms. Some gun rights activists may be unhappy with these suggestions, arguing that laws like this take away freedom. But it's worth noting that *every* law in the history of mankind limits freedom in some way. And while we conservatives believe that freedom should not be limited without some damn good reasons, we believe that on the issue of gun related violence, there are some damn good reasons for well-founded regulations. Going forward, we need a balance of rights and regulations that protect law-abiding citizens and punish criminals. We also need to be truthful enough to admit that no law is perfect; no law will prevent all crime. And while no amount of legislation can change human nature, our laws can at least be a reflection of the belief that our society seeks to protect both life and liberty.

10

BEFORE LIBERTY AND THE PURSUIT OF HAPPINESS

There is a popular political narrative spoken by some pro-choice advocates that goes like this: pro-life advocates are on the wrong side—the nonhumanitarian side. We want to take away women's rights (an entire hard-fought body of rights of which abortion is simply the tip of the iceberg) and we want to send women into "back alleys" for abortions. That trope doesn't work with me. My whole life revolves around women. I was raised by a single mom. I have five sisters. My wife and I raised a daughter. Even my cat is female. The toilet seat in my house is always down, even when I use it. It's just easier to sit. Most of my direct bosses starting at a young age have been women. The idea that I am somehow indifferent to the rights of women is laughable. However, I've been around politics long enough to know that most of the time, these criticisms are political in nature. Because in real life, I have never met a pro-life man who truly didn't care about mothers. In my experience, people who genuinely care about others tend to care about *all others*. Yet, defenders of unborn life are attacked as if they cared only about abortion prevention.

This type of argument often begins with some comment like, "Great, Rick, you're pro-life. Well, let me ask you something! Are you going to adopt all the kids?"

This is an empty claim that not only ignores the fact that there are long waiting lists of couples who want to adopt, but it is also a claim that could be made about any issue or stance. For instance, if I came out against caging children at the border (which I repeatedly have), someone could always say: "There's Tyler again talking about freeing kids at the border. Well, let me ask you something, Rick: Are *you* going to take care of all those kids!?!" If I come out in favor of flying humanitarian aid to oppressed nations, someone could say, "Are you planning on flying over there Rick!?!" You get the idea.

In 2018, an article appeared in *The New York Times* written by Michelle Oberman, a pro-choice law professor and self-described "lifelong feminist." For years, Oberman has researched and documented abortion laws and their effects in other nations, but she decided to investigate and delve into America's pro-life culture. To accomplish that research, she traveled to the state of Oklahoma, which has some of the strongest pro-life laws in America. There, she visited Birth Choice (it is now called Willow Pregnancy Support), a pro-life pregnancy counseling center. She seemed surprised by what she saw.

She explains that the organization sees as many as four hundred patients every month, even women who are in America illegally and speak only Spanish. Free of charge, they receive pregnancy tests, blood pressure tests, ultrasounds, prenatal vitamins, and referrals for medical care. Oberman witnessed they received something else as well: a friend who listened. One of the founders of the organization explained to Oberman that they come seeking someone who will listen: "Even if they think they want an abortion, they come to be heard."[1] Operated largely by volunteers, their mission reads: "Willow Pregnancy Support exists to empower pregnant women to choose the gift of life for herself and her unborn baby and provides the means to do so."[2] Befriending, empowering, and assisting women doesn't seem to correlate with the misogynistic narrative. Yet, there it is. Moreover, places like this exist all around the country. In fact, there are thousands of them.

Like millions of others, my wife and I give to a no-cost pregnancy center with the intention of helping pregnant mothers with the resources they need to make choices about their pregnancy. The center does not provide abortions or refer them, but if the mother does choose to have an abortion, post-abortion counseling is also offered. And there are countless other organizations like it that most people have never heard about.

One such organization is the Sisters of Life, which is a Catholic religious order that takes the traditional vows of poverty, chastity, and obedience, and adds a fourth: "the vow to protect and enhance the sacredness of human life." The sisters have locations in five cities in America and offer pregnant and new moms help with "housing, employment, medical assistance, legal advice" as well as "emotional and spiritual accompaniment."[3]

In addition to organizations like these, there are also individual churches that routinely provide for unwed mothers as well as people who open their homes to women in troubled situations with crisis pregnancies. The truth is that pro-life groups and individuals offer a wide array of help to pregnant women, both during and after the birth of their children, even after an abortion. People can always do more; there's no doubt about that. But to deny that much is being done to assist pregnant mothers and mothers of newborns is untrue, witnessed by the very existence of so many organizations. It is not the case that pro-life people care only about making abortion illegal or that they only care until the baby is born and then couldn't care less. That's a most unfair charge.

On that point, visit most any church, synagogue, or mosque in America and you will see people helping people every day. You will almost never see these people in the news. They don't seek publicity. They just quietly go about their ministries, visiting the sick, the elderly, and the lonely. My wife is one of these angels. Some make home repairs for the poor. Some drive people to appointments, drop off dinner, or shop for them. If only half the people in the United States would commit to helping just one other person, think how much more fulfilled we would be with far less need. People making a positive difference in the life of another to me is pro-life.

Pro-life groups are also trying to help women by bringing to light the link between abortion and subsequent depression. Over the past several decades, numerous studies have illustrated the increased likelihood of suicide after abortion. In a study based in Finland, the *European Journal of Public Health* illustrated that even with the new emphasis on post-abortion counseling, "The excess risk for suicide after induced abortion is still more than two-fold."[4] In a wide-ranging study of women ages fifteen to twenty-five, *The Journal of Child Psychology and Psychiatry* reported: "Those having an abortion had elevated rates of subsequent mental health problems including depression, anxiety, suicidal behaviors and substance use disorders."[5] It would be reasonable to assume that some of this depression pre-existed the abortion, but the report took that factor into account, finding: "This association persisted after adjustment for confounding factors."[6]

Planned Parenthood dismisses reports like these. In 2013, Planned Parenthood issued a two-page flyer that opened by stating: "For more than 30 years, substantive research studies have shown that legally induced abortion does not pose mental health problems for women."[7] The flyer states that the research that contradicts Planned Parenthood's position is the "most flawed," but the research that confirms Planned Parenthood's position is the "highest quality" research. (Obviously, anyone could use this tactic to disregard any position. In fact, the tobacco lobby insisted for years that despite the medical research illustrating the alarming rate of lung cancer and heart disease among smokers their own research showed no link whatsoever.) I'm not suggesting that any research is infallible, nor do I have particular reason to ascribe bias to medical journals like *The Journal of Child Psychology and Psychiatry*. Furthermore, if Planned Parenthood is correct, and post-abortion depression doesn't exist, then why are thousands of women seeking counseling for it every year? And shouldn't the groups that offer such free counseling get some credit for doing so?

When writing about the life issue, I want to be respectful not only of those who don't agree with me, but in particular, I keep in the front of my mind also those women who are facing or have faced a life-changing unwanted pregnancy and especially those who've had an abortion.

Though there was a time when championing the rights of the unborn was central to American conservatism, in recent times conservatives have decided to run from the pro-life issue or simply ignore it altogether. At least in prime time, the 2016 Republican Convention never mentioned the life issue at all, even though some of the speakers would have self-identified as pro-life conservatives. Even the Religious Right seems to have replaced the once-premier issue of abortion with illegal immigration. In his recent book outlining the history and philosophy of conservatism—a tome that runs 640 pages—George Will does not mention abortion. That's a curious omission. After all, conservatism is about liberty, and the right to life is the first liberty mentioned by Jefferson. Maybe conservative leaders just got tired; maybe they became weary of all the mockery and jabs that pro-life conservatives have come to count on. But if conservatism abandons the pro-life issue, can liberty be far behind? Conservatism will become a meaningless specter of an ideology long since dead and buried if life itself cannot be defended. If conservatives give up on life, how can the rest of the conservative issues not fall from the same mockery that pushed it off the table? The pro-life side deserves a better hearing than the one it's been getting, even—and in some ways, especially—by conservatives. This is the central issue for conservatives because, in profound ways, it affects all the others.

A SIMPLE PRINCIPLE

Over the years, conservatives like me have often been accused of being "one-issue voters," the one issue being abortion. Largely, the purpose of that accusation is to make it seem like the only thing I care about are fetuses (or, as I like to say, "unborn babies"). It is meant to imply that I don't care about women or their rights, and some have even implied that I hate women.

This tiresome argument is that I am so narrowly focused on this single issue that I lose sight and objectivity of all the others. That might make for some meaningful rhetoric on the pro-choice side, but it's not true. In fact, my pro-life position is not simply one single issue; it encompasses a broad array of political viewpoints.

I believe that the intentional taking or deliberate harming of an innocent human life is wrong, and it applies to preborn babies in the womb, children at the border, adults at the border, the people of foreign nations suffering under dictatorships, people who require medical care, men and women who need to defend themselves against attackers, people who need to trade freely to support themselves and their families, and so on. And to me it's clear: whether at the border, in foreign countries, or in the womb, I'm for life. Obviously, I believe there is consistency there. If you're for the cause of protecting innocent human life, then I'm with you. At a recent pro-life march, someone was carrying a sign that read: PRO-LIFE IN THE WOMB, AND AT THE BORDER. I'd like to think that my political views are too sophisticated to fit on a poster written with a wide Sharpie, but that sign comes much closer to my political stance than many writings and speeches of those in the current administration.

If you ask me if it's OK that a government forcibly separates families and cages children, I would answer that it's wrong because it deliberately harms innocent lives. For that same reason, I'd say it's wrong that North Korea routinely tortures people. I'd say sexual assault is wrong for the same reason. These are all pro-life positions. Does American soldiers killing Nazi troops in battle violate my principle? No, because Nazis troops are not innocent. What about deliberately bombing German civilians in the same war? That *does* violate the principle, because the civilians are innocent—that is, they are not personally guilty of any wrongdoing. What about bombing a munitions factory that produces Nazi weaponry, if you are pretty certain that innocent bystanders will be harmed in the process? My answer would be that you could bomb the factory because your intention is to strike the factory not innocent lives; in other words, you're not *deliberately* intending to harm innocents. Even in that case, striking the factory must be done when it is least likely to hurt innocents. We could throw questions at this principle all day, but all in all, I'd say that this principle holds up.

Ethics is the study of the morality of human action. The questions above dealing with government actions in wartime, we might call macro-ethics. But there is also what we might call micro-ethics, the study of individual moral choice. On that level, everyone with the use of reason has an ethical system. Should I lie on my taxes? Should I cheat on my wife? Should I steal money from my employer? A person might find these things ethically wrong. But what if he didn't? What if he thought nothing were wrong? That's an ethical system, too. His ethical system is that he can do whatever he wants.

Most people, however, have an ethical code in which they believe some things are wrong. Most people, perhaps for no greater reason than naked self-interest, try to avoid committing certain actions. For instance, a person might really enjoy pickpocketing his friends and kicking them in the groin, but he soon realizes that performing these actions results in chaos—most immediately for his social life. (Presumably, if you kick a friend in the groin and pickpocket him enough times, he'll simply stop wanting to be around you.) A higher motive might be that he desires the good of his friends: the happiness of his friends results in his own. Either way, groin kicking and pickpocketing have no place in his ethical system. Of course, ethics do not deal only with negatives. A positive aspect of ethics would be to develop a moral code that assists people in need: feeding the hungry, providing clothing for the poor, welcoming a stranger.

As it is for individuals, so it is for societies. Without ethics—without the ability to call something right or wrong—chaos ensues. Societies must have generally accepted ethical principles; otherwise, they really cannot function as societies. That doesn't mean we all have to agree on *everything*, but it does mean that we must agree on *some* things. If we cannot agree that armed robbery is wrong, we are all in greater danger (and so are our bank accounts). If we can't all agree to drive on the right side of the road, well, you get the point. These are pretty obvious and intuitive examples. But some questions are more difficult. Some things strike us as right or wrong for reasons we cannot immediately explain. At present, the people of our country have an ongoing debate as to the ethics of separating families at the southern border. Is it right or wrong? To answer that question, I simply apply the aforementioned principle and conclude that I am against it because the policy intended as a deterrent harms innocent people.

THE PRINCIPLE APPLIED

Now, let's see how this principle applies to abortion. Does elective abortion constitute the intentional taking or deliberate harming of an innocent human life?

Regarding the "intentional taking," I don't think there's any disagreement between the pro-life and pro-choice side that when a doctor performs an elective abortion, he or she has the surgical goals of termination and extraction of the fetus. And it must be in *that* order; otherwise, the physician could be in violation of partial-birth abortion restrictions. Thus, the essential difference between abortion and live birth is not the *extraction*, it is the prior *termination*. The intentional "taking" of the fetus is evident.

What about "deliberate harming?" That's an interesting topic of its own. As many Americans are well aware, medical professionals are increasingly performing fetal surgery. (The first prenatal surgery was performed in 1963, a full decade before the *Roe* decision.)[8] And not only is there open fetal surgery, but also there is now "minimally invasive fetoscopic surgery," in which an ultrasound and fetoscope precisely guide the surgeon. The Cardinal Glennon Children's Hospital of St. Louis is a leading performer of such surgeries, at which these medical wonder workers treat fetal heart issues such as "cardiac tumors," fetal lung issues such as "lesions" and "airway obstructions," and fetal spina bifida.[9] "In open fetal surgery," they explain, "the mother is placed under general anesthesia and given an epidural to help with pain control. The fetus is also given medications as needed for pain control and to prevent movement."[10] Pain control medications are considered standard care in the world of fetal surgery,[11] and a physician would no more operate on a fetus without administering it than a dentist would perform a root canal without novocaine.

To restate that, the top prenatal surgeons in the world deem pain-control medications necessary for fetuses in surgery. But if fetuses can experience pain during lung operations, how much more pain would they feel during an abortion? With that question in mind, pro-life advocates across America have attempted to pass bills that would require abortion doctors to administer pain medication to fetuses before abortion. Yet, that initiative has been condemned as a "slippery slope to overturning Roe," and many state legislators have voted against giving pain medication to fetuses. And so, in millions of cases across America, fetuses are given no pain medications or sedatives before they are aborted. That is deliberate harming. Just to highlight the point, I am not suggesting that women who abort their babies are deliberately inflicting pain. I am saying that this prenatal inhumane infliction of pain is the result of political pressure.

As to whether the fetus is "innocent," the contrary argument doesn't merit much time or attention. What crime has the fetus committed? Every once in a while, a libertarian will try to justify abortion by saying that the fetus is "trespassing" in the womb and may therefore be "evicted," even though eviction might mean certain death. Assuming for a moment that the libertarian is being serious, would he also be in favor of shooting someone who accidentally wandered onto his property? Don't answer that.

Now we come to the "human life" part of the equation: when does human life begin? It's curious how often this is framed as a religious question—curious, perhaps, because those who seem generally disinterested in religious matters are quick to call it a religious question. Even Justice Blackmun in his vaunted *Roe v. Wade* decision inferred that it was a question for theologians to help decide. The skeptic in me wonders whether classifying the beginning-of-life matter as a "religious" question is simply a way to dismiss the matter as innately unknowable. (Imagine for instance if I said, "We'll never really know if there's global warming; that's something for theologians to decide.) There are certainly theological questions that could be asked regarding the issue of life; for instance, questions about whether and when God imparts a soul to a baby is a religious question that should be left to religious scholars. But the question about when life begins is not religious in the least. Rather, it is a matter of basic bioscientific observation.

In 1981, Dr. Jerome Lejeune (dubbed "the Father of Modern Genetics") testified before the US Senate that it "is no longer a matter of taste or opinion" nor is it "a metaphysical contention" that life begins at conception; rather, "it is plain experimental evidence."[12] Back then, especially in light of the *Roe* decision, this might have been a controversial statement. But not today. For instance, pick up a copy of the 2016 edition of *The Developing Human,* a book with contributions from more than sixty accomplished obstetricians, fetal surgeons, and pediatricians— sort of the *Top Gun* school of prenatal medicine. Here's the opening sentence: "Human development is a continuous process that begins when an oocyte (ovum) from a female is fertilized by a sperm (spermatozoon) from a male."[13] The American College of Pediatricians explains that advances in medical technology in recent years have provided a much clearer window into the genesis of human life and how fast life begins: "During the first 24 hours, once the sperm and egg bind to each other, the membranes of these two cells fuse, creating in less than a second a single hybrid cell: the zygote, or one-cell embryo." They conclude: "The American College of Pediatricians concurs with the body of scientific evidence that corroborates that a unique human life starts when the sperm and egg bind to each other in a process of fusion of their respective membranes and a single hybrid cell called a zygote, or one-cell embryo, is created."[14]

At this point, I reiterate that this is not a religious argument but a biological one. At a public debate with political commentator/actor

Ben Stein, even the famous atheist Christopher Hitchens acknowledged this. Stein asked him if he was "opposed to abortion" and "involved in the pro-life movement?" Hitchens responded, "I believe
that the concept *unborn child* is a real concept, yes, and I've had a
lot of quarrels with some of my fellow materialists and secularists
on this point. I think that if the concept child means anything, the
concept *unborn child* can be said to mean something. And actually, all
the discoveries of embryology—which have been very considerable
in the last generation or so, and of viability—appear to confirm that
opinion, which is, I think, should be innate in everybody. It's innate
in the Hippocratic Oath. It's instinct in anyone who's ever watched a
sonogram, and so forth."[15]

For me, the scientific evidence is simply overwhelming that elective abortion is taking an innocent human life. I am tempted to call
it settled science, but I'll resist that temptation.

A DIFFERENT ARGUMENT?

Some will dismiss all of these findings about the beginning of life—
all this talk about zygotes, embryos, and single-hybrid cells. They
will not only dismiss the idea that life begins at conception but also
that life begins at anytime prior to birth. They dismiss the observa-
tional data that has been compiled by those who actually perform
prenatal surgery. But here is my question: on the level of medical
science, where is the conflicting evidence? Where is the scientific evidence that Lejeune and the pediatricians are wrong?

However, I don't think the core of this debate has ever really been
about science. Over the years, I've been interviewed many times on
various networks about the subject of abortion, and as the pro-life
guest, I often volunteer that I believe, based on scientific evidence, that
life begins at conception. Sometimes I challenge opposing guests as
to when *they* believe it begins. I think that's a fair question. Which-
ever side you're on, doesn't this matter to the argument? If we are

going to debate about abortion, isn't this central to the argument? But they never answer my question. Instead, they divert to a discussion of "women's rights," the presumption being that if I dare ask the question about the origin of life, I am somehow against women's rights. How does that follow? Presumably, about half of abortions terminate female fetuses, right? Last year, there were something like 56 million abortions worldwide. I'm trying to stand up for more than 20 million young girls who have no voice. That makes me the *bad* guy? There are those who say that as a man, I shouldn't even have a voice in this discussion. This is a women's issue only. No men allowed.

That position is even more telling than it seems, because the position illustrates why there is a refusal to answer that question in the first place. In the eyes of the pro-choice lobby—even at the highest levels of that leadership—there is no universal answer or even a suggestion as to when the fetus becomes human. Rather, it seems, each fetus has its own unique moment when "he" or "she" *becomes* human—or "it" *fails* to become human. In other words, the fetus becomes human at the very moment the baby is wanted by the mother. Not *before* the fetus is wanted by the mother and not *unless* the fetus is wanted by the mother. This is why fetal homicide laws (those laws that criminalize assault on a pregnant woman that results in the death or injury of the fetus) present such a difficult case for the pro-choice lobby: do they champion them or condemn them? Without first speaking to the mother, they really can't do either. I've never met an expectant mother who talks about the child she is carrying as an unviable tissue mass or a cluster of cells. She talks about her baby.

The argument of viability of the fetus outside the mother's womb used to be made before science destroyed that argument. Premature babies survive earlier and earlier thanks to medical technology; the earliest was 21 weeks and 5 days old. But even a full-term baby has no hope of survival outside the womb without care and that is true for at least several years to come.

"My body, my choice" is another popular pro-choice refrain. But are the mother and her unborn child really one? Are they not two separate and distinct bodies? Or does the mother temporarily have two hearts, two brains, four legs, four arms, and so on? Of course not. The argument then falls apart.

That may seem extreme, but either we recognize each person's right to own his or her own body or we do not. Pragmatically, we might also observe that if the history of liberty illustrates anything, it is that human rights tend to rise and fall together. Rights are bundled, and societies either accept rights or they don't. Either we all have a right to life or none of us does. Either we all have a right to liberty or none of us does. Either we all have a right to pursue happiness or none of us does. While fetal "personhood" is continually confirmed by science, the pro-choice arguments just get louder. And that has implications for every one of us. That is why we must seek to protect innocent life.

One last point on this. Whenever the topic of passing pro-life laws arises, there is the inevitable jab that pro-lifers are simply seeking to prosecute women. So let me be clear: I would not be in favor of prosecuting or persecuting women for having an abortion. Even prior to *Roe*, anti-abortion laws were designed not to prosecute woman but physicians.[16] As far as I know, no leading pro-life voice in the abortion debate is pushing for criminal penalties against a woman who has undergone abortion, making it all the more frightening when candidate Donald Trump told Chris Matthews he supported it.[17] The general belief in the pro-life movement, and it is universal among the most relevant pro-life voices, is that women who have undergone abortion have already suffered more than enough.

LOOKING FORWARD

In pro-life circles, it has become popular to say that when it comes to abortion, women deserve better. I agree.

If we are going to address the abortion issue in America, we have to understand why they are taking place. In some cases the underlying problem is poverty. In many cases, it is not that women want to undergo abortions; it is that they feel trapped in a desperate situation where they feel as though they cannot escape.

For many pro-choice individuals, the answer is abortion. That does not solve problems; it simply creates more.

For pro-life individuals, the answer is often more government assistance. I believe that more government assistance is part of the answer. As a conservative, I believe in limited government but not so limited that it cannot help a young woman keep her baby. Government can also help in other ways, starting with better policies. Earlier in this book, I passionately argued for free trade. One of the reasons is that free trade is a pro-life issue. When the government decides to tax incoming produce, that can make buying food that much harder for someone barely making it now. A free trade policy might literally mean the difference between eating today or going hungry. Our healthcare system is fraught with monopoly and fraud, but a more transparent healthcare system will save lives. It would also help if our tax code allowed a larger deduction for children. Every policy we have in America should exhibit a respect for life rather than contempt. So yes, there is more the government can do. But ultimately, the government cannot convey compassion. Even when it works perfectly, government is impersonal.

Much of the pro-life answer is going to be accomplished and is already being accomplished at the community level. As I've briefly addressed in this chapter, many pro-life groups over the past four decades have come to realize that the main struggle is poverty, and—more importantly—they have acted on it. They have recognized that helping poor women betters their lives and saves the lives of their unborn children. They have established free housing for pregnant women and young mothers, donated food, provided free medical care to them and their babies, assisted with job training and educational programs, and provided love and support to young mothers and families. It's noteworthy that so much of this has happened by private initiative with little or no government involvement. These are simply groups of people who want to help others, forming a coalition of caring. And they want to do more. Much of the answer to the abortion problem in America lies in expanding these private initiatives far and wide. Being pro-life is not a single issue; it encompasses many issues from conception to helping improve the quality of life for others until natural death.

II

THE FALSE GOD
OF POLITICS

Once abolish the God and the government becomes the God.

— G. K. Chesterton

In his 1979 essay "Unspeakable Ethics, Unnatural Law," former Yale Law School professor Arthur Leff reduces the whole question of morality into two words: "Sez who?" He writes:

> *Napalming babies is bad.*
> *Buying and selling each other is depraved.*
> *. . . Sez who?*

If you've read this far, it should not surprise you to learn that I am a follower of Christ. I found this chapter the most difficult to write, and if it troubles you, skip it. The book in your hands is not meant to serve as a manual of Christian theology but a defense of conservatism. While I believe that Christianity and conservatism are mutually supportive, they are not the same. And I'm using Leff's example above—whatever your religion or lack of religion—to make a political point that we all need to consider.

From my Christian perspective, there is an answer to Leff's "Sez who?" question: *God says*. Many people consider that an almost childish response—but there's nothing childish about it. If we believe that the Ten Commandments are not merely the "Ten Suggestions," there is an inescapable duty to grow up. These moral rules not only affect my personal relationship with God but also my personal relationships with others. There is a duty to treat others—*all others*—with respect, justice, honesty, dignity, and charity even when it's difficult to do so.

As C. S. Lewis put it, "moral rules are directions for running the human machine. Every moral rule is there to prevent a breakdown, or a strain, or a friction, in the running of that machine."[1] That's also true for society. A society with no moral rules—a society that finds no objection to lying or stealing—is not a society but collective chaos.

But most people seem to innately desire a perfect place, and this creates political disturbances. These are the two polar worldviews: one says this life on earth is not heaven, and therefore our situation is not perfectible; the other says that since there is no life after death, we must try to perfect the world we have while we have it. I'm not arguing that conservatives are all believers and liberals are atheists. Political ideologies don't align neatly with any particular religion, but they can correspond with these two worldviews. And there are central common themes. Both want heaven. Both seek the truth. Both seek justice either here or hereafter. Both really want the same thing. Yet, they work against each other. The desire to create Heaven on earth creates an earthly Hell. And whether in this life or the next, Hell is something we're trying to avoid.

It would be futile to suggest Christians don't have a worldview; we do. But some have suggested that it is inappropriate for Christians to bring that worldview into government either as a government employee, judge, or as an elected official. But everyone has a system of morality, and it is expected that when you take a position in government you would use those standards to make decisions as a government employee or official. So why would it be unacceptable for another person with a Christian worldview of morality to somehow check those beliefs at the door when they enter government? They shouldn't. More to the point, they can't. Christians are no more capable of setting aside their belief system than anyone else and therefore the Christian has as much right to work in government with their beliefs as anyone else does with theirs.

Nevertheless, the claim is made by many non-Christians that Christians are constantly seeking to grab governmental power and transform the American republic into an officially Christian state. But is that what Christianity is trying to accomplish? And beyond that question, it's time to recognize another truth. It's not that politics is being Christianized; it's that politics is becoming its own religion.

CHURCH VS. STATE?

The concern that Christians would attempt to turn America's republic into an officially Christian government, sometimes referred to as a theocracy is unwarranted. Let me begin with a concession: We Christians would certainly like Christianity to influence the hearts and minds of Americans, and we would like to see those ethical principles reflected in law. We would at least hope that the ethical principles expressed in the commandments are not contradicted in human law. But if the worry is that Christians want to establish a theocratic form of government, everyone can rest easy. Up until the current presidency, with the possible exceptions of Jefferson and Lincoln (historians disagree over the level of involvement in their respective faiths and churches), every single president in American history was Christian. Some were more serious than others about practicing the tenets of Christianity, but which of them tried to turn America into a theocracy? None. Aside from possibly Jefferson and Franklin, all the signers of the Declaration of Independence were Christian. That would have been their best chance—1776—to create a theocracy. Which one of them tried? None. But the worries persist, nevertheless.

When John F. Kennedy—America's first Catholic president—was running for office, this argument presented itself again. Some of Kennedy's opponents insisted that if America elected Kennedy, he would be constantly on the phone with the pope—the result being that the pope would be governing America from the Vatican. Even some non-Catholic Christians who were motivated by shopworn anti-Catholic tropes brought up this concern, as millions of anti-Catholic flyers and pamphlets were mailed to potential voters before the election.[2] (Ironically, it was not President Kennedy but Ronald Reagan, a lifelong Protestant, who developed the closest friendship with a pope in American history. Reagan's relationship with Pope John Paul II was forged by a common belief in human liberty, and when the two men spoke, their consistent topic was how to bring down Soviet Communism together, in which they were successful. Yet, like every single one of his predecessors, Reagan didn't abolish the American republic in favor a theocracy.)

This thinking continues to the present day. Here's an example. In 2017, President Trump nominated Amy Coney Barrett to the Seventh Circuit Court of Appeals. Barrett had three qualities that didn't seem to sit well with some of the senators: mother of seven, professor of law at the University of Notre Dame and Catholic. *Mother of seven* implied she was pro-life; *professor of law at Notre Dame* implied she was an originalist; and *Catholic* implied, well, that she was Catholic. There was the obligatory senatorial grilling of the nominee on her pro-life position, exhibited by the fact that Senator Richard Blumenthal spent his entire allotted time asking Barrett what she thought about *Roe* and abortion. Senator Amy Klobuchar cast aspersions on Barrett's view of originalism, which was effectively a roundabout way of asking Barrett about her opinion of *Roe*. But it was Barrett's Catholic faith that generated the most attention. It's important to note that there is one essential purpose of such a hearing: to determine the overall qualifications and ability of someone to serve as a circuit court judge. Keeping that in mind, consider the question Barrett was asked by Senator Dick Durbin: "Do you consider yourself an orthodox Catholic?"[3] It's surprising that no one in the room immediately objected, because Durbin was clearly out of order. Consider this. What if Barrett were not a Catholic but an atheist, and Durbin had asked her: "Do you consider yourself an atheist?" For that matter, what if Durbin had substituted "Catholic" for any other word? Are you an orthodox Jew? Are you a Muslim? Are you a Mormon? Are you a Buddhist? If the purpose of the hearing was to determine Barrett's qualifications for office, what—in Durbin's mind—was the right answer to his question? More to the point, what was the *wrong* one?

But Durbin's question never really made it to national media attention because of an even worse comment made by Senator Dianne Feinstein at the same hearing. Referring to Barrett's Catholic faith, Feinstein said, "When you read your speeches, the conclusion one draws is that the dogma lives loudly within you, and that's of concern."[4] Feinstein was essentially saying: "Oh, wait! You're one of those Catholics who actually goes to Mass and says the Rosary? How could someone like you interpret the Constitution and not feel compelled to impose your Catholic dogma on society?" In her comments, Feinstein claimed that she spoke for "so many of this side" (meaning so many Democratic senators on the committee). Is she correct? Many Democratic senators on the Judiciary Committee find a personal adherence to Catholicism irreconcilable with interpreting the Constitution? More to the point, are they worried that Catholics are trying to impose their religion on the rest of America? If so—given the strong Catholic representation on the Supreme Court over the years—how is it that eating fish on Fridays hasn't been made mandatory yet?

Jefferson wrote: "I have sworn upon the altar of God, eternal hostility against every form of tyranny over the mind of man." I believe Jefferson would have included the tyranny of a religious state. The idea that Christians are trying to meld church and government is not only without foundation, but it also ignores the fact that Christians are *against* such a union and have been for quite some time. As Russell Kirk points out, James Madison was in favor of the constitutional separation of church and state because, primarily, such separation protected the churches.[5] From colonial times forward, any establishment of religion in early America proved disastrous toward various Christians and the practice of their faith.[6] The hope of Christians is not to take over the government and impose their faith; rather, it is the hope that the government does not encroach upon the practice of Christianity. That was the concern of the Danbury, Connecticut, Baptists in their letter to Thomas Jefferson. Jefferson's famous reply was that there is a wall of separation between church and state, assuring the Baptists that the nascent government had no intention of interfering in worship. That might seem unrealistic to us today, but England had created a state-run church under Henry VIII. Every colonist was well aware of the power of the church, which was in many ways indistinguishable from the power of the state. The founders rejected the notion of state-established churches. In fact, the antiestablishment clause is line one of First Amendment in the Bill of Rights part of the Constitution. Moreover, a theocracy is not in line with biblical principles. Jesus did not start a revolution to overthrow the imperial Roman Empire. He started a revolution to change the heart.

If you look worldwide at existing theocracies where the political leader is also the titular religious leader, you can't distinguish who is kneeling in prayer because of political reasons or because of their devout faith. When patronage and patronage jobs are to be had, everyone will at least appear religious. Jesus said, "You hypocrites! Isaiah was right when he prophesied about you, for he wrote, 'These people honor me with their lips, but their hearts are far from me.'"

EVANGELICAL TAKEOVER?

Irrespective of everything mentioned above, there are those who worry about an Evangelical takeover of the Republican Party and government. If you're one such worrier, put your mind at ease. There was a time—in the not-too-distant past—when Evangelical leaders had a significant footing in the Republican Party. They even established formal and informal coalitions known collectively as the Religious Right.

At the height of their popularity, Jerry Falwell Sr. and Ralph Reed were able to politically guide and organize Evangelical Christians. But Jerry Falwell Sr. passed away in 2007. And Ralph Reed's influence evaporated after his organization was reportedly paid millions of dollars by gambling casinos to mobilize Christians to oppose the evils of gambling conducted by competing gambling interests.[7] Christians may vary on the morality of gambling, but Reed may have been the first Christian to suggest that the ethics of gambling were somehow either geographical in nature or in the case of opposing online betting that in-person bets were morally superior to those placed over the internet. Since that scandal, not only is Reed left with very little influence but his endorsements and speeches are often counterproductive. Jerry Falwell Jr., who currently holds his father's former position as president of Liberty University, eschewed his role as a Christian leader claiming he has "never been a minister" but a "UVA-trained lawyer and commercial real estate developer for 20 yrs."[8] Franklin Graham, son of Billy Graham has a fraction of the influence of his father. As important as the Christian vote is, there are no more Christian leaders that have enough influence to move them toward any candidate. The truth is, President Trump has more influence over the Evangelical vote than any of the self-proclaimed Christian leaders.

And speaking of counterproductive, it might turn out that the all-in stance that some Evangelicals took toward Trump's presidential campaign will do more harm than good to the remnants of the Religious Right.

One such incident stands out more than most. On June 21, 2016, Trump met with the self-proclaimed movers and shakers of the Christian Evangelical movement in an event jointly organized by two groups: My Faith Votes and United in Purpose. In some sense, it constituted what might be called a job interview. He was going to meet behind closed doors with one thousand Christian pastors from all around the country, collectively known as the Christian Right. I did not attend this event but have attended similar events with other candidates for president in past presidential elections. Ben Carson—who was later appointed as the secretary of HUD—was in attendance and insinuated that Trump's victory was divinely ordained. He did not indicate how he had come to this conclusion. Franklin Graham was there and reminded the audience that while Donald Trump had moral failings, so did Abraham, Moses, David, and the apostles. Mike Huckabee—whose daughter Sarah was later appointed as White House press secretary—assured Trump: "I don't think anybody here expects you to be theological today. I want to put you at ease. Because I don't think anyone's here thinking we're interviewing you to be our next pastor. This is not a pastoral search committee. So you're off the hook for deep theological questions."[9] (This was a point made not only throughout the day but also throughout the campaign season: we are not looking for a pastor; we are looking for a president—the insinuation being that if they were looking for a pastor, they would have to conduct a more serious investigation.) Another notable attendee at the meeting was Dr. James Dobson, former head of Focus on the Family.

But it was not just who was there that was noteworthy, it was who was *not*—and *why* not. One noteworthy omission was Michael Farris. As the founder and chairman of the Home School Legal Defense Association (HSLDA), Mike Farris may be the greatest champion of homeschooling—and its overall legal status—in America. Yet, Farris was not invited to the meeting. On June 21, Farris wrote an open letter in *The Christian Post* explaining why.[10] He said that the meeting's organizer came to Farris's office and explained to him that he was not invited because he had been "too vocal" in his criticisms of Trump; and it was made clear that his attendance at the meeting—which was essentially a Trump rally—was not desired.

Farris pointed out that he was a founder of the Christian Right, going back to 1980, the goal of which was to support "only candidates that reflected a biblical worldview and good character." He wrote that while the Christian Right was established so "that Christians could dramatically influence politics," this meeting was a sign that the roles had been reversed: politics was influencing and dramatically shaping Christians.

The man who may have most disagreed with Farris's assessment was an attendee at that meeting: Jerry Falwell Jr. had not only been at the June 21 meeting but he had also introduced Trump at that meeting, pontificating to the assembled throng that Donald Trump had everything a Christian could ask for in a leader (except, presumably, the practice of Christianity). He explained to the crowd that he and Trump had been friends for years. Though a friendship between the two might have seemed unlikely, the most obvious bond they share is that both men inherited institutions built by their fathers: Trump inherited a real estate business in New York City; for his part, Falwell inherited a nonprofit and now financially thriving university in Lynchburg, Virginia, for which he receives an annual salary of more than $900,000.

According to Falwell, this meeting of June 21 was a huge success. After the meeting, Falwell announced on Twitter: "Honored to introduce @realDonaldTrump at religious leader summit in NYC today! He did an incredible job!"

But it was not the words of the tweet that were notable; it was the picture that Falwell posted under his words. The picture had been taken in Trump's office against a cream-colored wall that was adorned with a few plaques and awards, but mostly gold-framed magazine covers that had featured Trump's photo over the years. In the middle of Falwell's picture stands a proudly smiling Donald Trump giving a thumbs-up sign. On his right stands Jerry Falwell Jr., dressed in a rumpled gray suit and wrinkled white shirt, also smiling and giving the thumbs-up sign. On Trump's left is Jerry's wife, Becki Falwell, smiling with hands curiously folded as though she had not received the message to extend the Fonzie thumbs-up sign. All in all, a remarkably boring photo—except for one small detail. One of the magazine covers in the photo contained a picture of Donald Trump wearing tuxedo pants, a tuxedo shirt, and black bow tie; on the left of the picture is a model in a provocative pose, loosely wrapped with his tuxedo jacket. The magazine: *Playboy*.

The optics seemed terrible. The non-Christian world found it hilarious, with one tweet reading: "I guess recreating the Playboy cover pose was too much to ask for." Some of Falwell's Christian Twitterati were less amused, with one tweet pondering: "Just curious how the Playboy cover squares with your morality."

And, as the *Huffington Post* quickly pointed out, what was on the inside that particular issue was far more interesting than what was on the cover: an interview with Donald Trump. In that *Playboy* interview, Trump said, "Every successful person has a very large ego."[11] Perhaps thinking that Trump must not have meant that statement universally, the reporter turned to two people—one who lived two thousand years ago and one contemporary, asking: "*Every* successful person? Mother Teresa? Jesus Christ?" Trump responded not only affirmatively but resolutely: "Far greater egos than you will ever understand." Thus, Trump was arguing that Mother Teresa and Jesus had egos that were not just inflated but were so lofty that they lay "far" beyond the comprehension of the interviewer. For some reason, still thinking that Trump must be aware of some exception to his stance on ego, the reporter followed up, "And the pope?" (Pope John Paul II at the time.) Trump's reply: "Absolutely."

One might argue that Falwell couldn't be expected to know the contents of a *Playboy* interview with Donald Trump. On the other hand, reviewing the contents of interviews is exactly the kind of research one might do before he endorsed a candidate in front of one thousand of his closest friends.

Some of Falwell Jr.'s Twitter followers made similar points, along with highlighting that whether we are choosing a president or a pastor, America is a nation founded on Judeo-Christian values. But in the minutes and hours following his tweet in which Christians objected to the picture and caption, Falwell concluded that it was the objectors who exhibited a lack of Christianity. Falwell tweeted that those who had an issue with his tweet were the "same hypocrites who accused Jesus of being a friend of publicans and sinners"[12] and followed up with "judge not lest ye be judged."

Falwell seemed to miss the point that his Twitter followers were not being critical of Trump; they were being critical of him. In an effort to illustrate the newfound friendship between the Evangelicals—the *invited* Evangelicals at least—and Donald Trump, Falwell found the need to tweet the picture. And if anyone had an issue with that, it was his own problem: not Falwell's, not Trump's, not *Playboy's*. This became the adopted position of the Evangelicals vis-à-vis Donald Trump: any questioning of candidate Trump would be seen not as evidence of one's Christianity but rather the lack of it. In the new Christian Right, there was room for Trump but no room for Mike Farris.

Ironically, I was in Donald Trump's office in Trump Tower for nearly an hour paying a courtesy call with Senator Ted Cruz in 2015. After the meeting, I asked Mr. Trump if we could take some pictures because, as I said to him, "After all, you are a genuine celebrity." He readily agreed and motioned us to the same wall where the Falwells would have their picture taken. After framing up the picture, I asked Mr. Trump and Senator Cruz if they could take just a few steps to their left so that the men's magazine cover would not appear in the photo. I did not hide my reasoning for moving them. I clearly said I didn't want the cover in the photo. They obliged. Trump rolled his eyes.

I won't let it go unmentioned that Ted Cruz announced his candidacy for president at Liberty University. It was a ready-made venue for Cruz's candidacy. I personally made the arrangements with Jerry Jr. He even canceled the Virginia governor's already-scheduled appearance for March 23, 2015—the same date we wanted to announce. We sought his endorsement. Rafael, Ted's father, said Jerry had told him he would endorse Cruz. I later called Jerry and asked him to make the endorsement. He demurred, saying his board was not going to allow him to endorse any candidate. He then endorsed The Donald instead.

One more point about this June meeting. To their credit, the Evangelical leaders seem to have convinced Trump that he needed their endorsements to win. If the leaders of the Christian Right had the widespread influence they claim, that meeting would have produced a marked upswing for Trump's poll numbers against Clinton; however, that didn't happen at all. On June 21, Trump polling numbers against Hillary were running at about 39 percent; about four months later, his numbers were virtually identical while Clinton's numbers had actually moved up a point. It's true that Evangelicals were not going to vote for Clinton. Nevertheless, those numbers mask a deeper problem. Evangelical influence may be at its lowest point in history. Though the Trump campaign sought to win the battle for white Evangelicals, it was observed that he was "conducting the campaign of the past, summoning the ghosts of past giants and faded institutions."[13] We might say that Evangelical leaders are having a problem moving Christians from the pews to the polls, but the truth is that they aren't even moving them to the pews. A cynic might observe that maybe that's part of the plan: it remains true that Trump's support is much stronger from self-identified Evangelicals who *do not* attend church services than from those who *do*. Hardly a bragging point for Evangelical leaders. In Iowa, where the Evangelical vote does matter in the Republican caucuses, Trump lost to Cruz.

But understand the point that Evangelical leaders were not interested in a moral president. They have their own purposes. To get what they wanted, they were willing to deceive Trump about their influence. Their objective was not spiritual but carnal. They weren't seeking proximity to God but proximity to the power of the presidency, even if that president lacks moral integrity. For their own selfish reasons, they seek to be important and influential. Its heady stuff being in the Oval Office laying hands on the most powerful man in the world and believing God put you there.

Pundits can forever speculate as to why the final election results occurred the way they did, but the effect of this meeting did very little to sway any significant numbers of voters. All it did was to shout down Christians like Mike Farris. The us-versus-them mentality that the Christian Right is accused of exhibiting is now directed at fellow Evangelicals. It's difficult to see how that furthers any movement. As Farris phrased it in his letter, "This meeting marks the end of the Christian Right." Farris is still right.

LOOKING FORWARD

Speaking as a Christian conservative, I will admit that we Christians often do a lousy job in promoting our faith. Though we preach virtue, we commit sin; and if that combination makes us hypocrites, then we're guilty as charged. But we try to act with the help of God's grace. Despite original sin and personal sin and all our defects and failings, we Christians are trying to spread the Good News of the Gospel to touch hearts and souls, to better the lives of others by being witnesses to God's love and mercy, to be a source of warm comfort in a world that is often cold. And for some of us, we feel called to serve others and to serve our nation by working in the government or the political world. But the suggestion that we are trying to create some sort of theocracy in America is simply without foundation. Going forward, it would help if our national discussion recognized that fact and that we Christians reciprocate with love, mercy, and understanding toward those of other faiths and those of no faith at all.

Believers and nonbelievers alike chase after the false god of politics, and in doing so, their political beliefs have become their religion. But it's a religion that seems to be very malleable. The truth is always the first casualty in politics. Spin, as it has become known, has been with us since the founding of the republic. But today, the truth is secondary to whether my team is winning or not. Let's suppose we are in a stadium watching Game 7 of the World Series. And let's suppose the fans are equally divided between the two league champions. It's the bottom of the ninth inning. The score is tied 2–2. There are two outs and a runner on second base. The batter swings and hits a grounder up the middle. The center fielder scoops it up and throws to home. The catcher receives the ball and tags the runner on the shoulder as he slides headfirst over home plate. The umpire calls him safe! The game appears to be over, but the call is challenged. The Jumbotron in the stadium shows the replay in high-def slow motion. Let's call the Jumbotron truth. Everyone can see clearly: the runner's hand touched home plate before the catcher tagged him. But you see, the truth doesn't matter. Half the stadium thinks it was a great call and half the stadium thinks it was a terrible call despite the fact that they are looking at the same event.

What matters is: does the call help my team or hurt my team. That's sadly where we are in politics today. The truth is, at best, a secondary consideration to the point. So entrenched are we to our positions and our teams that we can neither hear nor accept the truth.

If you follow politics closely, it seems every issue takes on a political significance. Everything is binary. On immigration, one side argues that the other side wants to close the border, round up everyone in the country illegally, and deport them. The other side argues that the other side wants open borders and lawlessness. The truth is there is a solution to the border crisis and the current irrational immigration system that doesn't involve either of these positions. You could say the same about guns, taxes, and the environment.

Moreover, the parties seem to have once again switched positions. It wasn't that long ago when Republicans were saying moral leadership was essential to hold elected office. Now Democrats are saying that, and Republicans are saying it's not important. Once Republicans were for free trade, balanced budgets, fiscal discipline, and immigration. Today, the Democrats defend immigration and trade. No one has yet taken up the cause for fiscal discipline.

You can wake up every morning in America, turn on the radio, read the paper, watch cable news, go online, and never encounter a liberal point of view; although I'm arguing throughout this book that you are not likely to hear the conservative philosophy either but rather a corrupted version of it. Similarly, you can do the same as a liberal and never hear a conservative point of view. We seek solutions that only reinforce what we either already believe or what our team says to believe. But it's even worse. Studies have shown that liberals and conservatives not only get their news from different sources but they also don't watch the same movies, eat at the same restaurants, shop at the same stores, or go on the same vacations. In our often-incoherent ideological isolation, we have let our politics become our religion, we look to politicians for salvation, and we allow unholy tribalism to trump truth.

12

THE FAILING GRADE OF
THE ELECTORAL COLLEGE

THE CONSERVATIVE CASE FOR A NATIONAL POPULAR VOTE

If the president of the United States were elected by popular vote, the candidate with the most votes would win. (In 2016's election, Hillary Clinton received 65,844,610 votes to Donald Trump's 62,979,636.) That is not, however, how our system works. In fact, Americans don't even vote for the president. Each state is granted a number of electors and only these electors vote for president. For instance, in November of 2016, when you checked the box for Trump or Clinton or wrote in Mickey Mouse (who performed quite well as a write-in candidate in 2016),[1] you actually weren't voting for that candidate, but rather for an elector, and the candidate who receives 270 electoral votes wins. The following month in a little-covered event, the electors gather in the US Capitol in Washington, DC, to vote for president. This elector process is a mere formality because the electors have already pledged to vote in accordance with the state's popular vote or in the cases of Maine and Nebraska where some electors are chosen in winner-take-all manner by congressional district. In other words, the electors can't disregard the election results and then vote for Mickey.

The convoluted electoral process is remarkably boring, but its final tally can yield some pretty interestingly lopsided results. For instance, in 2016, Donald Trump won the Michigan popular vote by less than a quarter of 1 percent to Hillary Clinton: roughly 2.28 million votes to 2.27 million votes. Though the vote was close, Trump took all sixteen electoral votes. Whether Trump had won by a million votes or by a single vote, the result would be the same: he would get all sixteen electoral votes.

In America, it's not a race for 66 million votes; it's a race for 270 votes. You can win the popular vote by nearly 3 million as Clinton did over Trump but still lose the presidency.

This fact is not lost on candidates or their campaign teams. This was the observation made by Kellyanne Conway to Donald Trump during the general election campaign of 2016.[2] The candidate was concerned about national poll numbers, but Conway explained to him that these numbers were irrelevant. The logic was that any Republican would carry Texas, and any Republican will lose New York. Those states aren't in play. Candidates aren't going to waste time and money in states that are foregone conclusions. Winning the presidency was about winning the swing states. Trump received the same advice from David Bossie (another longtime politico and adviser to the campaign), who told him to run the campaign as though he were running for governor of the important states.[3] Of course, Bossie and Conway were right, and Trump won despite having lost the popular vote decisively.

Presidential candidates spend as much as three-quarters of their money in a total of ten swing states; the rest is spread out in the other forty states.[4] The amount of time the candidates spend in the states can be even narrower. In the 2016 presidential race, between the party conventions and election day, the Clinton and Trump campaigns held seventy-one "campaign events" in the state of Florida, fifty-five in North Carolina, and fifty-four in Pennsylvania.[5] Texas and California—which both have more electoral votes than any of those three states—had a total of two presidential events between them.[6] New York State has a population of about 20 million people and twenty-nine electoral votes, but neither candidate held a single event in New York. In fact, neither campaign held a single event in twenty-four states.[7]

Why does all this matter? What difference does it make where politicians campaign? Here's the answer. The Electoral College system not only influences the way a campaign is run and where a campaign spends its resources, but it also influences the way the *entire country* is run and where it spends its resources. National policy—even international policy—is heavily dictated by whether that policy helps or hurts swing states like Florida, North Carolina, and Pennsylvania. It makes members of Congress from the swing states much more influential than members of deep red or deep blue states. It affects the way first-term presidents (in hopes of reelection) govern and the way in which challengers propose to govern. States—through their governors and state legislatures—constantly lobby for billions in federal money, and swing states are far less likely to get turned down.[8] Want more money for your state? Easy, just tighten up your voting gap and become a battleground state, and the money from campaigns and taxpayer money from the federal government will come pouring in.

Currently, only ten states dictate the fortunes of the other forty. And the state-by-state winner-take-all process even removes power from voters in these states by not having the electors proportionally allocated. The reason most states have winner-take-all is so that the respective parties in each state can deliver all the electoral votes for their party's candidate. Moreover, most states have taken the approach that winner-take-all makes their state more attractive to the general election candidates. But it's not true. Unless you live in a swing state, not only does your vote for president not matter, the issues that affect your state may hardly matter either.

If we're going to become a nation where each vote really is equal to the next, a state compact is needed so that each vote really does matter—whether it's cast in Florida, New York, or Texas. The process for winning presidential elections can be reformed without a constitutional amendment or getting rid of the Electoral College. The Constitution allows states to choose their electoral votes in a way consistent with the popular vote. A group of states is currently attempting to form a compact where the states who join will hold at least 270 electoral votes, the minimum number needed to win. Then each state would allocate all its electors to the candidate that wins the national popular vote, thus ensuring the candidate with the most actual votes would also win the Electoral College.

At this point, conservatives across the country are convinced I'm suggesting a strategy that would cost them countless national elections going forward. After all, if the popular vote decided elections, Hillary Clinton would be president right now. Right? (For that reason, many of the conservatives reading this have already thrown this book across the room.) Now that you've picked the book back up, let me explain why a conservative should support this and why Hillary might not be president right now after all. Not necessarily.

In the 2016 election, both candidates pursued a strategy to gain the majority of electors as have every candidate in every presidential general election. But if the popular vote were the goal, the strategy would clearly be different. In fact, it seemed evident that Hillary Clinton, confident of her win, was pursuing winning the national popular vote in the final weeks of the campaign in order to claim a mandate. Unfortunately for her, she wasn't paying close enough attention to the electoral strategy and lost.

A national popular vote would change the way that presidential elections are won and lost. Republicans would campaign in blue California and in red Texas, because getting 45 percent of the vote versus 40 percent would matter a great deal. A vote in a deep red part of California would have the equal weight of a vote in the deep blue part of Texas. Put another way, Republicans in California—or pick your favorite blue state—would have to be campaigned to, and their vote would count as much as any Democrat voting in California. Similarly, Texas Democrats—or Democrats in your favorite red state—would see the Democratic nominee actually campaigning in their state and their vote would count as much as any Republican voting in Texas.

The argument that Democrats would need to campaign only in deep blue cities and Republicans in larger, more sparsely populated areas doesn't hold. If you look at the red-blue map of presidential elections you can see that rural America mostly votes Republican and urban America mostly votes Democratic. If you look at the populations of rural versus urban, its roughly the same. Also, if you look at past general election campaign events for both nominees, they occur about equally in urban and rural areas but only in swing states.

The United States has 330 million people spread across huge areas. Those voters have many similar interests, but they also have many more dissimilar interests and issues. Most states have a diverse economic base, but most are strong in just a few: the Upper Midwest has had a strong history in manufacturing; the Midwest, agricultural; Appalachia, coal mines; the Northeast, fishing, agriculture, and high tech; California, high tech and agriculture including winegrowers; Alaska, fishing and oil; Hawaii, tourism. The list goes on. But the issues that get the most attention are the regional interests of swing states. Shouldn't the candidates' campaigns appeal to the interests of all Americans? Shouldn't the executive branch work for all the people in all the states and not just the ones that meet their political objectives?

Moving to a national vote while preserving the constitutional Electoral College would not only make every vote count equally, it would also force candidates to have a broader appeal as opposed to narrow regional appeals. It preserves the states' power to allocate electors as it serves the state's interests. And it would create a more responsive government that would better serve all Americans. To the point, it would change the way America is governed. For the better.

If you like the idea of a national popular vote that does not require changing the Constitution, you can visit National Popular Vote at www.nationalpopularvote.com. As of this writing fifteen states with 196 electoral votes have joined the compact. When the total reaches 270, the law will be triggered in all the compact states to allot their electoral votes of a presidential election to the winner of the national popular vote.

13

RECLAIMING THE CONSERVATIVE BRAND

I'm a conservative, but don't forget, this is called the Republican Party. It's not called the Conservative Party.

—Donald Trump, 2016

I mentioned this speech earlier, but it's worth revisiting here. On May 17, four months into his first term, President Ronald Reagan gave the commencement address to the University of Notre Dame graduating class of 1981. Reagan was not the first president to do so but rather the fifth. The press gathered as they do for any presidential address, but there was an enormous amount of speculation about what Reagan would say. It had been forty-nine days since a would-be assassin's bullet hit Reagan in the chest. Unknown for many years was how close Reagan was to death as a result of that assassination attempt. This was the first time he had left Washington since the March 30 shooting. Just four days earlier, there was also an attempt on the life of Pope John Paul II, who was himself recovering from a gunshot wound as the audience at the private Catholic university sat in anticipation of Reagan's remarks.

Reagan began his speech, reliving his connection with Notre Dame by entertaining the students with his role in a movie about the school's legendary football coach, Knute Rockne. He played George Gipp, from which Reagan acquired one of his many nicknames, the Gipper.

Told with his own brand of self-deprecating humor, Reagan offered a unique perspective to a story very familiar to the audience, giving his speech a surprisingly intimate feel.

Once he had the room, Reagan skillfully transitioned to his main message, saying, "Now, it's only a game. And maybe to hear it now, afterward—and this is what we feared—it might sound maudlin and not the way it was intended. But is there anything wrong with young people having an experience, feeling something so deeply, thinking of someone else to the point that they can give so completely of themselves? There will come times in the lives of all of us when we'll be faced with causes bigger than ourselves, and they won't be on a playing field."

Moving from football to founding fathers, Reagan continues: a small band "gave us more than a nation. They brought to all mankind for the first time the concept that man was born free, that each of us has inalienable rights, ours by the grace of God, and that government was created by us for our convenience, having only the powers that we choose to give it." Reagan points out that the concept of self-governance in the form of our constitutional republic is not an old way of thinking but an extraordinarily new one. If the time life has existed on earth were compressed into just one year, America would arrive within the last four seconds.

But in the last second of that compressed timeline, our system of checks and balances has been distorted. Reagan, giving the Notre Dame graduating class its final lesson says, "Central government has usurped powers that properly belong to local and State governments. And in so doing, in many ways that central government has begun to fail to do the things that are truly the responsibility of a central government."

All of this has led to the misuse of power and preemption of the prerogatives of people and their social institutions." Even Notre Dame, an independent university, cannot escape the reach of government from hiring, firing, construction, or fund-raising. Reagan warns that "if ever the great independent colleges and universities like

Notre Dame give way to and are replaced by tax-supported institutions, the struggle to preserve academic freedom will have been lost."

Then Reagan offers this prescient and optimistic prediction: "We need you. We need your youth. We need your strength. We need your idealism to help us make right that which is wrong. Now, I know that this period of your life, you have been and are critically looking at the mores and customs of the past and questioning their value. Every generation does that. May I suggest, don't discard the time-tested values upon which civilization was built simply because they're old. More important, don't let today's doom criers and cynics persuade you that the best is past, that from here on it's all downhill. Each generation sees farther than the generation that preceded it because it stands on the shoulders of that generation. You're going to have opportunities beyond anything that we've ever known."

Since the founding of the republic and the formation of the political parties George Washington sternly warned us about, there has been a debate about whether conservatism or liberalism should prevail, and that is as it should be. But since 2016, the most significant attacks on conservatism have not come from the Democratic Party but rather from the Republican Party. As we've seen in the previous chapters of this book, the Republican Party has shifted from a pro-immigration, pro-trade, pro-NATO party to one unrecognizable to a Reagan conservative. The Republican Party—the party of Lincoln and the party of Reagan—is not what it was just a few years ago. Republican Party politics has tabled any notion of furthering principle and has become all about winning. But from a conservative perspective, I've been asking: winning *what*? It used to be anti-Communist; now it is anti-conservative. Before you argue that point, consider this: the Republican Party has decided that building a wall to keep out immigrant children deserves far more attention than keeping a hostile nation from interfering in our heretofore free elections. That fact *alone* should cause alarm. But it's indicative of the fact that conservatives no longer have any voice in a party they once considered home. And if conservatives are going to get that voice back, it needs leadership. Ronald Reagan left us a blueprint. It seems to me that there are five skills and traits in particular that our next leaders of conservatism—when they emerge—must possess.

MORAL INTEGRITY

A famous Roman orator named Cicero wrote extensively about how to deliver a great speech. Cicero claimed that the "moral character of the speaker" (called *ethos*) was paramount in terms of persuasion. Absent the moral character of the speaker, the speech could be phrased perfectly with beautiful rhetorical flourishes and yet still fall flat. But that principle goes well beyond speeches. Broadly, if someone lacks moral character, he or she is unlikely to be taken seriously, even in unrelated matters. For instance, when Al Capone pleaded not guilty to tax evasion charges, no one took him seriously. Why? Because he was widely known to be a murderer, thief, and extortionist, people simply assumed that Capone was also a tax evader. Capone had championed so many vices that it became impossible to believe that he was scrupulously honest regarding taxes. Conversely, men and women of high moral character tend to be believed. Earlier, we looked at the trial of Oliver North and noted that when the American people considered North's overall decency, people were inclined to dismiss the charges made against him during the Iran–Contra hearings. "Character counts" is not simply a campaign slogan; it is human reality. (It's also a point that Republicans used to emphasize not too long ago.)

Reagan—like the rest of us—was not a man without faults, but audiences sensed that he was a decent, good, and caring man.

Reagan's speechwriters will forever be credited for writing with power and poignancy, as well they should. Still, a speechwriter can do only so much. The real essence of a speech lies not merely in the words but in the speaker and his ability to connect with the audience. Reagan did more than connect; he *befriended* the audience. He laughed when we laughed, and he cried when we cried. And as

Americans came to know Reagan, the reverse also happened: we cried when he cried.

Reagan's address to the nation after the terrible and shocking *Challenger* space shuttle tragedy on January 28, 1986, is yet another good example. That morning, millions of Americans were glued to their television sets watching the launch of the space shuttle, which contained a crew of five men and two women. Though those were exciting days for NASA and America, this mission was extra special because one of the crew members was a schoolteacher named Christa McAuliffe who was planning to teach class to America's schoolchildren from space on the mission. Nearly one-fifth of Americans—and a much higher percentage of schoolchildren across America—were watching the liftoff when only seconds into its flight *Challenger* exploded. In America, it was as though time stopped that morning; the nation was in a state of shock. Though he was scheduled to deliver his annual State of the Union speech that night, the word went out that Reagan would cancel that speech and instead address the nation from the Oval Office.

The speech Reagan delivered that night (which was written by Peggy Noonan) was somber and mourning, yet hopeful, reminding everyone that the crew were heroes in a country known for heroism. His conclusion is perhaps most famous: "The crew of the space shuttle *Challenger* honored us by the manner in which they lived their lives. We will never forget them, nor the last time we saw them, this morning, as they prepared for their journey and waved goodbye and 'slipped the surly bonds of earth' to 'touch the face of God.'" The speech was immediately hailed as one of the finest in American history, and every serious American speechwriter since then has studied it. Great words, yes. But without Reagan's *ethos*—the moral character of the speaker that Cicero spoke about—the speech would have had far less power.

And so it is with the overall message of conservatism. The idea that a leader must be one of moral integrity has fallen out of favor in recent times, but if the chosen leader of conservatism lacks moral character, we cannot blame people for rejecting conservative principles. If it's going to gain any traction, conservatism must be led by decent men and women with a integrity.

COMPASSION

Reagan's *Challenger* speech also exhibited compassion, a trait that will be necessary for conservatism's next champion. Compassion is needed in a leader because a leader must not only seek to understand the circumstances and suffering of others but also have the desire to alleviate that suffering.

At present, politics is sorely lacking in compassion. On the first point, too many don't even seem to want leaders who try to understand another's circumstances; we seem to just want leaders who will poke a finger in the eye of political opponents. Rather than listening, both parties shout down the other and attempt to discredit them on a personal level. On the second point, if there's a desire to eliminate suffering, it's an unfulfilled one, and one need look no further right now than our southern border.

Clearly, it wasn't always this way. Domestically—as was outlined earlier in this book—Reagan was a friend to the immigrant to America, recognizing that life, liberty, and the pursuit of happiness weren't the exclusive domain of a single set of humans. Ronald Reagan produced the most sweeping pro-immigrant legislation in history. Reagan was also emphatic about the need for humanitarian aid throughout his presidency. One such form of aid occurred in Sudan, where a widespread famine was putting as many as 6 million people in danger of starvation.[1] The Reagan administration sent not only money but also nearly 1 million tons of grain to the Sudanese.[2] Some, both then and now, have criticized this aid as a violation of conservatism. Ordered liberty, however, must not only be about punishing enemies but also about making friends before fights begin.

The conservative vanguard must be able to explain how conservative policies are consistent with compassion here, at our borders, and abroad. Though many conservatives often fail at properly conveying the logic of how conservative policies make life better. The next leaders of the conservative movement must be able to connect and convey that message.

COMMUNICATION

In the presidential race of 1984, Ronald Reagan—falling less than a quarter of a percentage point shy of victory—lost the state of Minnesota. He won the other forty-nine. Reagan also won the popular vote by more than 18 percent. In a red-versus-blue America, these are numbers that other candidates don't even fantasize about in their most unbridled moments of lust for power. Some might wonder why I keep going back to Reagan. Doesn't he represent the old conservatism? Is there nothing new? If I could point to a conservative leader since Reagan that exemplified how conservatism could be an attractive political philosophy, I would. Sadly, there really are not better examples than Reagan.

So how did Reagan do it?

Presidential historians and biographers have speculated and argued about it since the election night of 1984, but Reagan won because he communicated a message about America to Americans and who they were and what their potential could be. If you want to find a common thread running through all of Reagan's communications, it was a belief that America was a uniquely good nation and that Americans were a good and fine people. Even beyond, America was a true friend to freedom-loving people wherever they live. Standing in retrospective contrast to the xenophobia that is so common today, Reagan used the word "Americans" almost interchangeably with "freedom-loving people."

Reagan realized very early on that communication is about the audience: who the audience is, what motivates them, what they love, what they believe. Reagan's audience was Americans, regardless of party affiliation. He had an audience that far surpassed the Republican Party. Reagan's major criticism was not with individual Democrats;

rather it was with the Democratic Party leadership and the direction they wanted to take the country. (In fact, Reagan gained an affinity with Democrats, and a bastion of "Reagan Democrats" emerged.)

He encapsulated all these ideas in just a few words at a rally in 1984 where, having the ethos Cicero wrote about, he said, "I think there's a new feeling of patriotism in our land, a recognition that by any standard America is a decent and generous place, a force for good in the world. And I don't know about you, but I'm a little tired of hearing people run her down."[3] In that same speech, speaking to the immigrants, he said, "You didn't come here seeking streets paved with gold. You didn't come asking for welfare or special treatment. You came for freedom and opportunity." (That's how Republicans used to speak.)

During the 1984 campaign, Reagan was criticized for not using the word "Republican" enough in his speeches,[4] but he was trying to gain a much wider audience for his message. Anyone can appeal to his or her base; there's much less skill needed for that. Real communication is about going beyond that base. The next conservative leader will need to draw upon that Reaganesque ability to speak to everyone—to explain to a new generation why conservative ideals should again be embraced by America.

In August of 1996, President Bill Clinton signed into law the Personal Responsibility and Work Opportunity Reconciliation Act—welfare reform. Clinton had previously vetoed the bill passed by both houses twice, but the third time he would sign it and in his next State of the Union address declare it was "the end of welfare as we know it."

Clinton tried everything to not pass sweeping welfare reform and so did the Democrats, even though fully half voted for the measure. What had happened was that Gingrich and the Republicans had so decisively won the argument with the American people that the Democrats understood that if they didn't pass welfare reform, their constituents would find someone who would. You can agree or disagree with the welfare reform bill of 1996; what you can't disagree with is that Gingrich had won the argument. Prime Minister

Margaret Thatcher would explain: "First you win the argument, then you win the vote."

Gingrich understood that in order to get real change, you need to first get the country to agree to your change. If you don't do that hard work of communicating effectively to the American people, you simply won't get anything meaningful done in Congress.

We often refer to our representatives in Congress as "leaders," but they are really followers. They will not form a parade, but they will march in front of one already organized. And so it is. But what is amazing to me is how the politicians in Washington who actually want reforms haven't figured this out.

It takes a lot of work, but in a constitutional republic, it's the only way real reforms get done. Communication and compromise are the key ingredients to transformative legislations.

VISION

As I mentioned earlier, politicians often draw cheers from their base by poking a finger in their opponent's eye. But, uncomfortable and unfortunate cheers and jeers notwithstanding, eye poking is not a long-term strategy for advancing a worthwhile cause. Nor does it resemble anything that might be called leadership.

Great leaders appeal not to human vices but to human virtues—or as Lincoln once phrased it, "the better angels of our nature."

Vision is clearly forward-looking and seeks to address who we are as a people; therefore, a leader's vision must first entail overcoming blindness—the blindness of racism and bigotry. In a 1984 speech to Jewish community leaders in New York, Reagan stated, "We must never remain silent in the face of bigotry. We must condemn those who seek to divide us. In all quarters and at all times, we must teach tolerance and denounce racism, anti-Semitism, and all ethnic or religious bigotry wherever they exist as unacceptable evils. We have no place for haters in America—none, whatsoever."[5] This message is fundamental to the cause of freedom.

Beyond that, leadership is in part defined by how well it sees the future.

The longtime knock on conservatism is that it is stuck in the past; the reality, however, is that conservatism seeks to find the best way forward. While the statist and socialist approaches desperately seek to hang on to the status quo, we opt to grant men and women freedom to move forward. Demand-side governmental programs myopically look at the past. A free market by contrast is limited only by the individual's ability to invent, improve, and innovate.

Vision is also the product of hope.

If the Republican Party had stopped for a moment from criticizing Barack Obama in terms often vehement and vague, they could have learned a lesson from his messaging: hope works. Bush lost in 1992 to a man from the town of Hope, Arkansas (a theme that was consistently played up in the campaign), and Barack Obama campaigned on the same single word: hope. And yet, for various reasons, Republicans have a difficult time conveying hope.

But it was Reagan's specialty.

In 1980, Reagan was campaigning for the presidency during a time of stagflation, Soviet invasions, a hostage crisis in Iran, and a populace that was questioning its very identity. Reagan's election message was clear: defeat the enemies of freedom, grow our economy through the creative energy of a free people, and show Americans how to believe in themselves again. In his inaugural address, he assured Americans, "Your dreams, your hopes, your goals are going to be the dreams, the hopes, and the goals of this administration, so help me God." Future leaders must be able to convey that same message.

RESOLVE

During his or her time in office, a president will face a plethora of challenges both foreign and domestic, as well as those that are internal to the administration. Without resolve, the president will fail. Resolve is what happens when you encounter hardship and objection, but you deem them so important that you will do everything within your power to see them through. Reagan's leadership was a lesson in resolve.

There are hundreds of stories to prove this point but none better than a single line from a speech that Reagan delivered in Berlin in June of 1987. Four decades after the United States had saved a Soviet-strangled Berlin from starvation, Reagan stood at the Berlin Wall and spoke to not only the assembled audience in Germany but also to the television audience of the world. Reagan's choice of venue wasn't accidental: the Berlin Wall represented Communism, and he wanted the whole world to see it.

To that point, Soviet leader Mikhail Gorbachev was in the process of becoming a political media darling of some in the Western press for his political reforms in the USSR. But for all the talk of his reforms, he still had troops carrying out a vicious occupation of Afghanistan, he was still building up a bloated military, and he still had a policy of disallowing religious freedom in his own country. Gorbachev certainly desired to appear as a reformer to the world, but was he serious? If so, why not reunify Germany? Reagan wanted to call Gorbachev's bluff on an international stage.

Peter Robinson, a speechwriter for Reagan, traveled to Germany to get a sense of the country and what Reagan might say. At a dinner meeting with some local Germans, Robinson asked everyone what they thought about the wall, which had been part of their lives for two generations. One woman responded in anger that Gorbachev was getting so much credit for being a reformer, but if he were serious, he should tear down the wall.[6] When Reagan first read the line, "Mr. Gorbachev, tear down this wall!" he loved it. Not only was it what he wanted to say but he himself had already said it in another speech before he commanded world attention. The State Department and the National Security Council desperately wanted the line deleted, as did Secretary of State George Shultz and adviser Colin Powell. Robinson recounts that it was objected to because the statement would create "false hopes" and prove "needlessly provocative."[7] But

Reagan held firm. He believed that Gorbachev needed to hear it, that the long-suffering Berliners—once heroically saved from starvation by American planes and pilots—needed to hear it, and that the world needed to hear it.

So against all that advice, Reagan—a living symbol of freedom—stood in front of the Berlin Wall, a hideous and menacing monument to oppression, and delivered the line: "General Secretary Gorbachev, if you seek peace, if you seek prosperity for the Soviet Union and Eastern Europe, if you seek liberalization: Come here to this gate! Mr. Gorbachev, open this gate! Mr. Gorbachev, tear down this wall!" The Soviets were furious that Reagan had made such a statement just yards from Communist-controlled Germany, but Reagan inspired a nation. Every significant history of the fall of Communism references the importance of this speech and that line in particular. It's impossible to ignore: just two years later, the wall was reduced to rubble, as was Soviet Communism and Gorbachev's rule four years later on December 25, 1991. In a historical twist of irony, a governmental system that was founded on the denial of Christianity officially fell out of power on the birthday of its founder.

And, at least in large measure, it would not have been possible if Reagan had not been such a resolute believer in human freedom. Resolve is what happens when strength meets principle.

But as we've seen in recent years, lasting powerful political movements cannot be sustained or even defined by one person. They must be driven by principled ideas that promote and expand freedom.

LOOKING FORWARD

My goal in writing this book was to make a case for conservatism as an attractive way of thinking, especially to younger Americans trying to discern their own political identity. I've asked the reader to set aside preconceived notions about conservatives, and those who claim to be conservative, to simply consider conservatism itself as a governing philosophy.

As I mentioned in the opening of this book, conservatives were once the unwanted foster children of the Republican Party that eventually gained a seat at the table under Reagan. After Reagan, conservatives sat alone in the far corner in subsequent Republican administrations and campaigns. Today, we're no longer even invited to family dinners. Indeed, our chairs are now occupied by ideological imposters posing as conservatives. Some of us are still trying to figure out how it all happened. It's as if a very few of us at the 2016 Republican National Convention in Cleveland left to get some beers, while those that remained drank the adulterated Kool-Aid. How was the conservatism of Reagan, which was so enormously successful on so many fronts, abandoned? And why, on so many issues, has the Republican leadership rejected conservative policy prescriptions? We can speculate about how it all happened, but that shouldn't be the focus of our energies. Rather, we should dedicate ourselves to restoring what we once believed: on individual freedom, on race relations, on immigration, on free trade, on religious liberty, on free markets, on foreign policy, and on the protection of human life. In convincingly communicating that message, we have a lot of work to do.

We began by positing the question: what is it that conservatives believe? I hope this book answers that question and how conservatism approaches the challenges of a self-governing people called Americans.

ACKNOWLEDGMENTS

First, thank you to Peter Zorich from Best Guest Media. Peter is a longtime television professional who has worked for some of the biggest shows in cable news. It was Peter who sealed my deal with MSNBC. It was also Peter who introduced me to my book agent, Peter McGuigan of Foundry Media, who put all the right people together to make this book a reality. McGuigan introduced me to Stephen S. Power from Thomas Dunne Books. Here is the obligatory "this book would not have been possible" but it's true. It would not have been. Without Stephen, who not only took a chance on me but took the time to rework my original proposal into what this book has become. I didn't believe I had the status to write a book about conservative thought. But Stephen believed that I did. I'll leave it up to you to decide if he was right but his persistence and asking a lot of very hard questions, made me dig deeper to sharpen my arguments.

Thanks also to everyone at Thomas Dunne Books, especially Tom, Macmillan Publishing, and Macmillan Audio for all you do. You are very appreciated.

To help me explore all of those hard questions Stephen kept asking, a big thanks goes to John Clark who spent many hours with me on the phone, by text, and in person. John, who writes for the *National Catholic Register,* was truly a partner in shaping each of the chapters in this book. John also came up with the title.

Thanks to Phil Griffin from MSNBC for allowing me the extraordinary opportunity of bringing conservative thought to the MSNBC cable news audience. My conservative arguments were vastly improved by making them appealing to a left-leaning audience.

Thank you to my wife Tamara to whom this book is dedicated, for your unceasing support and encouragement.

My ten years with former Speaker of the House Newt Gingrich gave me invaluable experience. In that time, Newt wrote at least ten books. I played some role in each, mostly promotion, some research, editing, and writing. Newt was kind enough to list me on the title page along with Vince Haley of his *New York Times* eleven-week bestseller *Real Change*. That experience helped enormously in what to expect when writing my own book. For that and much more, I will always be grateful to Newt.

Thanks to Sam Dawson, who never stopped pushing me to get going and do more. Thanks to Bob McEwen for his pithy explanation of third-party purchasing. Thanks to Rick Wilson for his generous thoughts on how he become a bestselling author. Thanks to Georgia State Ashe Family Chair Professor of Law Eric Segall for convincing me about the best way to reform the Supreme Court. Finally, thanks to Saul Anuzis of National Popular Vote for educating me on how to keep the Electoral College while ensuring the winner of a presidential race is the candidate with the most votes.

ENDNOTES

INTRODUCTION:
CONSERVATISM—THE IDEOLOGICAL FOSTER CHILD

1 Jay Caruso, "16 Years Ago, William F. Buckley Wrote This About Donald Trump and It's Eerily Accurate," RedState, July 24, 2016, redstate .com/jaycaruso/2016/07/24/16-years-ago-william-f.-buckley-wrote -donald-trump-eerily-accurate.

2 William J. Bennett, "Become a 'Conviction' Party Once Again," *Washington Post*, November 10, 1992, https://www.washingtonpost.com /archive/opinions/1992/11/10/become-a-conviction-party-once-again /857a262e-dd1d-402c-af97-34bde53d282f.

3 Thomas Sowell, "Trump's Blather Dangerous for Troubled Nation," *Atlanta Journal-Constitution*, September 15, 2015, https://www.ajc .com/news/opinion/trump-blather-dangerous-for-troubled-nation /A22qk1TnFHjNH21JlKDXCL.

4 "Conservatives against Trump," *National Review*, February 15, 2016, nationalreview.com/magazine/2016/02/15/conservatives-against -trump.

5 This and the following quotations in this paragraph and the next two paragraphs are from Phyllis Schlafly, introduction to *The Conservative Case for Trump* (Washington, D.C.: Regnery Publishing, 2016), Kindle.

6 "Sarah Palin: Trump Will 'Kick ISIS' Ass,'" YouTube, January 19, 2016, https://www.youtube.com/watch?v=gzFNAoYGJ48.

7 Chris Cillizza, "Pat Buchanan Says Donald Trump Is the Future of the Republican Party," *Washington Post*, January 12, 2016, washingtonpost

.com/news/the-fix/wp/2016/01/12/pat-buchanan-believes-donald
-trump-is-the-future-of-the-republican-party.

8 Jim Rutenberg, "Sean Hannity Turns Adviser in the Service of Donald Trump," *New York Times*, August 21, 2016, https://www.nytimes
.com/2016/08/22/business/media/sean-hannity-turns-adviser-in-the
-service-of-donald-trump.html.

9 Paul Farhi, "Guess Who's Taking Aim at Fox News Now? Conservatives," *Washington Post*, September 5, 2016, washingtonpost.com/lifestyle
/style/guess-whos-taking-aim-at-fox-news-now-conservatives/2016/09
/05/e85807c2-7141-11e6-8533-6b0b0ded0253_story.html.

CHAPTER I WHAT IS CONSERVATISM AND WHERE DID IT COME FROM?

1 Edmund Burke, *Reflections on the Revolution in France*, MDB Oxford
Editions, Kindle.

2 Carroll Doherty, Jocelyn Kiley, and Bridget Johnson, "Obama Tops
Public's List of Best President in Their Lifetime, Followed by Clinton, Reagan," Pew Research Center, July 11, 2018, assets.pewresearch
.org/wp-content/uploads/sites/5/2018/07/11111653/Best-President-for
-release.pdf.

3 Whittaker Chambers, "Big Sister Is Watching You," *National Review*,
January 5, 2005, nationalreview.com/2005/01/big-sister-watching-you
-whittaker-chambers.

4 "Ayn Rand on Families and Children," *On the Issues*, September 10,
2018, ontheissues.org/Celeb/Ayn_Rand_Families_+_Children.htm.
Accessed March 3, 2020.

5 William F Buckley, interview by Brian Lamb, "William F. Buckley,
Jr. Interview on Books, Education, Family, Finance, Political Views
(2000)," *Book TV*, C-SPAN 2, youtube.com/watch?v=v8lTxJVZYWs.

6 Jesse Norman, *Edmund Burke* (New York: Basic Books, 2013), Kindle.

7 Edmund Burke, *Delphi Complete Works of Edmund Burke*, illus., Delphi,
7th ser., bk. 2 (Hastings: Delphi Classics, 2016), Kindle.

8 Alvin Felzenberg, "How William F. Buckley, Jr., Changed His Mind
on Civil Rights," Politico, May 13, 2017, politico.com/magazine/story
/2017/05/13/william-f-buckley-civil-rights-215129.

9 William F. Buckley, *God and Man at Yale: The Superstitions of "Academic Freedom"* (Washington, D.C.: Gateway Editions, Regnery Publishing, 2001), Kindle.

10 Ibid.

11 Arthur C. Brooks, *Who Really Cares: The Surprising Truth About Compassionate Conservatism—America's Charity Divide—Who Gives, Who Doesn't, and Why It Matters (New York: Basic Book, 2006), 3–5*

CHAPTER 2 THE MORALITY OF FREE TRADE

1 F. A. Hayek, *The Constitution of Liberty: The Definitive Edition* (Chicago: University of Chicago Press, 2011), 88–89.

2 Russell Kirk, *The Conservative Mind* (Washington, D.C.: Regnery Publishing, 1995 ed.), 10.

3 Adam Smith, *An Inquiry into the Nature and Causes of the Wealth of Nations* (New York: Modern Library, 1937), 462.

4 George Gilder, *Wealth and Poverty: A New Edition for the Twenty-First Century* (Washington, D.C.: Regnery Publishing, Inc., 2012), 11.

5 Adam Smith, *The Wealth of Nations*, 425–26.

6 Jeremy Hill, "As Steelmaker Shuts Plant, Governor Points to Tariffs," Bloomberg, October 1, 2019, https://www.bloomberg.com/news/articles/2019-10-01/as-bankrupt-steelmaker-closes-plant-governor-points-to-tariffs.

7 Frédéric Bastiat, trans. Arthur Goddard, *Economic Sophisms* (New York: Foundation for Economic Education, Inc., 1975 ed.), 75–76.

8 David Ricardo, *The Principles of Political Economy and Taxation* (London: J. M. Dent and Sons, Ltd., 1948), 81.

9 Ibid.

10 Thomas L. Friedman, "Foreign Affairs Big Mac I," *New York Times*, December 8, 1996, https://www.nytimes.com/1996/12/08/opinion/foreign-affairs-big-mac-i.html.

11 Thomas L. Friedman, *The Lexus and the Olive Tree* (New York: Farrar, Straus and Giroux, 1999), 196–97. Friedman notes that Montesquieu had made similar observations.

12 M. de Secondat Baron de Montesquieu, trans. Thomas Nugent, *The Spirit of Laws*, vol. 1 (Cincinnati: Robert Clarke and Co., 1873), 365.

13 Gary Galles, "Montesquieu on Commerce," Mises Institute, January 18, 2010, https://mises.org/library/montesquieu-commerce.

14 Chas. M. Morris, *Hon. Reed Smoot, Senior United States Senator from Utah: His Record in the Senate* (Salt Lake City, 1914), 7, https://play .google.com/books/reader?id=1wFQAAAAYAAJ&hl=en&pg=GBS .PA7.

15 U.S. Congress, *Tariff Act of 1930* (Washington, D.C.: United States Printing Office, 1930), cover, https://books.google.com/books?id =hX01AQAAIAAJ.

16 Ibid., 87.

17 Ibid., 8.

18 Charles P. Kindleberger, *The World in Depression 1929–1939* (Berkeley: University of California Press, 1986), 123.

19 Amity Shlaes, *The Forgotten Man: A New History of the Great Depression* (New York: Harper Perennial, 2007), 96.

20 Ibid.

21 William J. Bernstein, *A Splendid Exchange: How Trade Shaped the World* (New York: Atlantic Monthly Press, 2008), 352.

22 "U.S. Automobile Production Figures," Wikipedia, https://en.wikipedia .org/wiki/U.S._Automobile_Production_Figures.

23 Alan Reynolds, "What Do We Know About the Great Crash?" *National Review*, November 9, 1979, https://www.heartland.org/_template -assets/documents/publications/21226.pdf.

24 Shlaes, *The Forgotten Man*, 7.

25 Alan S. Blinder, "A Look Behind the Curtain of Trumponomics," *Wall Street Journal*, November 17, 2016, https://www.wsj.com/articles /a-look-behind-the-curtain-of-trumponomics-1479427674; see also: Karen Ruiz, "Steve Bannon Says Trump's Tariffs Will Put Up Prices of 'the Junk You Buy at Walmart' by as Much as 10 Per Cent," *Daily Mail*, September 20, 2018, https://www.dailymail.co.uk/news/article -6189469/Steve-Bannon-says-Trumps-tariffs-prices-junk-buy -Walmart.html; see also: Jessica Bursztynsky, "Bannon: Trump's New Tariff Threat Sends a Message that China Can No Longer 'Game the System,'" CNBC, August 2, 2019, https://www.cnbc.com/2019/08 /02/steve-bannon-trump-new-tariff-threat-sends-a-message-to-china .html.

26 Adam Nossiter, "'Let Them Call You Racists': Bannon's Pep Talk to

National Front," *New York Times*, March 10, 2008, https://www.nytimes
.com/2018/03/10/world/europe/steve-bannon-france-national-front
.html.

27 Greg Evans, "Steve Bannon Fires Back at Jeff Zucker: CNN a 'Disgrace
to Journalism,'" Deadline, March 22, 2018, https://deadline.com/2018
/03/steve-bannon-fires-back-jeff-zucker-cnn-disgrace-to-journalism
-1202351727.

28 Tony Lee, "Bannon to Charlie Rose: Elites Have Committed 'Economic
Hate Crime' Against Working-Class Americans," Breitbart, September 12, 2017, https://www.breitbart.com/politics/2017/09/12/bannon
-charlie-rose-elites-committed-economic-hate-crime-working-class
-americans.

29 "The Future of Bannonism," *Economist*, August 25, 2017, https://
www.economist.com/united-states/2017/08/25/the-future-of
-bannonism.

30 Richard Cohen, "Bannon's Origin Story Doesn't Add Up," *Washington Post*, March 20, 2017, https://www.washingtonpost.com/opinions
/bannons-origin-story-doesnt-add-up/2017/03/20/8f2ef9f8-0d90-11e7
-9b0d-d27c98455440_story.html.

31 Froma Harrop, "Froma Harrop: Bannon Failed His Father, not AT&T,"
Providence Journal, March 18, 2017, https://www.providencejournal
.com/opinion/20170318/froma-harrop-bannon-failed-his-father-not
-atampt.

32 Steve Holland, "Ex–Trump Aide Bannon: 'To Hell with Wall Street'
View on Trade Moves," *Reuters*, April 4, 2018, https://www.reuters
.com/article/us-usa-trade-china-bannon/ex-trump-aide-bannon-to
-hell-with-wall-street-view-on-trade-moves-idUSKCN1HB2LE.

33 Erica Pande and Jonathan Swan, "Peter Navarro's Radical Transfor-
mation," Axios, June 24, 2018, https://www.axios.com/peter-navarro
-free-trade-globalist-the-policy-game-book-7e2739be-104b-41cf
-a5b6-986ac66f213a.html.

34 Peter Coy, "Trump's Trade Warrior Is the Most Unpopular Economist in
the Class," *Bloomberg Businessweek*, May 2, 2017, https://www.bloomberg
.com/news/features/2017-05-02/trump-s-trade-warrior-is-the-most
-unpopular-economist-in-the-class.

35 This and the following quote from Erica Pandey and Jonathan Swan,
"Peter Navarro's Journey from Globalist to Protectionist, in His Own

Words," *Axios*, June 24, 2018, https://www.axios.com/peter-navarro-globalist-protectionist-china-trade-war-policy-c9822426-aa7c-4706-b1a4-3c16cab63098.html.

36 Peter Navarro, "The Era of American Complacency on Trade Is Over," *New York Times*, June 8, 2018, https://www.nytimes.com/2018/06/08/opinion/trump-trade-g7-russia-putin-navarro.html.

37 Wilbur Ross, "Revitalizing the U.S. Steel and Aluminum Industry Will Keep America Safe: Wilbur Ross (Opinion)" Cleveland.com, Updated Jan 30, 2019; Posted Jul 15, 2018, https://www.cleveland.com/opinion/2018/07/revitalizing_the_us_steel_and.html.

38 Sharon Lerner, "Before Pushing Tariffs, Wilbur Ross Had a Messy History with the U.S. Steel Industry," Intercept, March 5, 2018, https://theintercept.com/2018/03/05/steel-tariffs-wilbur-ross-pollution.

39 Bob Woodward, *Fear: Trump in the White House* (New York: Simon & Schuster, 2018), Kindle.

40 "Commerce Secretary Wilbur Ross on Tariffs and Trade Policy | CNBC," YouTube, March 2, 2018, https://www.youtube.com/watch?v=YrVADC083xk.

41 "Campbell Soup's (CPB) on Q3 2018 Results—Earnings Call Transcript," Seeking Alpha, May 18, 2018, https://seekingalpha.com/article/4175421-campbell-soups-cpb-on-q3-2018-results-earnings-call-transcript.

42 Woodward, *Fear*, 137.

43 Bureau of Labor Statistics, Consumer Price Index—April 2018 and May 2018, https://www.bls.gov/news.release/archives/cpi_05102018.pdf.

44 Sarah Nassauer and Heather Haddon, "Tariffs on Mexican Imports Would Hit More than Avocados in Grocery Stores," *Wall Street Journal*, June 1, 2019, wsj.com/articles/tariffs-on-mexican-imports-would-hit-more-than-avocados-in-grocery-stores-11559409197.

45 This and following Sasse quote by Dave Boyer, "Trump's Bailout Plan for Farmers Criticized by Some in GOP," *Washington Times*, July 24, 2018, https://www.washingtontimes.com/news/2018/jul/24/donald-trumps-bailout-plan-farmers-criticized-some.

46 Donald J. Trump (@realDonaldTrump), December 4, 2018, 10:03 a.m., https://twitter.com/realDonaldTrump/status/1069970500535902208.

47 Daniel J. Ikenson, "Why Trump's Tariffs on China Hurt Everyday Americans," Cato Institute, May 7, 2019, cato.org/publications/commentary /why-trumps-tariffs-china-hurt-everyday-americans.

48 Paul Ryan and Ted Cruz, "Putting Congress in Charge on Trade," *Wall Street Journal*, April 21, 2015, https://www.wsj.com/articles/putting -congress-in-charge-on-trade-1429659409.

49 Jon Greenberg, "I Opposed TPP (Trans-Pacific Partnership) and Have Always Opposed TPP," Politifact, March 10, 2016, https://www .politifact.com/factchecks/2016/mar/10/ted-cruz/ted-cruz-i-always -opposed-tpp-trans-pacific-partne/.

50 Team Fix, "The CNN Miami Republican Debate Transcript, Anno-tated," *Washington Post*, March 10, 2016, https://www.washingtonpost .com/news/the-fix/wp/2016/03/10/the-cnn-miami-republican-debate -transcript-annotated.

51 Aaron Blake, "The Final Trump-Clinton Debate Transcript, Anno-tated," *Washington Post*, October 19, 2016, https://www.washingtonpost .com/news/the-fix/wp/2016/10/19/the-final-trump-clinton-debate -transcript-annotated.

52 Mark J. Perry, "In 1970, Milton Friedman Called for Unilateral Free Trade Rather than Retaliation. We Still Haven't Learned That Sim-ple Lesson," FEE, July 16, 2018, https://fee.org/articles/in-1970-milton -friedman-called-for-unilateral-free-trade-rather-than-retaliation-we -still-haven-t-learned-that-simple-lesson.

53 Shlaes, *The Forgotten Man*, 7, 96–99.

CHAPTER 3 KNOWING OUR PLACE IN THE WORLD

1 Barry M. Goldwater, *Conscience of a Conservative* (Radford: Wilder Publications, Inc., 2014), Kindle.

2 "Russia Military Strength (2020)," Global Firepower, globalfirepower .com/country-military-strength-detail.asp?country_id=Russia.

3 Neil MacFarquhar and David E. Sanger, "Putin's 'Invincible' Missile Is Aimed at U.S. Vulnerabilities," *New York Times*, March 1, 2018, https://www.nytimes.com/2018/03/01/world/europe/russia-putin -speech.html; see also: Andrew Osborn, "Putin Warns NATO against

Closer Ties with Ukraine and Georgia," Reuters, July 19, 2018, https://www.reuters.com/article/us-russia-nato-putin-idUSKBN1K92KA.

4 Ronald Reagan, "Transcript of Address by President on Lebanon and Grenada," *New York Times*, October 28, 1983, https://www.nytimes.com/1983/10/28/us/transcript-of-address-by-president-on-lebanon-and-grenada.html.

5 Steven F. Hayward, *The Age of Reagan: The Conservative Counterrevolution* (New York: Crown Publishing Group, 2009), Kindle.

6 Ibid., 470.

7 Ronald Reagan, "Transcript of Address by Reagan on Libya," *New York Times*, April 15, 1986, https://www.nytimes.com/1986/04/15/world/transcript-of-address-by-reagan-on-libya.html.

8 Bernard Weinraub, "President Bars 'Concessions': Orders Antihijacking Steps; 3 More TWA Hostages Freed," *New York Times*, June 19, 1985, https://www.nytimes.com/1985/06/19/world/president-bars-concessions-orders-antihijacking-steps-3-more-twa-hostages-freed.html.

9 Caspar Weinberger, "Caspar Weinberger Interview," *Frontline*, PBS, September 2001, pbs.org/wgbh/pages/frontline/shows/target/interviews/weinberger.html.

10 Caspar Weinberger, "The Uses of Military Power," *Frontline*, PBS, November 28, 1984, https://www.pbs.org/wgbh/pages/frontline/shows/military/force/weinberger.html.

11 Francis Fukuyama, "Nation-Building 101: The Chief Threats to Us and to World Order Come from Weak, Collapsed, or Failed States. Learning How to Fix Such States—and Building Necessary Political Support at Home—Will Be a Defining Issue for America in the Century Ahead," *Atlantic*, January/February 2004, http://theatlantic.com/magazine/archive/2004/01/nation-building-101/302862.

12 Margaret Thatcher, *Statecraft* (London: HarperCollins Publishers, 2002), Kindle.

13 James Mackenzie, "Afghanistan Prepares for Election amid Fraud Allegations, Fear of Taliban," Reuters, October 6, 2018, https://www.reuters.com/article/us-afghanistan-politics-election-idUSKCN1MH01S.

14 "Over a Million Votes Invalid in Kabul General Election," *Der Spiegel*, https://www.spiegel.de/politik/ausland/afghanistan-stimmen-bei-parlamentswahl-in-kabul-ungueltig-a-1242228.html.

15 David Zucchino and Fahim Abed, "Afghan Government Fires Election Officials after Votes Tainted by Fraud Claims," *New York Times*, February 12, 2019, nytimes.com/2019/02/12/world/asia/afghanistan-election-voter-fraud.html.

16 Andrew Gawthorpe, "Nation-Building: A Forgotten Aspect of the Vietnam War," Defence In Depth, December 8, 2014, defenceindepth.co/2014/12/08/nation-building-a-forgotten-aspect-of-the-vietnam-war.

17 "The Berlin Airlift," *American Experience*, PBS, April 26, 2013, https://www.pbs.org/wgbh/americanexperience/films/airlift.

18 Matt Fratus, "Fighting Communism with Candy: The Berlin Candy Bomber," Coffee Or Die, December 8, 2018, https://coffeeordie.com/berlin-candy-bomber.

19 David Lauterborn, "Interview with Gail Halvorsen, the Berlin Candy Bomber," HistoryNet, https://www.historynet.com/interview-with-gail-halvorsen-the-berlin-candy-bomber.htm; see also: Gail S. Halvorsen, *The Berlin Candy Bomber* (Springville, UT: Horizon Publishers, 2010), https://www.amazon.com/Berlin-Candy-Bomber-Gail-Halvorsen/dp/0882903616.

20 John Lenczowski, "Advancing Human Rights to Combat Extremism: Testimony before the Subcommittee on Africa, Global Health, Global Human Rights, and International Organizations House Committee on Foreign Affairs," December 6, 2017, docs.house.gov/meetings/FA/FA16/20171206/106698/HHRG-115-FA16-Wstate-LenczowskiJ-20171206.pdf.

21 Ibid.

22 Ibid.

23 This quote and the next quote in this paragraph by Reagan are from Ronald Reagan, "Address at Commencement Exercises at the University of Notre Dame," speech delivered at South Bend, IN, May 17, 1981, https://www.reaganlibrary.gov/research/speeches/51781a.

24 Hayward, *Age of Reagan*, 95.

25 Ibid., 115.

26 Paul Kengor, *A Pope and a President: John Paul II, Ronald Reagan, and the Extraordinary Untold Story of the 20th Century* (Wilmington: Intercollegiate Studies Institute, 2017), Kindle.

27 Ibid.; see also: Newt and Callista Gingrich, *Nine Days that Changed the World*, written and directed by Kevin Knoblock, Regnery Publishing, February 22, 2011, amazon.com/Nine-Days-That-Changed-World/dp /1596982004.
28 Kengor, *A Pope and a President*, 185.
29 Theodore R. Bromund, "How Margaret Thatcher Helped to End the Cold War," Heritage Foundation, September 28, 2009, heritage.org /europe/report/how-margaret-thatcher-helped-end-the-cold-war.
30 This quote along with the following by Thatcher are from Margaret Thatcher, "the lady's not for turning," speech delivered at Brighton, UK, October 10, 1980, https://www.theguardian.com/politics/2007/apr/30 /conservatives.uk.
31 This and the following quote in this paragraph from John Lenczowski, "Advancing Human Rights to Combat Extremism."

CHAPTER 4 TAXATION WITH REPRESENTATION CAN BE WORSE

1 Hernando de Soto, *The Mystery of Capital: Why Capitalism Triumphs in the West and Fails Everywhere Else* (New York: Basic Books, 2000), 1.
2 Greg Weiner, "The Shallow Cynicism of 'Everything Is Rigged'" *New York Times*, August 30, 2019, https://www.nytimes.com/2019/08/25 /opinion/trump-warren-sanders-corruption.html.
3 Alvin Rabushka, *Taxation in Colonial America* (Princeton: Princeton University Press, 2008), Kindle.
4 Charles Adams, *For Good and Evil: The Impact of Taxes on the Course of Civilization* (Lanham: Madison Books, 2001 edition), 28–29.
5 Ibid., 28–31.
6 John Marshall, *McCulloch v. Maryland*, Legal Information Institute, https://www.law.cornell.edu/supremecourt/text/17/316.
7 David Burnham, *A Law Unto Itself: Power, Politics and the IRS* (Cleveland: Open Road Distribution, 2015), Kindle.
8 Ben Shapiro, *The People vs. Barack Obama: The Criminal Case Against the Obama Administration* (New York: Threshold Editions, 2014), https://www.amazon.com/People-Vs-Barack-Obama-Administration /dp/1476765138.
9 Judson Phillips, "Phillips: An opportunity to Abolish the IRS: Public

Opinion Is Ready to Eliminate this Temptation of Presidents," *Washington Times*, May 16, 2013, https://www.washingtontimes.com/news/2013/may/16/an-opportunity-to-abolish-the-irs.

10 "IRS Harassment of Pro-Life Groups Continues Despite Claims to Contrary," Thomas More Society, August 1, 2013, https://www.thomasmoresociety.org/irs-harassment-of-pro-life-groups-continues-despite-claims-to-contrary.

11 Bryan Preston, "IRS to Pro-Life Group: 'Tell Us About Your Members' Prayers,'" PJ Media, May 17, 2013, https://pjmedia.com/blog/irs-to-pro-life-group-tell-us-about-your-members-prayers.

12 Philip Bump, "Acting IRS Head Who Took the Fall This Week Has Few Answers for Congress," *Atlantic*, May 17, 2013, https://www.theatlantic.com/politics/archive/2013/05/acting-irs-head-who-took-fall-week-has-few-answers-congress/315153.

13 P. J. O'Rourke, preface to *Parliament of Whores: A Lone Humorist Attempts to Explain the Entire U.S. Government* (New York: Grove Press, 1991), Kindle.

14 George Gilder, *Wealth and Poverty: A New Edition for the Twenty-First Century* (Washington, D.C.: Regnery Publishing, 2012), Kindle.

15 Andrew Glass, "Lincoln Imposes First Federal Income Tax: Aug. 5, 1861," Politico, August 5, 2009, https://www.politico.com/story/2009/08/lincoln-imposes-first-federal-income-tax-aug-5-1861-025787.

16 Giovanna Breu, "Economist Milton Friedman Calls the Income Tax 'An Unholy Mess' and Wants to Reform It," *People*, April 5, 1976, people.com/archive/economist-milton-friedman-calls-the-income-tax-an-unholy-mess-and-wants-to-reform-it-vol-5-no-13.

CHAPTER 5 SAVING THE PLANET OR THE HUMANS?

1 Nick Holonyak, "Interview of Nick Holonyak" interview by Babak Ashrafi, Niels Bohr Library and Archives, American Institute of Physics, College Park, MD, March 23, 2005, https://www.aip.org/history-programs/niels-bohr-library/oral-histories/30533.

2 Ibid.

3 Laura Schmitt, *The Bright Stuff: The LED and Nick Holonyak's Fantastic Trail of Innovation* (Urbana: BookBaby Milton Feng, 2012), Kindle.

4 Ibid.

5 "LED Lighting," Department of Energy, energy.gov/energysaver/save
-electricity-and-fuel/lighting-choices-save-you-money/led-lighting.

6 Ibid. (accessed March 6, 2020).

7 George Gilder, *Knowledge and Power: The Information Theory of Capitalism and How It Is Revolutionizing Our World* (Washington, D.C.: Regnery Publishing, 2013), Kindle.

8 Charles Darwin, *The Descent of Man* (London: John Murray, Albemarle
Street, 1871), 316.

9 Ibid., 326–27.

10 "Hillary, Bernie Answer 6 NV Questions," *Reno Gazette Journal*, February 16, 2016, https://www.rgj.com/story/news/2016/02/16/caucus
-prep-hillary-bernie-answer-nevada-questions/80459848.

11 Jorge R. Barrio, "Consensus Science and the Peer Review," US National Library of Medicine National Institutes of Health, April 28,
2009, https://www.ncbi.nlm.nih.gov/pmc/articles/PMC2719747.

12 "Dr. Semmelweis' Biography," Semmelweis Society International, http://
semmelweis.org/about/dr-semmelweis-biography.

13 Barrio, "Consensus Science and the Peer Review."

14 Gus Lubin, "49 Former NASA Scientists Send a Letter Disputing Climate Change," Business Insider, April 11, 2012, businessinsider.com
/nasa-scientists-dispute-climate-change-2012-4.

15 Roy Spencer, *An Inconvenient Deception: How Al Gore Distorts Climate
Science and Energy Policy* (Huntsville: Roy W. Spencer, 2017), Kindle.

16 Ibid.

17 Dr. Patrick Michaels, director of the Center for the Study of Science
at the Cato Institute, "The Truth about Global Warming," interview
by Mark Levin, Fox News, October 21, 2018, youtube.com/watch?v
=fA5sGtj7QKQ&t=320s.

18 This quote and those that follow in this paragraph from 116th Congress, "H.Res.109—Recognizing the Duty of the Federal Government to Create a Green New Deal" (Washington, D.C., February 7,
2019).

19 David Montgomery, "AOC's Chief of Change," *Washington Post Magazine*, July 10, 2019, https://www.washingtonpost.com/news/magazine
/wp/2019/07/10/feature/how-saikat-chakrabarti-became-aocs-chief-of
-change.

20 Frank Newport, "Americans View Government as Nation's Top Problem in 2017," Gallup, December 18, 2017, news.gallup.com/poll/224219 /americans-view-government-nation-top-problem-2017.aspx.

21 Drew Johnson, "Al Gore's Inconvenient Reality: The Former Vice President's Home Energy Use Surges Up to 34 Times the National Average Despite Costly Green Renovations," *National Policy Analysis 679* (August 1, 2017), nationalcenter.org/ncppr/2017/08/01/al-gores-inconvenient -reality-the-former-vice-presidents-home-energy-use-surges-up-to-34 -times-the-national-average-despite-costly-green-renovations-by-drew -johnso.

22 James Taylor, "Is Al Gore a Fossil-Fuel Industry Mole?," *Forbes*, June 29, 2011, forbes.com/sites/jamestaylor/2011/06/29/is-al-gore-a-fossil -fuel-industry-mole/#45d76597d150.

23 Robert Rapier, "Al Gore's Hypocrisy: The Climate Crusader Profits from Fossil Fuels," Oil Price, February 6, 2013, oilprice.com/Energy /Energy-General/Al-Gores-Hipocrisy-The-Climate-Crusader-Profits -from-Fossil-Fuels.html.

24 "Effects of a Carbon Tax on the Economy and the Environment," Congressional Budget Office, May 2013, 2.

25 Ibid., 8.

26 Ibid., 2.

27 Ibid.

28 Aaron Wudrick, "Lessons from Australia—Carbon Tax Failure," *Canada Free Press*, December 5, 2016, canadafreepress.com/article/lessons -from-australia-carbon-tax-failure.

29 Margaret Wente, "Why Australia's Carbon Tax Bombed," *Globe and Mail*, May 11, 2018, theglobeandmail.com/opinion/why-australias -carbon-tax-bombed/article19704906.

30 "Another Carbon Tax Defeat," editorial, *Wall Street Journal*, April 17, 2019, wsj.com/articles/another-carbon-tax-defeat-11555542235.

CHAPTER 6 IMMIGRATION: AMERICA'S GREATEST STORY

1 "El Salvador Events of 2018," Human Rights Watch, hrw.org/world -report/2019/country-chapters/el-salvador.

2 John Carlos Frey, "Inside the 'Pure Hell' of Honduras's Rising Tide

of Domestic Violence," *News Hour*, PBS, October 24, 2015, pbs.org /newshour/show/inside-pure-hell-violence-women-honduras.

3 David Bier, "Travel Ban Separates Thousands of U.S. Citizens from Their Spouses and Minor Children," Cato Institute, January 29, 2019, cato.org/blog/travel-ban-separates-thousands-us-citizens-their-spouses -minor-children.

4 Ibid.

5 Roger Daniels, *Guarding the Golden Door* (New York: Hill and Wang, 2005), Kindle.

6 Ibid.

7 "US: 20 Years of Immigrant Abuses," Human Rights Watch, April 25, 2016, hrw.org/news/2016/04/25/us-20-years-immigrant-abuses.

8 Betsy Cooper and Kevin O'Neil, "Lessons from the Immigration Reform and Control Act of 1986," *Policy Brief* (Washington, D.C.: Migration Policy Institute, August 2005), 2.

9 Dolia Estevez, "Debunking Donald Trump's Five Extreme Statements about Immigrants and Mexico," *Forbes*, September 3, 2015, forbes.com /sites/doliaestevez/2015/09/03/debunking-donald-trumps-five-extreme -statements-about-immigrants-and-mexico/#4d6fb92d1e81.

10 Matthew Feeney, "Walling Off Liberty: How Strict Immigration Enforcement Threatens Privacy and Local Policing," Cato Institute, November 1, 2018, cato.org/publications/policy-analysis/walling-liberty -how-strict-immigration-enforcement-threatens-privacy.

11 Daniel T. Griswold, *Cato Journal*, "Is Immigration Good for America?" Cato 32, no. 1 (2012), Kindle.

12 Bob Woodward, *Fear: Trump in the White House* (New York: Simon & Schuster, 2018), Kindle.

13 Tim Hains, "Trump to Illegal Immigrants: The Country Is Full, So Turn Around," RealClear Politics, April 5, 2019, https://www.realclearpolitics .com/video/2019/04/05/trump_to_illegal_immigrants_sorry_our _country_is_full_so_turn_around.html.

14 Rosalind S. Helderman, "Stephen Miller's 'Cringeworthy' Campaign Speech for Student Government," *Washington Post*, February 15, 2017, https://www.washingtonpost.com/news/post-politics/wp/2017 /02/15/stephen-millers-cringeworthy-campaign-speech-for-student -government.

15 Stephen Miller, "Political Correctness out of Control," *Surf Santa Monica*, March 27, 2002, surfsantamonica.com/ssm_site/the_lookout/letters /Letters-2002/MARCH_2002/03_27_2002_Political_Correctness _Out_of_Control.htm.

16 This and the following quotes from this paragraph are from Stephen Miller, "Welcome to the Durham Petting Zoo," *Chronicle*, April 5, 2006, https://www.dukechronicle.com/article/2006/04/welcome-durham -petting-zoo.

17 McKay Coppins, "The Outrage over Family Separation Is Exactly What Stephen Miller Wants," *Atlantic*, June 19, 2018, theatlantic.com/politics /archive/2018/06/asdaq-miller-family-separation/563132.

18 Woodward, *Fear*, 321.

19 Julie Hirschfeld Davis and Somini Sengupta, "Trump Administration Rejects Study Showing Positive Impact of Refugees," *New York Times*, September 18, 2017, https://www.nytimes.com/2017/09/18/us/politics /refugees-revenue-cost-report-trump.html.

20 Jonathan Blitzer, "How Stephen Miller Single-Handedly Got the U.S. to Accept Fewer Refugees," *New Yorker*, October 13, 2017, newyorker .com/news/news-desk/how-stephen-miller-single-handedly-got-the-us -to-accept-fewer-refugees.

21 John Paul II, *Centesimus Annus*, 1991, http://www.vatican.va/content/john -paul-ii/en/encyclicals/documents/hf_jp-ii_enc_01051991_centesimus -annus.html.

22 Bryan O. Walsh, "The History of Operation Pedro Pan," *Bishop Accountability*, March 1, 2001, bishop-accountability.org/news5/2001_03 _01_Walsh_TheHistory.htm.

23 Ibid.

24 Dick Lobo, moderator of "Operation Pedro Pan—The Largest Recorded Exodus of Unaccompanied Minors in the Western Hemisphere," YouTube, May 6, 2011, youtube.com/watch?v=vT0ItwvcQMI.

25 Walsh, "The History of Operation Pedro Pan."

26 *Cato*: "Is Immigration Good for America?"

27 Daniels, *Guarding the Golden Door*, 18.

28 Joanna Michal Hoyt, *A Wary Welcome: The History of US Attitudes toward Immigration* (Lacona: Skinny Bottle Publishing, 2017), Kindle.

29 This and the following quote are from Gerald R. Ford, "Text of Statement

and Proclamation," *New York Times*, September 17, 1974, https://www
.nytimes.com/1974/09/17/archives/text-of-statement-and-proclamation
-statement.html.

CHAPTER 7 COST-DRIVEN HEALTHCARE MAY PUT YOUR HEALTH AT RISK

1   Glenn Kessler, "Michele Bachmann's 'Bombshell' on a 'Hidden' $105
    Billion," *Washington Post*, March 8, 2011, https://www.washingtonpost
    .com/blogs/fact-checker/post/michele-bachmanns-bombshell-on-a
    -hidden-105-billion/2011/03/08/Abn7GRP_blog.html.

2   M. J. Lee, "10 Best Pro and Con Health Care Quotes," Politico, March 29,
    2012, https://www.politico.com/story/2012/03/10-best-pro-con-health
    -care-quotes-074638.

3   Sean Sullivan, "Ben Carson: Obamacare Worst Thing 'Since Slavery,'"
    Washington Post, October 11, 2013, https://www.washingtonpost.com
    /news/post-politics/wp/2013/10/11/ben-carson-obamacare-worst-thing
    -since-slavery.

4   Steven Brill, *America's Bitter Pill* (New York: Random House Publish-
    ing Group, 2015), Kindle.

5   Dylan Scott, "The Untold Story of TV's First Prescription Drug Ad,"
    Stat News, December 11, 2015, statnews.com/2015/12/11/untold-story
    -tvs-first-prescription-drug-ad/.

6   Joanne Kaufman, "Think You're Seeing More Drug Ads on TV? You
    Are, and Here's Why," *New York Times*, December 24, 2017, nytimes
    .com/2017/12/24/business/media/prescription-drugs-advertising-tv
    .html.

7   Centers for Medicare and Medicaid, "OpenPaymentsData.CMS.gov,"
    openpaymentsdata.cms.gov/company/100000000286/summary.

8   Bob Herman, "Think Drug Costs Are Bad? Try Hospital Prices," Axios,
    July 25, 2018, axios.com/hospitals-drug-prices-trump-pharma-223585c8
    -f085-454d-8e17-078177274d24.html.

9   Reed Abelson, "When Hospitals Merge to Save Money, Patients Often
    Pay More," *New York Times*, November 14, 2018, nytimes.com/2018
    /11/14/health/hospital-mergers-health-care-spending.html; see also:
    Avik Roy, "Hospital Monopolies: The Biggest Driver of Health Costs

That Nobody Talks About," *Forbes*, August 22, 2011, forbes.com/sites /theapothecary/2011/08/22/hospital-monopolies-the-biggest-driver-of -health-costs-that-nobody-talks-about/#5029fcc62ce8.

10 Stella Roque, "Open Markets Publishes Exclusive Concentration Data Exposing the Monopoly Problem in Health Care," Open Markets Press Release, June 10, 2019, openmarketsinstitute.org/releases/open-markets -publishes-exclusive-concentration-data-exposing-monopoly-problem -health-care.

11 Chris Newmarker, "BD Stuck with Antitrust Suit over Syringes," MD-DiOnline, July 20, 2015, mddionline.com/bd-stuck-antitrust-suit-over -syringes.

12 Zacks Equity Research, "Becton, Dickinson Ordered to Clarify False Syringe Claims," Nasdaq, November 13, 2014, nasdaq.com/article/becton -dickinson-ordered-to-clarify-false-syringe-claims-analyst-blog -cm413833.

13 Ibid.

14 Brill, *America's Bitter Pill*.

15 Robert Pearl, "Why Patent Protection in the Drug Industry Is Out of Control," *Forbes*, January 19, 2017, forbes.com/sites/robertpearl/2017 /01/19/why-patent-protection-in-the-drug-industry-is-out-of-control /#1fefa2ff78ca.

16 Denise Roland, "At $2 Million, New Novartis Drug Is Priciest Ever," *Wall Street Journal*, May 24, 2019, wsj.com/articles/at-2-million-new -novartis-drug-is-priciest-ever-11558731506.

17 Liyan Chen, "The Most Profitable Industries in 2016," *Forbes*, December 21, 2015, forbes.com/sites/liyanchen/2015/12/21/the-most-profitable -industries-in-2016/#5aa79a805716.

18 Value Line, "PFIZER INC. NYSE-PFE," http://www3.valueline.com /dow30/f7040.pdf.

19 Alexander Zaitchik, "How Big Pharma Was Captured by the One Percent," *New Republic*, June 28, 2018, newrepublic.com/article/149438 /big-pharma-captured-one-percent.

20 Alex Tabarrok, *Launching the Innovation Renaissance: A New Path to Bring Smart Ideas to Market Fast*, bk. 8 (New York: TED Books, 2011), Kindle.

21 Robin Feldman and Evan Frondorf, *Drug Wars: How Big Pharma Raises*

Prices and Keeps Generics Off the Market (New York: Cambridge University Press, 2017), Kindle.

22 Ibid.

23 Michael Hiltzik, "The Government Quashes a Nasty Stunt Used by Big Pharma to Keep Drug Prices High," *Los Angeles Times*, February 20, 2019, https://www.latimes.com/business/hiltzik/la-fi-hiltzik-fda-generics-20190220-story.html.

24 "Pharmaceuticals / Health Products: Long-Term Contribution Trends," Open Secrets, opensecrets.org/industries/totals.php?cycle=2018&ind=H04.

25 Congressional Research Service, "Medicare: Insolvency Projection," Federation of American Scientists, July 3, 2019, https://fas.org/sgp/crs/misc/RS20946.pdf.

26 "The Burdens of BernieCare," editorial, *Wall Street Journal*, May 5, 2019, wsj.com/articles/the-burdens-of-berniecare-11557091123.

27 Seema Verma, "Remarks by CMS Administrator Seema Verma at the American Hospital Association Annual Membership Meeting," Colorado Medical Society, May 7, 2018, cms.gov/newsroom/fact-sheets/speech-remarks-cms-administrator-seema-verma-american-hospital-association-annual-membership-meeting.

28 Chad Reese, "'Medicare for All' Plan Would Cost Federal Government $32 Trillion," *Bridge*, July 30, 2018, https://www.mercatus.org/bridge/commentary/medicare-all-plan-would-cost-federal-government-32-trillion; see also: "From Incremental to Comprehensive Health Reform: How Various Reform Options Compare on Coverage and Costs," Research Report, Urban Institute, October 16, 2019, https://www.urban.org/research/publication/incremental-comprehensive-health-reform-how-various-reform-options-compare-coverage-and-costs.

29 Brill, *America's Bitter Pill*; see also: "UPDATE 1-Sanofi-Aventis Settles US Claims Case for $190 Mln," Reuters, September 10, 2007, https://www.reuters.com/article/idUSN1032848920070910; see also: "Aventis Pays More Than $190 Million to Settle Drug Pricing Fraud Matters," Department of Justice, September 10, 2007, https://www.justice.gov/archive/opa/pr/2007/September/07_civ_694.html.

30 James Doubek, "Feds Charge 24 in Alleged $1.2 Billion Medicare Fraud Scheme," NPR, April 10, 2019, https://www.npr.org/2019/04

/10/711688988/feds-charge-24-in-alleged-1-2-billion-medicare-fraud
-scheme; see also: U.S. Attorney's Office Eastern District of Michigan,
"Thirteen Individuals Indicted in Health Care Fraud and Drug Distribution Scheme: Five Doctors, Four Pharmacists, and Home Health
Agency Owner among Those Indicted in Follow-up to the Babubhai
Patel Case," Justice.gov, March 19, 2013, https://www.justice.gov/usao
-edmi/pr/thirteen-individuals-indicted-health-care-fraud-and-drug
-distribution-scheme.

31 Brian McNeal, "Drug Distribution Investigation Uncovers Massive
Health Care Fraud," press release, United States Drug Enforcement
Agency, August 2, 2011, https://www.dea.gov/press-releases/2011
/08/02/drug-distribution-investigation-uncovers-massive-health
-care-fraud.

32 U.S. Attorney's Office Eastern District of Michigan, "Thirteen Individuals Indicted in Health Care Fraud And Drug Distribution
Scheme," https://www.npr.org/2019/04/10/711688988/feds-charge
-24-in-alleged-1-2-billion-medicare-fraud-scheme.

33 "Indian-American Jailed for 17 Years for Healthcare Fraud," NDTV,
https://www.npr.org/2019/04/10/711688988/feds-charge-24-in-alleged
-1-2-billion-medicare-fraud-scheme.

34 Katherine Skiba, "24 Charged in Alleged Massive Medicare Fraud,"
AARP, April 10, 2019, aarp.org/money/scams-fraud/info-2019/feds
-crackdown-medicare-fraud.html.

35 Heather Landi, "DOJ Charges Telemedicine Executives, Doctors in
$1.2B Medicare Fraud Scheme," Fierce Healthcare, April 10, 2019,
https://www.fiercehealthcare.com/tech/doj-charges-telemedicine
-executives-doctors-1-2b-medicare-fraud-scheme.

CHAPTER 8 EVENING OUT THE SUPREME COURT

1 John Roberts remarks, "Roberts: 'My job is to call balls and strikes
and not to pitch or bat,'" CNN, September 12, 2005, cnn.com/2005
/POLITICS/09/12/oberts.statement.

2 Ibid.

3 Tyler O'Neil, "Blame the Left for Making the Supreme Court Too

Political," PJ Media, July 10, 2018, pjmedia.com/trending/blame-the -left-for-making-the-supreme-court-too-political; see also: Randolph J. May, "Woodrow Wilson's Case against the Constitution," *Washington Times*, May 30, 2018, washingtontimes.com/news/2018/may/30 /woodrow-wilsons-case-against-the-constitution.

4 Bernard Schwartz, *A History of the Supreme Court* (New York: Oxford University Press, 1993), 215–16; see also: *Oxford Companion to the Supreme Court* (New York: Oxford University Press, 2005), 83–85.

5 *Oxford Companion to the Supreme Court*, 85.

6 John Roberts, "We do not speak for the people, but we do speak for the Constitution," YouTube, October 17, 2018, youtube.com/watch?v =oWzfDCb_dIw.

7 Jonah Goldberg, *Suicide of the West* (New York: Crown Forum, 2018), 180.

8 James Reston, "Washington; Kennedy and Bork," *New York Times*, July 5, 1987, https://www.nytimes.com/1987/07/05/opinion/washington -kennedy-and-bork.html.

9 Ted Kennedy remarks, "Flashback: Ted Kennedy freaks out over Ronald Reagan's Supreme Court nominee Robert Bork," YouTube, September 23, 2018, youtube.com/watch?v=ITo8HuKiOIQ.

10 Mark Gitenstein, *Matters of Principle: An Insider's Account of America's Rejection of Robert Bork's Nomination to the Supreme Court* (New York: Simon & Schuster, 1992), 30.

11 Robert Bork, *The Tempting of America: The Political Seduction of the Law* (New York: Free Press, 1990), 292.

12 Suzanne Garment, "The War Against Robert H. Bork," *Commentary*, January 1988, commentarymagazine.com/articles/the-war-against-robert -h-bork.

13 Ibid.

14 Bork, *The Tempting of America*, 281.

15 Gitenstein, *Matters of Principle*, 191.

16 Ibid., 193.

17 Ibid.

18 Michael Dolan, "Borking Around," *New Republic*, December 20, 2012, newrepublic.com/article/111331/robert-bork-dead-video-rental-records -story-sparked-privacy-laws.

19 Tom Murse, "The Joe Biden Plagiarism Case," ThoughtCo., July 3, 2019, thoughtco.com/the-joe-biden-plagiarism-case-3367590.

20 Matt Flegenheimer, "Biden's First Run for President Was a Calamity. Some Missteps Still Resonate," *New York Times*, June 3, 2019, nytimes .com/2019/06/03/us/politics/biden-1988-presidential-campaign.html.

21 James Ryerson, "'America's Constitution': A Liberal Originalist," *New York Times*, November 6, 2005, nytimes.com/2005/11/06/books/review /americas-constitution-a-liberal-originalist.html.

22 Antonin Scalia, "Trump's Supreme Court Pick Is a Disciple of Scalia's 'Originalist' Crusade," NPR, February 2, 2017, https://www.npr.org /transcripts/512891485?storyId=512891485?storyId=512891485.

23 Antonin Scalia, "Law and Justice with Antonin Scalia," interview by Peter Robinson, YouTube, March 16, 2009, youtube.com/watch?v =zE9biZT_z1k; see also: Antonin Scalia, *Scalia Speaks: Reflections on Law, Faith, and Life Well Lived* (New York: Crown Forum, 2017), 195.

24 Edward A. Hartnet, "Ties in the Supreme Court of the United States," *William and Mary Law Review 44*, no. 2, article 4 (2002), scholar- ship.law.wm.edu/cgi/viewcontent.cgi?referer=&httpsredir=1&article =1360&context=wmlr.

25 Gary M. Galles, "Why Packing the Supreme Court Is a Bad Idea," Foundation for Economic Education, March 19, 2019, fee.org/articles /why-packing-the-supreme-court-is-a-bad-idea.

26 Hartnet, "Ties in the Supreme Court of the United States."

27 Ibid.

28 Sarah Turberville and Anthony Marcum, "Those 5-to-4 Decisions on the Supreme Court? 9 to 0 Is Far More Common," *Washington Post*, June 28, 2018, washingtonpost.com/news/posteverything/wp/2018 /06/28/those-5-4-decisions-on-the-supreme-court-9-0-is-far-more -common.

29 Robert Baldwin III, "Maybe a Supreme Court with 8 Justices Isn't So Bad after All," HuffPost, June 1, 2016, https://www.huffpost.com/entry /supreme-court-eight-justices_n_574da49ce4b0dacf7ad56e7e.

CHAPTER 9 THE RIGHT TO KEEP AND BEAR CHILDREN

1 Jason Whitlock, "In KC, It's No Time for a Game," *Fox Sports*, December 1, 2012, https://www.foxsports.com/nfl/story/jovan-belcher-kansas -city-chiefs-murder-suicide-tragedy-girlfriend-self-leave-orphan -daughter-why-still-playing-sunday-120112.

2 Jeff Labrecque, "Bob Costas Takes Heat for Gun-Control Commentary on 'Sunday Night Football,'" *Entertainment Weekly*, December 3, 2012, https://ew.com/article/2012/12/03/bob-costas-jovan-belcher-gun -control.

3 Daniel W. Webster, *Updated Evidence and Policy Developments on Reducing Gun Violence in America* (Baltimore: Johns Hopkins University Press, 2014), Kindle.

4 Greg Corombos, "Stupid, 'Totalitarian' Judges Scorched for Anti-Gun Ruling," Gun Owners of America, June 10, 2016, https://gunowners.org /news06092016.

5 Vin Suprynowicz, "Second Amendment: Changing of the Guard," Gun Owners of America, February 19, 1998, gunowners.org/op9802.

6 "Larry Pratt," Southern Poverty Law Center, https://www.splcenter .org/fighting-hate/extremist-files/individual/larry-pratt.

7 Erich Pratt, "GOA Welcomes Kentucky to the Constitutional Carry Club!," Gun Owners of America, March 11, 2019, gunowners.org/goa -welcomes-kentucky-to-the-constitutional-carry-club.

8 Gun Owners of America, IRS Form 990, 2016, https://pdf.guidestar .org/PDF_Images/2016/521/256/2016-521256643-0ece76dc-9O.pdf.

9 Adam Winkler, *Gunfight: The Battle Over the Right to Bear Arms in America* (New York: W. W. Norton and Company, 2011), Kindle.

10 Ibid.

11 Clayton E. Cramer, *Armed America* (Nashville: Thomas Nelson, 2006), Kindle.

12 Winkler, *Gunfight*.

13 Ibid.

14 Ibid.

15 Cramer, *Armed America*.

16 Winkler, *Gunfight*.

17 Stephen P. Halbrook, *That Every Man Be Armed: The Evolution of a Constitutional Right* (Albuquerque: University of New Mexico Press,

2013), Kindle. see also: Tho Bishop, "The Racist History of Gun Control," Mises Institute, May 22, 2018, mises.org/wire/racist-history-gun -control-1#footnote1_0j9t4or; Allen W. Trelease, *White Terror: The Ku Klux Klan Conspiracy and Southern Reconstruction* (Baton Rouge: Louisiana State University Press, 1995); Clayton E. Cramer, "The Racist Roots of Gun Control,"1993, claytoncramer.com/scholarly/racistroots .htm.

18 Bishop, "The Racist History of Gun Control."

19 Winkler, *Gunfight*.

20 Cramer, "The Racist Roots of Gun Control."

21 Winkler, *Gunfight*.

22 Trelease, *White Terror*. This point is well-documented in various sections of the book.

23 Stephen V. Ash, *Middle Tennessee Society Transformed, 1860–1870* (Knoxville: University of Tennessee Press, 2006), 194.

24 Cramer, "The Racist Roots of Gun Control."

25 Stephen King, *Guns* (Bangor: Philtrum Press, 2013), Kindle.

26 Jayme Deerwester, "Piers Morgan Signs Off with Gun-Control Plea," *USA Today*, March 29, 2014, usatoday.com/story/life/tv/2014/03/29 /piers-morgan-last-show/7052009.

27 Nicholas Kristof, "Some Inconvenient Gun Facts for Liberals," *New York Times*, January 16, 2016, nytimes.com/2016/01/17/opinion/sunday/some -inconvenient-gun-facts-for-liberals.html.

28 Winkler, *Gunfight*.

CHAPTER 10 *BEFORE* LIBERTY AND THE PURSUIT OF HAPPINESS

1 Michelle Oberman, "The Women the Abortion War Leaves Out," *New York Times*, January 11, 2018, https://www.nytimes.com/2018/01/11 /opinion/sunday/abortion-crisis-pregnancy-centers.html.

2 "Our Mission," Willow Pregnancy Support, willowpregnancy.org/our -mission (accessed March 8, 2020)

3 "Moving Forward: You Are Not Alone," Sisters of Life, sistersoflife.org /what-we-do/pregnancy-help/abortion-alternatives/.

4 M. Gissler, E. Karalis, and V-M Ulander, "Suicide Rate after Induced Abortion Decreased in Finland after Current Care Guidelines," *European*

Journal of Public Health 24, issue supplement 2 (October 24, 2014), https://doi.org/10.1093/eurpub/cku163.045.

5 David M. Fergusson, L. John Horwood, and Elizabeth M. Ridder, "Abortion in Young Women and Subsequent Mental Health," *Journal of Child Psychology and Psychiatry 47* (January 24, 2006), eric.ed.gov/?id=EJ950852.

6 Ibid.

7 "The Emotional Effects of Induced Abortion," Planned Parenthood Federation of America, 2013, https://www.plannedparenthood.org/files/8413/9611/5708/Abortion_Emotional_Effects.pdf.

8 Kathleen O'Connor and Erica O'Neil, "Fetal Surgery," Arizona State University, November 1, 2012, embryo.asu.edu/pages/fetal-surgery.

9 Cardinal Glennon Children's Hospital, "Fetal Surgery," SSM Health, ssmhealth.com/cardinal-glennon/fetal-care-institute/advanced-procedures/fetal-surgery.

10 Ibid.

11 Jeff Guo, "Should We Give Fetuses Painkillers before We Abort Them?" *Washington Post*, March 26, 2015, washingtonpost.com/blogs/govbeat/wp/2015/03/26/montana-lawmakers-want-fetuses-to-be-anesthetized-before-theyre-aborted.

12 Randy Alcorn, "Why Life Begins at Conception," NAACP, naapc.org/why-life-begins-at-conception.

13 Keith L. Moore, *The Developing Human* (Philadelphia: Elsevier Health Sciences, 2016), Kindle.

14 "When Human Life Begins," American College of Pediatricians, March 2017, acpeds.org/the-college-speaks/position-statements/life-issues/when-human-life-begins.

15 Editor, "An Unexpected Ally: Did You Know Atheist Christopher Hitchens Was Pro-Life?" ChurchPop, January 25, 2017, churchpop.com/2017/01/25/an-unexpected-ally-did-you-know-atheist-christopher-hitchens-was-pro-life.

16 Clarke D. Forsythe, *Abuse of Discretion: The Inside Story of* Roe v. Wade (New York: Encounter Books, 2013), Kindle.

17 Callum Borchers, "How Chris Matthews Tripped Up Donald Trump on Abortion," *Washington Post*, March 31, 2016, https://www.washingtonpost.com/news/the-fix/wp/2016/03/31/how-chris-matthews-tripped-up-donald-trump-on-abortion/.

CHAPTER II THE FALSE GOD OF POLITICS

1 C. S. Lewis, *Mere Christianity* (New York: HarperCollins E-Books, 2009), Kindle.

2 Colleen Carroll Campbell, "The Enduring Costs of John F. Kennedy's Compromise," Catholic Culture, catholicculture.org/culture/library/view .cfm?recnum=7572.

3 Sohrab Ahmari, "The Dogma of Dianne Feinstein," *New York Times*, September 11, 2017, https://www.nytimes.com/2017/09/11/opinion/the -dogma-of-dianne-feinstein.html.

4 Ibid.

5 Russell Kirk, *The Roots of American Order* (Wilmington: Intercollegiate Studies Institute, 2014), Kindle.

6 Ibid.

7 Alex Gibney, "The Deceptions of Ralph Reed," *Atlantic*, September 26, 2010, https://www.theatlantic.com/politics/archive/2010/09/the -deceptions-of-ralph-reed/63568; see also: Michal Shermer, "Religion Is Disappearing. That's Great for Politics," Politico, June 10, 2015, https:// www.politico.com/magazine/story/2015/06/pew-survey-religion-118834; Sean Flynn, "The Sins of Ralph Reed," *GQ*, July 12, 2006, https://www .gq.com/story/ralph-reed-gop-lobbyist-jack-abramoff; "Ralph Reed: The Crash of the Choir-Boy Wonder," Right Wing Watch, July 2006,|https:// www.rightwingwatch.org/report/ralph-reed-the-crash-of-the-choir-boy -wonder.

8 Brandon Ambrosino, "'Someone's Gotta Tell the Freakin' Truth': Jerry Falwell's Aides Break Their Silence," Politico, September 9, 2019, https:// www.politico.com/magazine/story/2019/09/09/jerry-falwell-liberty -university-loans-227914; see also: Jerry Falwell, Twitter post, June 4, 2019, 7:05 p.m.

9 Jon Ward, "Transcript: Donald Trump's Closed-Door Meeting with Evangelical Leaders," Yahoo, June 22, 2016, https://news.yahoo.com /transcript-donald-trumps-closed-door-meeting-with-evangelical -leaders-195810824.html.

10 Quotes in this and the next paragraph from Michael Farris, "Trump's Meeting with Evangelical Leaders Marks the End of the Christian Right," *Christian Post*, June 21, 2016, https://www.christianpost.com

/news/trump-meeting-evangelical-leaders-end-of-the-christian-right
.html.

11 This and all quotes in this paragraph from Donald J. Trump, "Play-boy: Interview with Donald Trump—March 1, 1990," https://factba.se
/transcript/donald-trump-interview-playboy-march-1-1990.

12 Michael Gryboski, "Jerry Falwell Jr. Blasts Critics as 'Hypocrites' for Judging His Pro-Trump Photo in Front of *Playboy* Cover," *Christian Post*, June 22, 2016, https://www.christianpost.com/news/jerry-falwell
-jr-hypocrites-trump-photo-playboy-cover.html.

13 Tom Roberts, "'The End of White Christian America' Explains Protes-tants' Diminishing Dominance," *National Catholic Reporter*, September 14, 2016, ncronline.org/books/2016/09/author-examines-how-white
-protestant-dominance-diminishing-america.

CHAPTER 12 THE FAILING GRADE OF THE ELECTORAL COLLEGE

1 Mike Donila, Jim Matheny, "Presidential Write-Ins Skyrocket in 2016; Names Serious and Silly," WBIR-TV, November 10, 2016, https://
www.wbir.com/article/news/local/presidential-write-ins-skyrocket-in
-2016-names-serious-and-silly/51-350803984.

2 Bob Woodward, *Fear, Trump in the White House* (New York: Simon & Schuster, 2018), Kindle. 17-18.

3 Ibid., 5.

4 Brennan Hoban, "Why Are Swing States Important?" Brookings, Sep-tember 28, 2016, brookings.edu/blog/fixgov/2016/09/28/why-are-swing
-states-important.

5 "Two-Thirds of Presidential Campaign Is in Just 6 States," no date, na-tionalpopularvote.com/campaign-events-2016. It explains: "'Campaign events' are defined here as *public* events in which a candidate is soliciting the *state's* voters (e.g. rallies, speeches, fairs, town hall meetings). This count of campaign events does not include visits to a state for the *sole* purpose of conducting a private fund-raising event, participating in a presidential debate or media interview in a studio, giving a speech to an organization's national convention, attending a noncampaign event (e.g. the Al Smith Dinner in New York City), visiting the campaign's own offices in a state, or attending a private meeting."

6 Ibid.

7 Ibid.

8 Christian Britschgi, "California Politicians Want More Federal Money to Keep Doing a Terrible Job with Homelessness," *Reason*, July 3, 2019, Reason.com/2019/07/03/California-politicians-want-more-federal -money-to-keep-doing-a-terrible-job-with-homelessness.

CHAPTER 13 RECLAIMING THE CONSERVATIVE BRAND

1 Tom Guettler, "Why Ronald Reagan Was a Strong Advocate of For- eign Aid," Global Citizen, August 11, 2016, globalcitizen.org/en/content /reagans-legacy-on-foreign-aid; see also: Gerald M. Boyd, "U.S. Releas- ing $67 Million for Sudan," *New York Times*, April 2, 1985, nytimes.com /1985/04/02/world/us-releasing-67-million-for-sudan.html.

2 Boyd, "U.S. Releasing $67 Million for Sudan."

3 Ronald Reagan, "Remarks at a Reagan-Bush Rally in Hammonton, New Jersey," September 19, 1984, https://www.reaganlibrary.gov/research /speeches/91984c.

4 Steven F. Hayward, *The Age of Reagan: The Conservative Counterrevolu- tion* (New York: Crown Publishing Group, 2010), Kindle.

5 Ronald Reagan, "Remarks to Members of the Congregation of Temple Hillel and Jewish Community Leaders in Valley Stream, New York," October 26, 1984, reaganlibrary.gov/research/speeches/102684a.

6 Peter Robinson, "How Top Advisers Opposed Reagan's Challenge to Gorbachev—But Lost," *Prologue 39*, no. 2 (Summer 2007), archives.gov /publications/prologue/2007/summer/berlin.html.

7 Ibid.

ABOUT THE AUTHOR

RICK TYLER is a leading conservative political analyst for MSNBC. He was also a contributing author to the *New York Times* bestsellers *Real Change: From the World That Fails to the World That Works* and *To Save America*. He lives in Northern Virginia.